In Faith and In Doubt

In Faith

and

In Doubt

*How Religious Believers and Nonbelievers Can
Create Strong Marriages and Loving Families*

DALE McGOWAN

AMACOM AMERICAN MANAGEMENT ASSOCIATION
New York I Atlanta I Brussels I Chicago I Mexico City
San Francisco I Shanghai I Tokyo I Toronto I Washington, D.C.

This publication is designed to provide accurate and authoritative information in regard to the subject matter covered. It is sold with the understanding that the publisher is not engaged in rendering legal, accounting, or other professional service. If legal advice or other expert assistance is required, the services of a competent professional person should be sought.

Library of Congress Cataloging-in-Publication Data

McGowan, Dale.
In faith and in doubt : how religious believers and nonbelievers can create strong marriages and loving families / Dale McGowan.
    pages cm
Includes index.
ISBN-13: 978-0-8144-3372-0 (pbk.)
ISBN-10: 0-8144-3372-3 (pbk.)
ISBN-13: 978-0-8144-3373-7 (ebook)
1. Interfaith marriage. 2. Interfaith families. I. Title.
HQ1031.M3945 2014
306.84'3—dc23

2014010124

About AMA
American Management Association (www.amanet.org) is a world leader in talent development, advancing the skills of individuals to drive business success. Our mission is to support the goals of individuals and organizations through a complete range of products and services, including classroom and virtual seminars, webcasts, webinars, podcasts, conferences, corporate and government solutions, business books, and research. AMA's approach to improving performance combines experiential learning—learning through doing—with opportunities for ongoing professional growth at every step of one's career journey.

Printing number
10 9 8 7 6 5 4 3 2 1

For Becca, who taught me how easy the mix could be

Contents

PART THREE
Meet the Issues

Acknowledgments

Thanks first and foremost to the more than 1,000 people who let me pry into their lives and marriages through the survey and interviews. Special thanks to Tom and Danielle, Arlene and Nate, Anna and Gary, Andrew and Lewis, Scott and Dhanya, Hope and David, Cassidy and Bill, and Evan and Cate, as well as Julie and Matthew and Kevin and Nora, the couples who were so generous in sharing their stories with me. You know your real names.

Special thanks to Cassidy McGillicuddy and Alise Wright for permission to reproduce first-person excerpts from their brilliant and insightful blog posts on this topic.

Mary Ellen Sikes was an invaluable partner in creating the McGowan-Sikes survey and analyzing the data. Without her brains and stamina, this book would be a ghost of itself.

Thanks to the staff at AMACOM, including Christina Parisi, who acquired the title, my patient editors, Ellen Kadin and Erika Spelman, project reviewer Chris Murray, and copyeditor Holly Fairbank, who stilled the waters of my citational chaos. My agent, Uwe Stender of TriadaUS, was excellent as always in securing the project.

Dave Muscato brought the University of Tennessee nonbeliever typology study to my attention, which provided the essential backbone for an entire chapter. Thanks as well to Christopher Silver and Thomas Coleman, the lead researchers in that seminal study, as well as Bruce Hunsberger and Bob Altemeyer, two of the pioneers in research on religious nonbelievers.

Many thanks to the staff of Foundation Beyond Belief for keeping things running and growing while my attention has been sorely split. A very special shout-out to my colleague Dr. Brittany Shoots-Reinhard for pointing to several good resources on the science of relationships, social psychology research on such key concepts as "re-fencing," and for creating the Shared Values Quiz in Chapter 13.

Readers of my blog, The Meming of Life, were once again invaluable as sounding boards, including Rajat Jha, who helped me understand the complexities of both Hinduism and Hindi, and Caprice Niccoli, who coined the beautiful and economical word *mixistential* for the secular/religious mixed marriage. I chickened out of using it in the book, but I continue to think it's the perfect word.

I am grateful as well to Dave Becker and Anna Minaya for help in unexpected ways, and to Mark Hulings for introducing me to Scrivener, which honestly saved my neck on this complex project.

Finally, all thanks and love to my wife, Becca, for endless support and a huge editorial contribution, as well as Connor, Erin, and Delaney, our terrific kids.

In Faith and In Doubt

Introduction

If major religious differences doom a marriage, mine should have been toe-tagged at the altar. Our religious differences were arguably as major as they could get.

Ours wasn't a marriage of people with two different religions. That has real challenges, of course, but there's also a clearer starting point for two believers—namely, God. As one religious friend of mine in an interreligious marriage told me years ago, "We both believe in God. The rest is fine print." When two religious traditions are blended, graces become less denominational, "Jesus" might be replaced with "our Lord," shared history and practice are emphasized, and differences are minimized. The Christmas tree sprouts a Star of David. It's not always easy, but there are well-trod bridges across that kind of divide.

Ours was different. We were squinting at each other across an even bigger belief gap—the one between religious belief and disbelief, between a committed Christian believer and an equally committed atheist.

I was never a conventional religious believer, and by the time I approached that altar in a century-old church in San Francisco, I'd identified as an atheist for 15 years. I read the Bible critically at 13 and debated preachers in the college plaza at 19. I was a vocal critic of many aspects of religion and still am.

The young woman approaching down that long aisle, on the other hand, was a born and bred Southern Baptist. I'd recently witnessed the adult baptism ceremony that confirmed her in the faith. Her stepfather, uncle, and grandfather were Southern Baptist ministers. Her parents met at a Baptist college. She attended church and planned to continue doing so once we were married. And the Bible is plenty clear about marriages between believers and nonbelievers: *Do not be yoked together with unbelievers*, it warns. *For what do righteousness and wickedness have in common? Or what fellowship can light have with darkness?*[1]

Given all of those alarm bells, why was I crying tears of joy as she came down the aisle? Why was she smiling as she approached me? And why are we still happily married 23 years and three children later?

The short answer is that people are more interesting than their labels. The long answer is this book.

Don't think that we entered this mixed marriage with eyes open and a plan in hand. We were both oblivious to the garment-rending literature on mixed-belief marriage, the scores of articles and books that would have told us just how terrible an idea it is to marry someone whose answers to ultimate questions differ dramatically from yours.

We'd been happily married about ten years when I stumbled on the first of the articles telling me we shouldn't be. Marrying outside of your own belief system is an epic blunder, it said, one that leads inevitably to unhappiness, divorce, and bitter regret.

Well that's strange, I thought. *We must be doing it wrong.*

Sure, we'd had some disagreements and frustrations around religious questions, especially once the kids came along. But our marriage was far from unhappy, and I've never felt anything like "regret" for having married someone with different beliefs. She says the same. And I know many other couples whose mixed-belief marriages are also successful and happy.

But not everyone is so lucky. I've also known many people, including close friends, whose mixed-belief marriages have been painful and unhappy. Some have ended in divorce, and some of those breakups were caused directly by their different religious beliefs.

Curious, I started digging into the literature on mixed-belief marriage and came away stunned. Book after book presented interfaith marriage as (to quote some actual passages) a uniformly "regrettable" choice made by starry-eyed young people "who think that love will conquer all" and so ignore the "slow catastrophe" of an interfaith marriage, leading inevitably to "tragic results" including unhappiness, shattered families, and bitter separation and divorce. They tend to include phrases like, "If you're determined to intermarry . . ." followed by advice for getting the best out of a terrible situation. And these dire warnings concern interfaith couples who both believe in God! One can imagine what they might say about secular/religious couples.

These dire warnings aren't all quaint echoes from long ago. In a 2010 *Washington Post* opinion piece ominously titled "Interfaith Marriages Are Rising Fast, but They're Failing Fast Too," author Naomi Schaefer Riley said, "Interfaith marriages often come with a heavy price. They are more likely than same-faith unions to be unhappy and, in some circumstances, to end in divorce."[2]

Read that again: Interfaith marriages are more likely, "in some circumstances, to end in divorce."

It's a sentence almost entirely without meaning.

Saying interfaith marriages are more likely to end in divorce "in some circumstances" is like saying men named Steve are more likely to get divorced "in some circumstances." It's both true and meaningless. Before you delete all of the Steves from your eHarmony account, you might want to find out what those circumstances are. Steves who commit serial infidelity might be expected to divorce more often, but their Steveness would have nothing to do with it. Walters and Jills and Davids with the same habits would also be more likely to divorce.

The same is true of interfaith marriages. The question is, Is it the religious difference that increases the risk of failure? And sure enough, a close examination of the research shows that the effect has been greatly exaggerated—mostly by folks who would simply rather not see you marrying outside of the fold. Other risk factors are almost always in play, factors that usually have little or nothing to do with the religious difference.

Riley, for example, cherry-picks two particular scenarios from a study in which certain interfaith marriages have higher divorce rates, then ignores the overall conclusion of the study: "Theological beliefs and the belief dissimilarity of spouses have little effect on the likelihood of dissolution [of marriage] over time."[3]

Even if they don't end in divorce, Riley says, interfaith marriages are "more likely than same-faith unions to be unhappy." It's a trope repeated by clergy in many denominations. Rabbi Kalman Packouz, author of *How to*

Prevent an Intermarriage, uses premarital counseling of interfaith couples to talk them out of it, saying they *will* have a higher likelihood of divorce and *will* be less happy. Period![4]

Though some studies have shown a small difference in average satisfaction for interfaith couples, others show no difference whatsoever. In addition to the quoted Vaaler and Ellison study, Dr. Janice Aron, the author of a 2009 interfaith marriage satisfaction study, found "absolutely no difference in marital satisfaction between people who were married to partners of the same faith, and people married to partners of a different faith."[5]

> *Theological beliefs and the belief dissimilarity of spouses have little effect on the likelihood of dissolution [of marriage] over time.* —Vaaler and Ellison study (2005)

So why would so many authors on interfaith marriage cherry-pick data to make such marriages look more problematic? The answer may lie in Riley's statement that interfaith marriages "tend to diminish the strength of religious communities, as the devout are pulled away from bonds of tradition and orthodoxy by their nonmember spouses."[6]

Rabbi Packouz makes his intentions even clearer: He's less interested in marital happiness and stability than in preserving Jewish identity. The first line in his book is, "Intermarriage is a recognized threat to the survival of the Jewish people." That's a valid concern for a rabbi. But casting a fearful cloud over all interfaith marriage with misleading statements seems a dishonest way to go about this.

Much of the interfaith literature takes a similar approach, concerned not about individuals and their marriages, but about the effect interfaith marriage has on religious institutions. That's a discussion worth having. But it should proceed honestly, not by claiming without evidence that interfaith marriages are themselves doomed to fail.

The religious aren't alone in their desire to preserve and expand their belief communities. I've had some atheists tell me quite directly that atheists should marry only atheists and raise their children as atheists because (to quote one), "Our retention rate is not good." That's exactly the argument made by shrinking religious denominations!

Most atheists don't support that kind of impersonal "group benefit" approach to choosing a life partner—and neither do most religious believers.

A close look at the research shows that differences in life-satisfaction indicators between same-faith and interfaith couples, always small, have almost vanished in recent years. In research for their phenomenal book *American Grace*, Robert Putnam and David Campbell noted that sharing a religious perspective has become less and less important to marital stability and satisfaction over the last two decades.

Though in her book *'Til Faith Do Us Part* Riley notes correctly that "some religious combinations are significantly more likely to end in divorce than others," later in her book she admits that overall "when we compare the likelihood that a Christian married to a non-Christian will be divorced to the likelihood that two Christians will be divorced, there is no discernible difference."[7]

So when you pull back the curtain and clear the smoke, it turns out that people with different religious perspectives generally have about the same shot at marital happiness as those who share the same religion.

That's good news, because interfaith marriage and mixed-belief marriage are becoming more common, with 27% of all U.S. married couples now claiming different religious (or nonreligious) identities. And it's going to keep rising rapidly. About 20% of marriages in the 1950s were between people of different religious identities. In the past decade, that's risen to 45%.[8]

So if even the naysayers seem to know that some mixed-belief marriages succeed brilliantly and some fail miserably—just like any other marriages—that leaves an interesting question: *Why do some mixed-belief marriages succeed while others don't?*

The Secular/Religious Mix

However challenging an interfaith marriage is, you might assume that a marriage joining someone who believes in God with someone who doesn't would be even more so. But there's been almost nothing written about these marriages.

A comment by an atheist friend of mine years ago captured the usual assumption that such a marriage is a terrible idea. "Interfaith marriage" doesn't quite describe my own marriage, since my worldview isn't a faith, so I asked if he knew of a word for the marriage of a religious believer and a nonbeliever.

He smirked and said, "Short."

That's adorable. But in our case, it's also not true. So I had to wonder: Was our marriage an exception? Was there something special about us or our situation, some vaccine that inoculated us against some virus that dooms others in the same mix?

I doubted we were quite that special. And sure enough, over the years I've met countless others in my exact situation—atheists, agnostics, humanists, and other nonreligious friends in successful and happy marriages with religious partners.

It doesn't always go that well, of course. I know others whose marriages have been made miserable or killed off entirely by the secular/religious difference.

So again, that better question pops up: *Why do some succeed and others fail?*

The process of answering that question is a fascinating one. It requires a careful look at the changing landscape of religion and irreligion, as well as the nature of marriage itself and our growing understanding of the science of relationships. It's also helpful to look closely at the brow-knitted warnings of the "heavy price" supposedly paid when spouses don't agree on religion—warnings that turn out to be grossly exaggerated, reliant on cherry-picked data, and agenda driven.

I'll explore the big-picture questions in the first section of the book, then pull in tight to look at real people in secular/religious marriages to see what works and what doesn't in bridging that divide. The last section looks at specific topics in this particular mix.

When I became part of the growing secular/religious trend 23 years ago, it was still a blip on the radar. The religiously unaffiliated ("Nones") were only 8% of the U.S. population in 1990. Now that number is 19.6%, meaning nearly one in five Americans have no religious affiliation.[9] And 59% of the unaffiliated who are married have partners who are religious.[10]

The issues encountered in those secular/religious marriages aren't always the same as those in other mixed-religion marriages, yet there have been almost no resources dealing with the secular/religious mix. Though research and expert opinion are brought to bear whenever possible, much of the insight emerges from the stories of real people who have experienced the mix firsthand. In some of these marriages, the belief mix is a nonissue. In others, it's a challenge, but not an insurmountable one. In still others, the challenge is too great, and the marriage falls apart.

The issues vary from one combination and situation to another, but at the same time, they are variations on unchanging themes of communication, identity, respect, family, community, parenting, and working out the fit and misfit of day-to-day practices.

Measuring the Mix

Religion in America has been measured and described from every angle. Even irreligion has gained more attention from researchers in recent years. But marriages between religious and nonreligious partners have gone almost completely unexplored.

To address this gap, I asked Mary Ellen Sikes of American Secular Census to help create a comprehensive survey of individuals in secular/religious mixed marriages. Conducted in June and July 2013, the online survey asked 87 questions of nearly 1,000 self-selected respondents in current or former secular/religious marriages, including residents of 46 U.S. states, seven Canadian provinces, and more than 20 other countries. The results appear throughout this book, providing the first in-depth look at the state of the secular/religious mixed marriage. The picture is imperfect, but it's a good initial snapshot that we hope will inspire further research.

Coming to Terms

One of the greatest challenges in writing this book has been terminology. Some of the most important terms and labels in this area mean very different things to different people.

Start with the basics: religious and nonreligious. Most people think of someone as religious if that person believes in the existence of a supernatural God or gods. But many Unitarians, Buddhists, Humanistic Jews, and others consider themselves religious but do not believe in God. They embrace aspects of religion unrelated to theistic belief, including identity, shared values, community, and tradition.

On the other side is a good friend of mine who believes deeply in God, prays daily, attends church weekly, and has Psalm texts painted around the border of her living room—but says she is "little if at all religious." She's not alone in this. Several top surveys show that millions of Americans believe in God but consider themselves nonreligious. Even more surprising are the 6% of respondents who identified as atheists in a 2007 Pew survey but said they believe in God—something philosopher and neuroscientist Sam Harris likens to someone claiming to be "a happily married bachelor."[11]

This categorical mess is captured nicely in a message I received during the writing of this book from Miriam Jerris, a nontheistic humanist rabbi whose husband, Steve, is an agnostic Catholic. She said that Steve would describe them as a secular/religious couple, "and I'm the religious one!"—even though she doesn't believe God exists.

It's hard to talk about the issues that arise in marriages between religious and nonreligious partners when we can't even agree on the meaning of the word *religious*. But as you'll see, that highlights one of the key points of this book: One reason that secular/religious marriages work is that religion itself is changing.

The terminological issues certainly don't stop with "religion." I'll also be using the word *secular* to denote things or people with no religious or spiritual basis. "Secular" should not be thought of as antireligious—it's just not religious.

Then there's "doubt." In its narrow popular meaning, doubt means "mild uncertainty." This might irritate some atheists whose convictions are strong. But the broader meaning takes in everything outside of religious faith, from mild uncertainty about the existence of God to the Richard Dawkins level of confident atheism.

Finally, there's that need for a term to describe a marriage that joins a religious believer and a nonbeliever. As I previously mentioned, *interfaith marriage* doesn't quite describe my own marriage, since my worldview isn't a faith by any traditional understanding of that word. After wrestling with many options, I decided that clarity was more important than poetry, opting for *secular/religious marriage*. It's a mouthful, but it's as close to clarity as we're likely to get.

So there's an overview of terms. In the topic of religion and irreligion, multiple meanings are impossible to avoid. I'll do my best to clarify when necessary, and I apologize in advance for anything that grates on your ears or your preferences.

How and Why You Should Read the Book

In Faith and In Doubt puts the secular/religious mixed marriage in a cultural context, counters the hair-pulling naysayers, tells the stories of real couples who have succeeded as well as some who've failed (and why), and offers suggestions and strategies for ending up in the success column. Readers may be considering a relationship that crosses this gap, or they may currently be in such a relationship and hoping to navigate it well. Or maybe you have a child entering a secular/religious relationship and the hair-pulling naysayers have you worried. Or maybe you're just interested in one of the most fascinating and understudied corners of the age-old dialogue between faith and doubt.

I hope the whole book is useful and interesting for believers and non-believers alike, but you'll be the best judge of what works for you. Read straight through or head for the sections that matter most to you. Here's the map:

Part One covers the big picture—how marriage, religion, and irreligion have changed over time, and the ways religious believers and nonbelievers are different from the stereotypes we carry in our heads. If you're a believer married to a nonbeliever or vice versa, this section can help you see your relationship through a wider lens, as part of a fascinating wave of social change.

Part Two puts the secular/religious marriage in the context of real life through the stories of the following eight actual couples:

Tom and Danielle. Married as an agnostic and a liberal Southern Baptist, Tom and Danielle had to survive a rough patch as Tom moved into a more activist atheism and struggled with what he could and could not respect.

Scott and Dhanya. A nonreligious American and a Hindu born and raised in South Africa, Scott and Dhanya's religious difference is only one of many bridges they've had to negotiate.

Hope and David. Parents of five, Hope and David were both born, raised, and married as conservative Baptists. Then David, who had been headed for the ministry, lost his beliefs entirely, sending the marriage into a tailspin.

Arlene and Nate. Already Southern Baptist and atheist from the start, Arlene and Nate were always able to be light and playful about their religious differences—until their son was born, and things got serious.

Evan and Cate. An atheist and a disaffected Catholic find common ground and a welcoming community in a Unitarian Universalist fellowship.

Anna and Gary. She was Catholic and he was an atheist at their wedding. Within a few years, she was an atheist and he was a born-again Baptist.

Cassidy and Bill. Both were Evangelical Pentecostals when they were married, but Cassidy's loss of faith and assertion of a new personal autonomy was not well received by Bill, who saw it as the breaking of a sacred promise.

Andrew and Lewis. A moderate atheist and a moderate nondenominational Christian, Andrew and Lewis have found that their differences are dwarfed by the common ground between them.

With the exception of Cassidy and Bill, each of the couples reappears in Part Three to illustrate their approaches to specific issues. A dotted arrow with the couple's name and chapter will appear to jog your memory.

Part Three breaks down the common issues—the first discussion, weddings, specific practices, identity, communication and respect, extended family, parenting, and divorce—drawing insights from the featured couples and many others, as well as expert opinion and social science research.

If all goes well, you'll end up with a new perspective on the secular/religious marriage. It isn't so strange after all.

PART ONE

Getting Perspective

1

The Big Picture

The way we talk about culture war, the booming Religious Right, and the pushback of the "New Atheists," you'd think the collision of faith and doubt was a new thing. It's not. It's a conversation—okay fine, an argument—that was already under way 3,000 years ago. When the author of Psalm 14 said, "The fool says in his heart, 'There is no God,'" he gave evidence that religious doubt was alive in some form in ancient Judea.

And it didn't end there. Writings from ancient Greece, Rome, China, and India all testify to the presence of both religious and irreligious points of view, and secular and religious ideas about who we are and how we should behave continue to contend for the soul of human culture straight down through the centuries—not as a sideshow, but as one of the defining conversations about what it means to be human. As daring as it seems to us, it's old hat for humanity.

This book is about the most fascinating possible meeting place of faith and doubt—not in public debate, not even in private conversation or friendship, but in the intimacy of marriage, the joining of people from different sides of this age-old divide in a lifelong commitment of love, respect, and shared purpose.

But before we narrow the focus, let's look at the bigger context in which these marriages happen.

So many of our assumptions about religion, irreligion, and the meeting of the two are colored by our own biases. That includes a natural tendency to see the nuance and variety on our own side of the aisle while underestimating the nuance and variety on the other side or sides.

It's not just a problem for the secular/religious boundary, of course. Both political liberals and conservatives tend to see themselves in high definition and full color while seeing those on the other side of the spectrum as a pencil sketch cartoon. Same with nationality, race, gender, sexual orientation—just about any categories we put ourselves into.

As bad as this kind of cartooning is in public life, it's even worse for a marriage. If an atheist and a Christian are headed for the altar, let's say, and the atheist believes her Christian fiancé is a dumb, fearful dogmatist, and he in turn thinks she's an immoral, joyless, hell-bound wretch—well, be sure to keep your gift receipts.

Sure, there are believers and nonbelievers who hold those opinions of the other side. They will tend to marry their own anyway, and that's probably wise. But most people on both sides of that belief gap have more moderate, flexible views of people on the other side of the gap. One of the main purposes of this book is to show that even as deep a difference as religious belief and disbelief is not the showstopper people often think it is. That in turn should make it much less puzzling that marriages between religious and secular people can and often do work brilliantly.

Almost every variable that impacts the secular/religious marriage—cultural attitudes, social blending, definitions of marriage, even what it means to be religious or secular—has undergone profound change in recent years. This chapter explores those changes and the ways they have made marriage between believers and nonbelievers more common and less surprising.

The Biggest Gap of All?

Marriages joining two existing faiths often bring a challenge that the secular/religious mix doesn't have: the loud collision of two long-established traditions. It isn't just abstract beliefs that collide for couples from two religions, it's the practical problems that arise when their traditions give different instructions about what to do on December 25, or when your child is born or turns 13, or before dinner on any given Thursday, or when a loved one dies. Or if you want eternal life.

Still, there's a pretty fundamental difference between the religious and nonreligious ways of seeing the world. Even if there is common ground, each perspective still has an inherent rejection of the other at its core. Making a secular/religious marriage work doesn't require us to deny that conflict, only to place it among the many differences that every couple carries into marriage. As the humanistic rabbi Adam Chalom once put it, every marriage is a mixed marriage, bringing difference of a hundred kinds together. When a believer and a nonbeliever come together, the mix is there, it's real, but it doesn't have to overwhelm the common ground. This is true in part because religion, irreligion, and marriage itself have undergone tremendous changes in recent generations.

Changing Marriage

In the early 2010s, as the scale of American public opinion tipped rapidly in favor of legalizing same-sex marriage, many conservatives worried that we were changing an institution that had been the "the essential and unchanging foundation for home, family, church and society."[1]

But marriage has always changed as the society around it has. As recently as the 19th century, even women in developed Western countries ceded all rights and property to their husbands upon marriage, and husbands wouldn't face legal consequences for beating their wives. Most people would agree that the changes since then have been good ones.

In 1947, interracial marriage was still illegal in 38 U.S. states and well over 90% of the population opposed it. After the Supreme Court made interracial marriage legal in all states in 1967, opposition dropped to 80%. By the mid-1990s, opposition to interracial marriage had dropped below half, and by 2010, it was down to 15%—fewer than the percentage who think the sun orbits the earth.[2]

As acceptance of interracial marriage increased, so did frequency. In 1970, of all U.S. marriages, 0.7% were interracial. By 2008, the percentage of couples who were interracial had risen to 4%, and a record 14.6% of new marriages that year were interracial.[3]

Same-sex marriage is just the most recent change. In 1996, only 25% of the American public supported the idea. By 2001 it was up to 35%. Three years later, Massachusetts was the first state to legalize same-sex marriage. As of December 2013, the Public Religion Research Institute shows 53% in favor, and 17 states and the District of Columbia have legalized same-sex marriage.[4]

This support crosses religious lines. Though white Evangelicals continue to overwhelmingly oppose gay marriage,

→ 38% of white Mainline Protestants supported it in 2001, and 62% do today

→ 40% of Catholics supported it in 2001, and 59% do today

→ 61% of the religiously unaffiliated supported it in 2001, and 77% do today[5]

Then there's mixed-belief marriage. If you're in one today, it's an arresting thought to realize that you probably wouldn't have been if you'd married in the 1950s. Even differences that seem pretty small now—a Methodist marrying a Catholic, say—just didn't happen all that often then. In the late 1950s, as few as one in five marriages was between people with different religious beliefs. Two generations later, the frequency of mixed-belief marriages has skyrocketed. Nearly half of the weddings since 2000 (45%) have joined people with different religious views.[6]

Faith in Flux

Religions address the biggest and most difficult questions of all: Does a God or gods exist? What is the origin and fate of the universe? What is the meaning and purpose of our lives? What is the nature and cause of goodness and evil? What happens to us after we die? It would take much more than a human lifetime to consider these questions in all of the detail they deserve.

That's not to say we can't form opinions about what the answers are, and we certainly do. But over the course of a lifetime, our opinions on these huge, complex questions often change.

Still, we usually think of religious identity in fixed terms: My friend *is* a Mormon; my sister *is* a Hindu; my uncle *is* an atheist. This wasn't far off the mark in the past, as people tended to stick with the religion they were born into. That's not so anymore: 44% of Americans now have a different religious (or nonreligious) identity than the one they were born and raised in. They also change religions "early and often," according to the Pew Research Center, most changing before they're 24 and many changing more than once.[7]

As a result of this game of musical pews, religious identity for most people is no longer tied as tightly to personal identity and family roots as it once was. This relaxes one of the longstanding barriers to mixed-belief marriage. If you left your family's faith community yourself, it's not as unthinkable to marry outside of that community as it would otherwise be.

The dynamic is every bit as true for those with no religious affiliation—the "Nones." Nones are a very fluid category, says Robert Putnam in *American Grace.* He and his coauthor, David Campbell, conducted the landmark Faith Matters Survey in 2006, then checked in again with the same cohort in 2007. Of those who called themselves "Nones" in the 2006 survey, only 70% said the same in 2007. Almost a third had picked up a specific religious identity. But they were replaced by a roughly equal number who started calling themselves Nones. Intriguingly, they most often step in and out of the unaffiliated category without changing *anything* else about themselves. Very few people who discarded or acquired a religious affiliation between 2006 and 2007 experienced any other significant change in religious belief or practice. "The only thing that changed," say Putnam and Campbell, "was how they described their religious identity."[8]

It's like a giant religious Hokey Pokey.

"These folks seem to be standing at the edge of a religious tradition, half in and half out," says Putnam. "Sometimes we catch them thinking of themselves as a 'something' (Baptist or Catholic or whatever), and other times they think of themselves as a 'None.'"[9]

Even those who stay nonreligious often pass through a number of "types" in their lives. One nonbeliever might begin by describing himself as an agnostic, then redefine as an atheist (or even antitheist) for many years, becoming more confrontational with religious ideas, before adopting a more conciliatory, humanistic approach. Others reverse that curve, or turn it inside out. "The typology of nonbelief is fluid," says Christopher Silver, a University of Tennessee researcher who established the first comprehensive type model of nonbelievers. "Based on our interviews, we suspect people transverse the various types over the course of their lives."[10] As we'll see in Chapter 3, nonbelief is every bit as flexible and changeable an identity as belief.

Another change—often overlooked but arguably even more common than complete changes of religious identity—is a change in the intensity of engagement with one's religious or nonreligious identity. A cradle Catholic becomes nonpracticing as a young adult, only to reengage her Catholicism with the birth of her child, sometimes more deeply than ever before. An agnostic teenager becomes more of an active atheist in his twenties, or an aggressive atheist becomes a more moderate, coexisting secular humanist. A staunch Mormon or Baptist gradually becomes more progressive in time, or a progressive Mormon or Baptist becomes more conservative.

There's no end to the possibilities and the ways these changes can influence a secular/religious mixed marriage. Sometimes a change widens the gap between partners, and sometimes it decreases it. Fewer than one-third of individuals in these mixed marriages report no change in identity or intensity since marriage. One-third changed from religious to nonreligious or vice versa, and one-third reported a change in the intensity of their engagement.

Changing Labels and Intensities in the Secular/Religious Mixed Marriage

→ *No change in religious identity or intensity since marriage: 29%*

→ *Changed identity completely (religious to nonreligious or vice versa): 33%*

→ *Kept identity but became less intense: 5%*

→ *Kept identity but became more intense: 29%*[11]

It's Who You Know

In the past it wasn't unusual for someone to grow up, go to school, live, play, work, and die surrounded only by people with the same religion. Though the United States likes to think of itself as a melting pot, for most of its history it's really been more of a mosaic. Instead of melting into each other to create a new amalgam, different racial, cultural, and religious pieces have tended to keep their own shape while resting (sometimes uncomfortably) next to other identities, interlocking without mixing. As each wave of immigrants settled in, they tended to group with others of their national origin, which usually also meant a shared religion. This was sometimes by choice, sometimes by economic necessity, and sometimes by law or to escape persecution—Jewish immigrants in New York City, Catholics in Maryland, Quakers in Pennsylvania, and on and on.

Imagine a Catholic girl growing up in South Boston in the 1950s. She could get well into her twenties before meeting anybody who didn't go to Mass every Sunday and have a saint's name. She'd probably have all Catholic peers, teachers, and family members. So when it came time to marry—age 20 on average at that time—it stands to reason that she'd almost always marry a Catholic. How could she not? But it would have much less to do with any conscious rejection of people of other faiths than with their absence from her daily life.

This is self-perpetuating, of course. If you were born Catholic, and every Catholic you knew was married to a Catholic, you'd see Catholics as marriageable and others as unthinkable. Same with any religion, race, or almost any other human difference.

American mobility has changed this picture dramatically. The average American now moves 11.7 times in a lifetime.[12] Combine that with social and economic mobility, and the churning of American society starts to look more like the melting pot we always thought we were. We now live, work, and play in the midst of difference unimaginable to our grandparents.

College is another powerful mixer, the first place many people experience a real diversity of religious and nonreligious (and racial and political) identities. College attendance has more than tripled since the 1950s, meaning a lot more people are surrounded by peers of other perspectives right around the age they're thinking about potential mates.

As a result of all this mixing, most Americans are now exposed to a variety of religious and nonreligious perspectives. Only 7% now say all of their neighbors share the same religion, and only 16% say most of them do. That leaves an astonishing 77% who report that most of their neighbors have a different religion from their own.[13]

That's not your granddaddy's America.

Family understandably lags the larger society, but it's still less uniform than you'd think. Fewer than a third of respondents in the Faith Matters Survey said their family members all share the same religious identity— 29% said most do, but not all, whereas a full 40% said only some or none of their family members have the same religion.[14]

Fewer than one in three Americans are in a family with a uniform religious identity, and more than three-fourths have at least one close friend of a different religion.

The same is true of our close friends. When asked how many of their five closest friends had the same religion they did, only 24% said they all shared a religion. That means more than three out of four Americans now have at least one close friend of another religious perspective—a dramatic change from two or three generations ago.[15]

Putnam and Campbell put it succinctly. We don't just have a vague awareness of religious difference: Unlike previous generations, most Americans are now intimately acquainted with people of other faiths and with no faith at all. This leads to something social psychologists call "re-fencing"—a first step in abandoning a stereotype. If you dislike or distrust a certain group, then find out someone you know and love is part of that group—gay, Muslim, atheist, Democrat, Mets fan, whatever—you may not immediately tear down the fence that separates you from the disliked group. Instead, you see your friend as an exception, and you "re-fence" just a bit so he or she is on your side after all. The Faith Matters researchers call this the "Aunt Susan Principle":

> We all have an Aunt Susan in our lives, the sort of person who epit-omizes what it means to be a saint, but whose religious background is different from our own. Maybe you are Jewish and she is a Methodist. Or perhaps you are Catholic and Aunt Susan is not reli-gious at all. But whatever her religious background (or lack thereof), you know that Aunt Susan is destined for heaven. And if she is going to heaven, what does that say about other people who share her reli-gion or lack of religion? Maybe they can go to heaven too.[16]

If your social and family connections include religious diversity, you will tend to think more positively about other religions. As Putnam and Campbell put it, "When birds of different feathers flock together, they come to trust one another."[17]

The nonreligious and Mainline Protestants are the most likely to live in that religious mix. Latino Catholics, Mormons, and black Protestants are the least likely to have friends and relatives of other religions.

Who Intermarries Whom?

Given all that mixing, it's not surprising that 27% of all couples currently married or in long-term relationships have two different worldviews.[18] And given the rapid rise of the unaffiliated—from 8% in 1990 to 19.6% in 2012—it's also clear that a large and growing number of these mixed cou-ples include a nonreligious partner. In fact, the religiously unaffiliated are the most likely to intermarry—59% of married Americans who claim no religious affiliation are married to someone who does.[19]

Buddhists are next in line: 55% of married Buddhists in the United States have a partner who isn't Buddhist, and 27% are married to someone who is religiously unaffiliated.

Mainline Protestants come in third. Just under half (46%) are married to non-Protestants, and 8% have an unaffiliated spouse.

The religiously unaffiliated are the most likely to intermarry: 59% of married Americans who claim no religious affiliation are married to someone who does.

Mormons and Hindus are the least likely to marry a partner outside their own faith (17% and 10%, respectively), and only 5% of Mormons and 3% of Hindus are married to someone who is unaffiliated.[20]

One result of the U.S. Religious Landscape Survey that seems surprising at first is the intermarriage rate for Jehovah's Witnesses. "Most Witnesses tend to think of society outside their own community as decadent and corrupt. . . . This in turn means to Jehovah's Witnesses that they must keep themselves apart from Satan's 'doomed system of things,'" says James Penton, a scholar of Witness history. "Thus most tend to socialize largely, although not totally, within the Witness community."[21] Marrying outside of the religion is discouraged, and marrying an outright nonbeliever is strongly discouraged—yet 36% of Jehovah's Witnesses are married to non–Jehovah's Witnesses, including 15% with religiously unaffiliated partners. But there is some sense to this. Witnesses don't practice infant baptism, and even those raised as Witnesses aren't bound to Witness restrictions unless and until they choose to be baptized. Because so many join the religion as adults, many Witnesses belonged to other religions or no religion prior to becoming a Witness, and many were already married to someone of a different belief system.

Seeing Past the News Paradox

Despite the growing interactions among people of different faiths and between the religious and nonreligious, and the lessening intensity of religious believers, the stereotypes of nonbelievers as extremists and intransigents continue, in large part because of what I call the "news paradox."

When you see something in the news, it's natural to think it represents reality. But the fact that something is in the news means it's *newsworthy*, which almost always means it is *not common*.

Hundreds of stories about mad cow disease in the 1990s had American consumers terrified of their burgers, despite just three confirmed U.S. cases of the disease. Stories about child abductions make us watch our kids like hawks, even though the rate of child abduction—always incredibly small—is currently at its lowest rate ever.[22]

Car crashes happen every day, so they are rarely in the news. But plane crashes are incredibly rare, so we hear about each and every one in graphic detail. The result? We race down the freeway without a care in the world, risking a very common death, but fear air travel, the safest travel of all.

The same thing applies to religion and atheism. Stereotypes of believers and nonbelievers are reinforced because both are brought to our attention not when they do something typical, but when they do something extremely atypical.

Every religious believer who burns a Qur'an, kills an abortion provider, or carries a sign reading "God Hates Fags" is brought to our attention, while the vast majority of moderate religious people remain out of view, most of them shaking their own heads at the extremists.

Several religious blog groups do more than shake their heads. One of my favorites, at christianstiredofbeingmisrepresented.blogspot.com, is called Christians Tired of Being Misrepresented. It isn't misrepresentation from the outside they are tired of, but misrepresentation by other Christians. "We are Christians who are tired of being misrepresented by right-wing fundamentalists who have hijacked Christianity and over the course of many years made it into the complete opposite of Christ's teachings."[23] They are tired of the fact that religious fundamentalism has come to define their worldview in the popular mind, thanks in large part to the news paradox. Another group called the NALT (Not All Like That) Christians Project is specifically devoted to showing that not all Christians are homophobic or oppose equal rights for gays and lesbians.

Of course, the news paradox distorts the other side, too. When a prominent atheist picks up dog feces using a Bible or calls religious believers "Christards" (a doubly ignorant and offensive slur), the media pick it up and the stereotype of the angry, intolerant atheist is reinforced—even though most atheists are equally outraged at this kind of thing. But just as with the religious, the moderate, tolerant atheists are drowned out by the newsworthy nonsense.

Among my favorite blogs working to counter the stereotype of angry, intolerant atheism is Non-Prophet Status (nonprophetstatus.com). NPS is the brainchild of Chris Stedman, one of the leaders of a movement within atheism that emphasizes common ground with the religious and the constructive expression of secular values. Stedman still has his differences with religion—he simply chooses to emphasize the common ground, believing that is the best path forward.

Regardless of your own perspective, reading these two blogs, as well as the other blogs they link to, is a good first step in getting past the stereotypes reinforced by the news paradox—even the stereotypes we carry of those who share our own views.

Seeing Past Doctrines

When I ask others if they know what their partner believes, I always get a puzzled expression. "Of course I do. He's a Christian," they'll say, or, "Sure, she's an atheist." We take these labels to be statements of belief, but they fall well short of that. Even if you get more specific—"He's a Missouri Synod Lutheran"—you won't necessarily be any closer to understanding what the person actually believes, only the doctrines of his denomination— or in the case of the atheist, the bare-bones definition of atheism. Most people never get around to actually asking their partners what *exactly* they believe is true.

As we'll see in the next chapter, most people who claim a religious label diverge dramatically from the official beliefs of their churches, and more so all the time. Even if it was once safe to assume a higher level of continuity between the written doctrines of a belief system and the actual beliefs of the people in the pews, that assumption no longer holds up. This doesn't mean the average religious practitioner is "less religious," just that she's more likely to express her beliefs in ways that are more fluid and individual, less orthodox and doctrinaire.

Seeing Purple

Ask just about anyone about polarization in American politics and you'll hear that we are more polarized than ever. The middle has dropped out, leaving two extremes—liberal and conservative, red states and blue—with little common ground.

But an eye-opening *Economist* article noted that when you look through any demographic lens other than party, the gap between liberals and conservatives is no wider today than it was decades ago, with individuals spread all the way through the middle of the spectrum. But when you have only two major political parties offering candidates and positions that are diametrically opposed, you get the false appearance of a wide gap in attitudes. It's called "party sorting": Liberals and left-leaning moderates all head over to the Democratic candidates, while conservatives and right-leaning moderates head over to the Republican side, leaving a big, misleading gap in the middle. If there was a political party in that middle, the huge number of political moderates might have a better home for their actual views.[24]

Think of the red state/blue state political map, which reinforces the same idea. Barack Obama won Florida with 50.01%, and Romney earned 49.13%. North Carolina flipped just slightly the other way: 50.1% Romney, 48.4% Obama. But because of our winner-take-all electoral system, Florida went bright blue and North Carolina went bright red. Two states that were almost identical to each other were painted as polar opposites on the map.

To show how false this polarization is, Princeton mathematician Robert Vanderbei created a map that colored every county in the United States not red or blue, but an appropriate shade of *purple* depending on the margin of victory in that county. The resulting map, dubbed "Purple America," is a much better representation of the real diversity of political opinion in every corner of the country. As a blue voter in a "red" state, I appreciated that.

Seeing Purple in Major Social Issues

With the exception of white Evangelicals, majorities of all major religious groups say they identify to some degree with both the "pro-life" and "pro-choice" positions.[25]

So what on earth does all this have to do with religion, or with mixed-belief marriage?

Religious labels create the same false impression of polarization. "Christian" and "atheist" are the equivalent of red and blue, implying a polar difference between individuals that's almost never true.

One of the best tools to bring out the "purple" in our religious beliefs is the Belief-O-Matic quiz at Beliefnet.com. The quiz asks 20 multiple-choice worldview questions, then generates a list of belief systems and the percentage of overlap your beliefs have with each one. It's a powerful and fun way to show that we all have more in common with each other than we ever would have guessed.

I take the quiz every year. Last time I was 100% secular humanist and 92% Unitarian Universalist, but also pretty darn Buddhist (73%). I shared 60% of the beliefs and values of Mainline Protestants—none of the theology, of course, but much of the rest. For some reason I'm less Jewish than I was a few years ago, but a little more Catholic (up from 16% to 18%). Not sure what that's about, but there it is.

A Southern Baptist friend of mine took the quiz and found that her beliefs lined up better with Orthodox Quakerism (100%) than with her own church (94%). And she was surprised to learn that she shares 54% of her beliefs and values with the creedless Unitarians—an interesting bridge between the two of us.

Overlapping Beliefs

If you're in a mixed-belief marriage of any kind, and even if you aren't, drop everything and take the Belief-O-Matic quiz at Beliefnet.com. Compare your results to your partner's or your friends' and relatives'. It brings out the purple in everyone.[26]

Getting the Secular/Religious Picture: The McGowan-Sikes Survey

Many of the results of the McGowan-Sikes survey of 994 people in secular/religious marriages ran counter to common assumptions about this mix—and often in a very good way.

The length of marriage among the survey respondents varied from couples in the first year of a relationship to those in their 45th year, with an average of 10 years—two years longer than the current U.S. average. And note that the 10-year figure for the secular/religious marriage isn't even marking the average *end* of those marriages, but the average *length so far*. Most of those are still going strong, blowing even further past the national average of eight years.

There are at least two reasons to believe this interpretation is on target:

1. Later marriages tend to be more stable, and the later you marry, the more likely you are to marry outside of your own belief community.

Age at marriage turns out to be a crucial number in the staying power of a marriage and the risk of divorce. Get married at 19 and your odds of divorce are about 40%. Wait until you are 25 and that risk drops sharply to 24%.[27]

In 1960, the average age at first marriage was 20 for women and 23 for men. By 1990 it was 24 for women and 26 for men. Today it's 27 for women and 29 for men, well beyond that crucial line. And sure enough, as the average age at marriage has risen, the divorce rate has steadily dropped for the past 20 years.

Average age at marriage for respondents to the McGowan-Sikes survey: 27.

Now add to the rising average age at marriage the fact that the older you are when you marry, the more likely you are to marry someone with different beliefs:

→ Of those who married at age 16–25, 48% are in mixed-belief marriages.

→ Of those who married at age 26–35, 58% are in mixed-belief marriages.

→ Of those who married at age 36–45, 67% are in mixed-belief marriages.[28]

That may seem strange at first, since younger generations are more likely to be comfortable with mixed marriages of all kinds, including race and religion. So why would older newlyweds be mixing it up at higher rates?

Again, it's who you know. When you're young, you're less likely to have mingled with people of different backgrounds and beliefs. Your pool of prospective partners gets more diverse during and after college or once you start your career than it was when you were 18. Add the fact that orthodox religious believers (who tend to marry within the faith) are often encouraged to marry young, and the older average age of mixed-belief couples—and the stability that comes with that later start—makes perfect sense.

2. Research suggests that mixed-belief couples often communicate better than same-belief couples.

Marriage researchers call it "dyadic consensus"—the ability to communicate effectively and come to agreement about important issues—and several studies indicate that mixed-belief couples show greater strength in dyadic consensus than couples who share the same beliefs. Researchers hypothesize that couples with different religious backgrounds confront issues that call for effective communication right out of the gate. They tend to develop effective communication skills because they have to, and those skills carry over into other aspects of the relationship. (More on dyadic consensus in Chapter 17.)

The Bottom Line

Marriages and other relationships between religious and nonreligious partners take place in a context that's constantly changing in ways that make those relationships less unusual and more likely to succeed. That doesn't mean that there are no real challenges—and sometimes unresolvable hurdles—in mixed-belief marriages. But there is cause for optimism.

The next two chapters continue filling in the big picture by introducing religious believers and nonbelievers as they really are, not as their most newsworthy public faces make us *think* they are.

2

Meet the Believers

The early days of a new papacy have to be a little bit nerve-wracking for the Vatican. It must take time and practice for someone to make the mental transition to one of the most unique jobs on earth. Once in a while, the opinions of the pre-papal man peek out from behind the miter.

One such moment happened on May 22, 2013, when during a homily just ten weeks into his pontificate, Pope Francis said, "The Lord has redeemed all of us, all of us, with the Blood of Christ: all of us, not just Catholics. Everyone! 'Father, the atheists?' Even the atheists. Everyone!"

The idea that everyone is redeemed by the sacrifice of Christ regardless of his or her beliefs is called *universalism*—and it's an absolute heresy in the Catholic Church. *Extra Ecclesiam nulla salus* ("Outside the Church there is no salvation") is one of the principles on which Catholicism stands. So the media naturally went wild with shock and delight at the new pope's apparent willingness to flout orthodoxy.

Within 24 hours, the Vatican rolled the statement back, quoting from the Catechism, a detailed statement of official Catholic doctrine: " 'Outside the Church there is no salvation' . . . means that all salvation comes from Christ, the Head, through the Church which is his body. Hence they cannot be saved who, knowing the Church as founded by Christ and necessary for salvation, would refuse to enter her or remain in her."

Bummer. But as the story played out in the media, I noticed that most of the surprise over what the pope said had come from non-Catholics. My Catholic friends mostly shrugged. This was just a high-profile example of something most Catholics already know—that "Catholic beliefs" and the beliefs of Catholics are often very different things. Many still hold to the traditional doctrines of the Church, of course, including the pope on most days. But you can't just read the Catechism and think you've understood what's in the mind or heart of any given Catholic. And that matters a lot in mixed marriages.

A diversity of opinion in the ranks goes way beyond Catholicism. The purpose of this chapter is to introduce religious believers of all kinds in a way most of us rarely see them, challenging the idea of religion as a monolith. Taking a close look at the wide range of actual beliefs and practices among the religious dispels the simple cartoon of believers, making it easier to picture a religious person building a successful and happy marriage with a nonbeliever.

Like many misconceptions, the cartoon is based on the loud, extreme examples of the faithful who crowd out the quieter, more moderate majority, or it comes from reading official doctrines instead of asking flesh-and-blood people how they see the world.

It isn't only nonbelievers who make this kind of generalization. Many religious believers also see their own worldview through the distorting lens of the extremists and consider themselves exceptions.

Americans Are Getting Less Extreme, Not More

It's helpful to picture every worldview label or statement of doctrine with an asterisk leading to a footnote saying, *Your results may vary.* Though nine in ten Americans hold religious beliefs of some kind, most don't remotely identify with the Religious Right or the loud intolerance of fundamentalists like Pat Robertson and Jerry Falwell, much less the hate-mongering of Fred "God Hates Fags" Phelps.

Given the huge success of the "Moral Majority" in the 1980s and the political clout of Evangelicals, it's easy to think that religious fundamentalism in the United States is on the rise, but by several measures it's actually losing ground. A survey of 35,000 Americans by the Pew Forum on Religion and Public Life found that most Americans are steadily trending away from religious fundamentalism and the intolerance and inflexibility that goes with it. Biblical literalism overall is down from 66% in 1963 to 30% in 2008, and most religious believers, including majorities of almost every denomination, do not believe that their religion is the only way to salvation—a major indicator of tolerance and the ability to play well with others.[1] Only in Mormonism and Jehovah's Witnesses (2.4% of the U.S. population combined) do most members still think theirs is the only path to salvation.

All of this tolerance doesn't mean religious believers are becoming "less religious." The same survey shows that more than half of Americans say that religion is very important in their lives, that they attend religious services regularly, and that they pray every day.

If you want to see a clear illustration of this change in what it means to be religious, look no further than Muncie, Indiana, a town so typical and reflective of average American attitudes and opinions that it's been dubbed "Middletown USA" and studied more than any other town in the country. Every year for the past 90 years, all high school graduates in Muncie have been surveyed, and many of the questions have been identically worded. In 1924, 94% of respondents agreed with the statement, "Christianity is the one true religion and all people should be converted to it." By 1977, agreement had dropped to 38%—even though Muncie was more religious in the 1970s than in the 1920s *by every measure.*[2]

That's an illustration of one of the key points of this book: Marriages between religious and nonreligious partners aren't more common and successful because religious people are "less religious" than they were in the past. It's (in part) because *being religious* is different today than it was in the past. There are still plenty of dogmatic religious conservatives out there, but study after study shows a rising trend in the direction of liberal, progressive expressions of religion—the kind that embrace beliefs without necessarily holding that everyone else has to do the same. The kind where bumper stickers say "Coexist" instead of "Real Men Love Jesus."

Maybe you can see why this trend is good news for the secular/religious mix.

Meet the Catholics

I started the chapter with a story about Pope Francis coloring outside of the Vatican lines and implied that he's far from alone among Catholics in doing that. Now let's look at the research to support that idea.

When it comes to correcting our misconceptions about what religious people actually believe, Catholicism is a good place to start. For one thing,

Catholicism comes with an owner's manual—the Catechism of the Catholic Church, a clear set of official doctrines and beliefs against which the actual beliefs of individuals can be compared. And because Catholics make up 25% of the U.S. population, including people in every region and every level of income, class, education, and race, a clearer picture of actual, individual Catholic belief will be a big step toward understanding religious belief in the United States generally.

Catholicism also has special relevance to the secular/religious marriage. Whether currently religious or not, 22% of those in secular/religious marriages were raised in Catholic families—more than twice the number who were raised Baptist, the second most common upbringing (10%). And 20% of those in secular/religious marriages were Catholic at the time of their marriage, more than double the second most common (Independent Christian, 8%).[3] A Pew Research Center study on religion switching found that 27% of the religiously unaffiliated overall were raised Catholic—again, the largest by a mile among denominations.[4]

If someone's knowledge of Catholics and Catholicism is limited to the news and *The Da Vinci Code*, it's easy to think of the whole religion as hidebound ritual and inflexible beliefs—two things that would seem to make it a poor fit for a secular/religious marriage. To see why that's not the case, we need to compare the beliefs of U.S. Catholics with the doctrines of the Catholic Church as found in that "owner's manual": the Catechism of the Catholic Church.

The current Catechism isn't some ancient medieval treatise. It's a modern document, a teaching tool first published in 1992—the year Bill Clinton was elected president and Miley Cyrus was born. Because it's a statement of Catholic beliefs, you might assume that it also represents what your Catholic friend, neighbor, relative, or partner believes. If that were the case, your friend/neighbor/relative/partner would (among other things) believe that:

→ "[H]omosexual acts are intrinsically disordered" matters of "grave depravity" that are "contrary to the natural law . . . under no circumstances can they be approved."

→ Birth control is "intrinsically evil."

→ "[D]ivorce is a grave offense against the natural law," and a "remarried spouse is then in a situation of public and permanent adultery."

→ Abortion is without exception a "moral evil" that is "gravely contrary to the moral law."[5]

Those are among the official beliefs and positions spelled out in the Catechism. If they were also the beliefs of all U.S. Catholics, it wouldn't bode well for a Catholic/nonreligious mixed marriage. Most secular Americans strongly support gay rights, believe that birth control is a good thing and should be widely available, believe that divorce and remarriage should carry no stigma, and feel that abortion should be safe and legal (though opinions on additional restrictions vary). These are deeply felt social issues, and several studies show that couples who differ substantially on key social and political issues are at greater risk of divorce from that difference than from almost any other risk factor.

Fortunately for the Catholic/nonreligious marriage, American Catholics tend to be much closer to the nonreligious on these issues than they are to the Catholic Catechism. Despite the Catechism's strict antigay stance, American Catholics overall are even more progressive in their attitudes toward lesbian, gay, bisexual, and transgender (LGBT) rights than the U.S. average,[6] 82% of U.S. Catholics consider birth control "morally acceptable,"[7] 69% consider it acceptable to differ from the teachings of the Church on divorce and remarriage, and American Catholics closely mirror the general population on abortion rights.[8] In fact, there's a good chance a progressive Catholic will clash more with a conservative Catholic than with another progressive entirely outside of her faith.

Belief That Humans and Other Living Things Have Evolved over Time[9]

Unaffiliated	85%
Mainline Protestant	66%
Catholic	65%
Evangelical	35%
General	61%

Conservative Catholics often complain that this kind of "cafeteria Catholicism" isn't Catholicism at all—that the catechetical doctrines lie at the heart of what it means to be Catholic. You can't just pick and choose, they say. But it's important to note that differing from the doctrine doesn't make the respondents any less Catholic in their *own* eyes. Quite the opposite: 77% of American Catholics say they are proud to claim that identity, even those who depart dramatically from the official positions of their church.[10] As Anna LaNave, national coordinator of Landings International, a ministry to inactive Catholics, puts it, "Once you're baptized into the Catholic faith, anyone who says 'I am Catholic' is Catholic."

Even when the topic is God and the Bible, the difference between Catholics and seculars is not nearly as absolute as you might think. According to the U.S. Religious Landscape Survey:

→ More than one in four U.S. Catholics (26%) are "agnostic Catholics"—less than certain God exists.

→ Just 23% of U.S. Catholics believe the Bible is God's literal truth.[11]

Agnostic and nonpracticing Catholics are by no means the only Catholics who make successful secular/religious marriages. But their existence shows how far the spectrum extends, and that a much larger swath of that spectrum includes common ground between the religious and the non-religious than either side tends to realize. As a result, the idea of a Catholic marrying someone who is nonreligious isn't half as problematic as it seems.

Meet the Protestants

It's even harder to capture the beliefs of Protestants in a single net than Catholics. Catholicism at least has an official unifying doctrinal statement, even if most Catholics don't adhere to it. But no catechism covers all of the denominations under the Protestant banner, much less the tens of millions of individuals in those denominations.

Pollsters usually divide Protestants into at least three broad categories:

1. Mainline Protestants. These include the United Methodist, Presbyterian, Episcopal, and American Baptist churches, as well as the United Church of Christ and several others. Despite its name, the Evangelical Lutheran Church in America, the largest of the Lutheran denominations, is not Evangelical but Mainline in its orientation. Mainline churches tend to put more emphasis on social justice than Evangelical churches.

For most of U.S. history, Mainline Protestants were the religious majority. Their numbers peaked in the 1950s but have declined since then.

As of 2009, about 15% of American adults (about 20 million) identify with a Mainline Protestant denomination.[12]

2. Protestant Evangelical. These churches are generally built on four priorities:

→ Spiritual rebirth—becoming a "born-again Christian"

→ A high degree of biblical literalism

→ A focus on redemption through Christ

→ Sharing of faith to convert others (evangelism)

Evangelicals tend to place a greater emphasis on theology and salvation (as opposed to social justice) than Mainline churches, though even that tendency varies. Evangelical denominations include Southern Baptist, Southern Methodist, Pentecostal, and Missouri Synod Lutheran.

3. Black Protestant. These are churches in which congregations are predominantly African American. Some entire denominations fall into this category, including the African Methodist Episcopal (AME) Church, the National Baptist Convention, and the Church of God in Christ, while some black Protestant churches fall within mostly white denominations.

Though not unified under a single set of doctrines, black Protestant churches tend to have a greater focus on social justice issues than white Evangelicals, though the two do overlap in some areas, including a tendency to oppose gay rights.

Biblical literalism overall dropped from 66% in 1963 to 30% in 2008.[13]

The key to understanding all this diversity is to go beyond doctrines to see what individuals actually hold true. Even if the official beliefs of this or that denomination continue to show an abyss between their members and nonbelievers, surveys of individuals show a great overlap in values between Protestants and their secular friends and neighbors—much larger than either seculars or Protestants tend to realize. Simply put, moderate and liberal Protestant values and even beliefs have more in common with secular values and beliefs than they do with the values and beliefs of Protestant fundamentalists.

The implications for the secular/religious marriage are huge.

If a Protestant believes that only his or her religion leads to eternal life and that every word of the Bible is literally true, opposes gay rights and abortion rights, supports capital punishment, and thinks that religious nonbelievers are beyond redemption, he or she isn't as likely to have a successful marriage with a nonbeliever as a liberal Protestant would be. Many Protestants do hold these more conservative views, even in the Mainline churches, but they are in the minority, as the following statistics show.

Among Mainline Protestants:

→ Just 22% believe every word of the Bible is literally true.

→ Just 12% believe that only his or her own religion leads to eternal life.

→ More than three-quarters (79%) believe that even non-Christians can go to heaven.

→ Over half (62%) say even someone who is nonreligious can go.

→ Nearly half (46%) say that even an outright atheist can go to heaven.[14]

(For more on why this idea matters, see "Accepting the Ultimate Compliment" near the end of this chapter.)

Mainline Protestants are also close to the national average and not far from secular Americans on the key social issues of our time. Among Mainline Protestants:

→ 70% support stem cell research.[15]

→ 63% think abortion should be legal in most cases.[16]

→ 62% support gay marriage.[17]

→ 66% believe humans and other living things have evolved over time.[18]

But what about Evangelicals? You might assume that the common ground falls away for Evangelical Protestants, leaving that old familiar abyss. Most people think of the Christian Right and the "Moral Majority" when they hear that term, including divisive, high-profile figures like Jerry Falwell and Pat Robertson. "Evangelical" mostly gets airtime when someone demands the Ten Commandments be posted in a courtroom, or claims that God endorsed him for Congress, or agitates to get creationism into the science classroom or prayer into a high school graduation. These aren't positions held by the average nonreligious person, and if they reflected the beliefs of all Protestant Evangelicals, we could safely put the secular/Evangelical marriage on the endangered list.

And though many Evangelicals tend toward fundamentalism, many defy the stereotype and even find common ground with the nonreligious.

One such Evangelical was the woman I married.

My Wife, the Evangelical

There is a Southern Baptist church in Fort Worth, Texas, that holds the Letter of Baptism for my wife, Becca. She was baptized into the church as an adult, as is the practice in the denomination. In technical terms, she wasn't just a Protestant when I married her—she was a Protestant Evangelical.

I love Becca for many reasons, among them her values and the things she holds true. If she ascribed fully to the Baptist Faith and Message, her church's creed,[19] we could still easily have been friends, but I doubt we would have dated, much less married.

She agreed with many elements of the creed, but the Baptist Faith and Message also includes a few important things that she did not agree with one bit. I asked her to go through the creed and indicate, to the best of her recollection, which things she did and did not hold true when we were first married.

This, then, is the reconstructed religious creed of my wife at the time I decided to spend my life with her:

She believed that there is only one God, that he is perfect, all-powerful, and all-knowing, and that man was made in his image. But she never believed that man brought sin into the human race by disobedience, nor that "as soon as [people] are capable of moral action, they become transgressors and are under condemnation."

She believed that Christ was the son of God, but not that he was born of a virgin, nor that salvation is available only through him.

She did not agree that "all Scripture is totally true and trustworthy," nor that "Christianity is the faith of enlightenment and intelligence," and she didn't agree that Sunday should have any special restrictions on behavior that the other days of the week didn't enjoy.

She did believe that baptism is "an act of obedience symbolizing the believer's faith in a crucified, buried, and risen Saviour, the believer's death to sin, the burial of the old life, and the resurrection to walk in newness of life in Christ Jesus," as well as a testimony to "faith in the final resurrection of the dead." But she didn't believe it is "the duty and privilege of every follower of Christ" to evangelize others to the faith, and she didn't think the world would end as described in the Book of Revelation.

She agreed that "Christians should oppose racism, every form of greed, selfishness, and vice"; "work to provide for the orphaned, the needy, the abused, the aged, the helpless, and the sick"; and "do all in their power to put an end to war." But she did not agree that homosexuality is a form of "sexual immorality," that Christians should "speak on behalf of the unborn," nor that the strict definition of marriage should be "the uniting of one man and one woman."

One of the statements of the Baptist Faith and Message that surprises outsiders—and insiders, come to that—is the clear support for church-state separation. "Church and state should be separate," it says, and "the state has no right to impose penalties for religious opinions of any kind." It was a position born in the early years of the denomination, back when Southern Baptist was a minority faith. They knew that any imposed version of God was not likely to be their own. A century later, after Southern Baptists had become the largest Protestant denomination in the country, Baptist politicians began to forget that part of their own creed.

Though Becca didn't know the Baptist Faith and Message embraced separation, she happened to agree with it.

As for marriage and parenting, she never believed that it was her place to "submit herself graciously to the servant leadership of her husband even as the church willingly submits to the headship of Christ," nor that she had "the God-given responsibility to respect her husband and to serve as his helper in managing the household and nurturing the next generation." But she did have a somewhat more conservative parenting approach in the beginning than she would have later, including the belief that children should be taught moral values based on "biblical truth" and should "honor and obey their parents."

By the doctrines she accepted and the ones she rejected, Becca showed herself to be a member of the Evangelical Left.

People on the Evangelical Left generally agree with the basic theology of the church—that God exists, that Christ was his incarnation, and that

Christ died for our sins and will return. They also tend to accept the Bible as the source of church authority, though they differ substantially on how literally it is to be taken. Two very different sets of social and political beliefs flow from that crucial difference. Most on the Evangelical Left (like Becca) oppose war and capital punishment and support gun control, abortion rights, and same-sex marriage just as passionately as their counterparts on the right oppose them—positions that put them in sync with most secular progressives.

If I tallied up my own agreements and disagreements with the Baptist Faith and Message at the time of our marriage, Becca and I would have overlapped by about three-quarters.

"Sure," you might say, "but that remaining quarter includes some pretty big stuff, like God and Jesus, and what happens when we die. Doesn't get much bigger than that."

And there's the question at the heart of the secular/religious marriage: Even if there is some common ground, aren't the remaining differences just too big for the relationship to work? How could any question be bigger than God's existence, how the universe will end, or what happens when we die?

This isn't about the way I see the world—it's about whether I can be in a loving, enduring relationship with someone who sees it differently.

These are indeed huge questions. But *"big" and "important" aren't always the same.* This isn't about the way I see the world—it's about whether I can be in a loving, enduring relationship with someone who sees it differently. And when the question is framed in that way, the "big" theological questions are actually smaller and less important than the social values questions. On those, this atheist and his Evangelical wife had a solid match.

The Many Faces (and Minds) of Judaism

Judaism is a bit of a paradox in the secular/religious marriage, at once welcoming and hostile to the idea.

There's a long history in Judaism of opposing intermarriage of any kind, which makes sense given the history of Jewish religion and culture. From pogroms in the Middle Ages to the Nazi Holocaust to the quieter threat of assimilation, Jewish identity has often faced the possibility of disappearing entirely. Fewer than 14 million people now claim Jewish identity worldwide—just 0.19% of the global population—and only 5.2 million in the United States (1.71%).[20] That's why maintaining the existence of their religious culture has been a higher priority for Jews than for any other major religious group.

So it's not surprising that Jewish voices are among the most prominent opponents of religious intermarriage. Rabbi Kalman Packouz, the author of *How to Prevent an Intermarriage*, mentioned in the introduction, advises Jewish parents of children who enter interfaith marriages to "sit shiva," acting as if their children are dead. He even offers a script:

> Understand that this is not the way we raised you, this is not what we stand for. You have free will, but there are consequences. If you drop a glass, it breaks. Know that you are cutting yourself off from your family. There are other children and we want them to marry Jews. This is what we did for 150 generations. We gave up our lives rather than convert. Don't think you'll be able to drive a wedge into this family. You do what you want, but you have to live with the consequences you create.[21]

Sounds pretty bad for the secular/Jewish mixed marriage, right? But just as with Catholicism and Protestantism, the key to understanding how secular/Jewish intermarriage can work is looking at the full spectrum of the religion, not just the conservative end. As it happens, Judaism contains a stronger acceptance of secularism, including outright religious disbelief, than any other major Western faith.

The structure of Judaism is different from Christianity or Islam. There's no central authority, and there are many separate movements or "streams" within the religion. Of these, five main branches are generally recognized:

1. Orthodox—The most conservative and traditional of the branches, adhering closely to the letter of the Torah.

2. Conservative—A branch much more liberal in practice than the Orthodox but still more conservative (especially in belief) than the reform, reconstructionist, and humanistic branches. I'll return to this one shortly.

3. Reform—A progressive movement that often infuriates the Orthodox by challenging any Jewish traditions, laws, and beliefs that don't fit with modern life. Emphasizes individual autonomy. This is the largest Jewish movement in the United States.

4. Reconstructionist—Even more liberal than Reform, this branch declares that advances in science and society require many of the claims and practices of Judaism to be thrown out. Secular morality trumps Jewish morality, and elements of Jewish religious law are now considered optional "folkways," not laws. God is generally not held to be a conscious being and is not believed able to communicate with us.

5. Humanistic—Unique among the Abrahamic religions, Judaism has a formal branch that is nontheistic. Rituals and ceremonies are more completely purged of theistic language while retaining elements related to Jewish human identity and culture.

That quick summary of the spectrum of Judaism manages to be even more incomplete than my summaries of Catholicism and Protestantism, which is saying something. But remember that my goal is limited: I want to show how surprisingly wide the spectrum of belief and practice is for an assortment of faiths so you can see how each faith fits reasonably into the picture of the secular/religious marriage.

> *I became secular again after talking with the rabbi and gaining insight that I could identify culturally as Jewish but still be an atheist.* —Christopher, secular Jew

You can see from that list that knowing someone is Jewish tells you just as little about what that person actually holds true as knowing that the individual is Catholic or Baptist. Judaism runs a vast spectrum, from the sidelocks and 613 commandments of Orthodox Jewry to Jews who follow only the traditions that speak to them and believe God is nonresponsive or even nonexistent. In fact, the whole spectrum leans hard to the left. Women, gays, and lesbians may serve as rabbis all the way up to the conservative branch, and as of 2012, same-sex marriage is permitted for all but the Orthodox.

Intermarriage has moved a lot more slowly, even among the liberal Jewish movements, but there's progress. Until recently, most rabbis were forbidden to perform intermarriages or even to attend as a guest. Today, though the Orthodox remain entrenched, most reform and reconstructionist rabbis will perform interfaith marriages, attend them, and not even pressure the non-Jewish spouse to convert—though they often still encourage the couple to raise their children as Jews.

Remember that these are all "denominational" or rabbinical positions. Just as American Catholics tend to be much more liberal than their church, so most American Jews are way ahead of the rabbinical doctrines and rules.

The Islamic Spectrum

Islam easily has the worst public perception problem of any religion today. For most non-Muslims in the West, terrorism, intolerance, beheadings, suicide bombings, repressive regimes, and the suppression of women all spring to mind more readily than any positive or even neutral impressions. But like almost all religions, Islam has a wide spectrum in practice and outlook, and although a conservative, traditional Muslim is probably not an ideal match for a secular partner, a large and growing liberal movement within the faith includes many of the same values as other religious and secular progressives.

According to the formal mandates of Islam, Muslim men may marry Muslim, Jewish, or Christian women, but Muslim women may marry only Muslim men, and neither can marry someone who is nonreligious. So for any Muslim conservative enough to embrace that doctrine, the secular/religious marriage is out.

One reason Muslim/secular is worth watching: Compared to other worldviews, Muslims and the unaffiliated are both relatively young. About 3 of 10 Muslims and seculars are under age 30—which means they are also much more likely to embrace liberal, nonexclusive attitudes, including intermarriage.[22]

But more liberal Muslims are not quite so doctrinaire. Like those of any liberal religious wing, followers of progressive Islam tend to wave off such categorical restrictions, relying instead on their own judgment. It's one reflection of a tension in Islam between *taqlid* (following authority) and *ijtihad* (thinking independently). Conservative Muslims lean more heavily on *taqlid*, whereas liberals are more likely to value and practice *ijtihad*. As a result, verses from the Qur'an are interpreted allegorically or even set aside completely by liberal Muslims when they conflict with modern knowledge or values—much like the progressive end of Judaism.

Most liberal Muslims therefore support the equality of all humanity, including full gender equality and LGBT rights. Nonviolence is a key concept, and interfaith dialogue is embraced. Most prefer secular government and the separation of church and state.

Muslim Americans are one of the fastest-growing sectors of the U.S. religious landscape. Even as mainstream Protestants have lost 12% of their members in recent decades, adherents of Islam have seen an estimated growth of 66% in 10 years to a current 2.6 million. And a 2011 Pew Center survey found that these U.S. Muslims are closer to the average American in their situation and values than they are to Muslims worldwide:

→ Whereas 95% of Muslims worldwide report that all or most of their close friends are Muslim, just 50% of U.S. Muslims say the same.

→ Most U.S. Muslims (56%) believe that many religions can lead to eternal life, a percentage approaching that of the general U.S. population (65%). Globally, just 18% of Muslims agree.

→ 59% of U.S. Muslims see religion and science as compatible—far more than U.S. Christians (39%) or the general public (37%).[23]

LGBT acceptance is one area in which Muslims lag the U.S. public— 39% of U.S. Muslims consider homosexuality "acceptable," compared with 60% of the general public.[24]

→ → →

By now the pattern should be clear: The attitudes and values of any religious person can't be assumed to match the scriptures or official doctrines of their faith. Every major faith has a large and growing liberal expression—millions of people whose attitudes and values overlap those of secular friends and neighbors more than traditionalists of their own religion.

Not all denominations are good candidates for the secular/religious mix. Though individuals still vary, Mormons and Jehovah's Witnesses are among the religious identities that show the highest levels of tension and conflict in relationships with nonreligious partners. They are also among the least likely to believe that atheists are candidates for eternal life—at least not the good kind.

Going East—Hinduism and Buddhism

Most religions have a single founding moment, then splinter into factions. Hinduism was just the opposite. It began as a huge umbrella bringing together many different Indian traditions under a single name. And unlike the Christian church, which held conclaves in the early days to decide on a core of beliefs, the many religious groups under the Hindu umbrella didn't lose their different traditions and beliefs. Individual freedom of belief is a given in Hinduism, and heresy is pretty much unheard of. A Hindu may believe in one god or many gods—up to 320 million by one count—or no gods at all.

Such variety can make for an interesting mix. One friend of mine described the strange dynamic in his own family: "My mom is a Hindu who detests rituals and temples, and my dad is an atheist who appreciates ritual and comes from a temple-loving family."

> *Hinduism is a very flexible, personal set of beliefs and rituals, so like most Hindus, Dhanya doesn't impress her beliefs on others. She eats vegetarian food on Mondays and Thursdays and no beef or pork at any time, and she prays every morning, lighting incense and a candle and singing a few Sanskrit hymns. It's very much a ritual and not a prayer as in asking a god for something. When somebody is born or dies, there are other rituals to be done following the occasion.* —Scott (nonreligious), on the Hinduism of his wife, Dhanya

A religion with all that diversity in its own ranks, including agnostic and atheistic branches, doesn't present much in the way of doctrinal opposition to intermarriage. But interestingly, Hindus in the United States are still among the least likely to intermarry—90% of Hindus marry other Hindus—though this is mostly for cultural rather than religious reasons.[25]

Buddhism offers one of the easiest fits with a nontheistic partner, in part because Buddhism was nontheistic from its founding. Some forms of Buddhism today include reference to superhuman beings, or *devas*, but these have neither the powers nor the other characteristics typical of gods in most other religions. Some Buddhist teachings even caution that theistic beliefs and the desires that accompany them can get in the way of achieving *nirvana*, the total freedom from suffering that is the goal of Buddhist practice. Instead, like several other Indian and Chinese philosophies, Buddhism emphasizes the effect our actions have on the people and world around us.

Departing from Doctrine

→ *Two-thirds of Evangelicals (67%) said they could differ with church teaching on abortion, and just under half (47%) said the same about homosexuality.*

→ *Legal abortion services are supported by majorities of white Mainline Protestants (72%), the religiously unaffiliated (71%), white Catholics (58%), and black Protestants (56%).*

→ *Significant majorities of Mainline Protestants (85%), Catholics (78%), black Protestants (74%), and Evangelicals (62%) support comprehensive sex education in public schools.[26]*

Accepting the Ultimate Compliment: Who Goes to Heaven?

When Pope Francis said even atheists are redeemed and go to heaven, some atheists asked why they should care whether they are admitted to a place they don't believe exists. I thought that entirely missed the point. It was a great compliment and a lovely gesture, expressed using language and concepts that are meaningful to the speaker, even if they aren't to me.

Americans who think:

→ *At least one non-Christian religion can go to heaven: 80%*

→ *The nonreligious can go to heaven: 56%*

→ *Atheists can go to heaven: 42%[27]*

Here's an analogy: Suppose while visiting a mountain-dwelling tribe in Peru you hear that they believe all people who are truly good at heart exude a blue aura that's visible only to the elders of the tribe. As you sit down to your first meal with them, one of the elders announces that you are clearly good at heart because you have the blue aura. The other elders around the table nod in agreement.

My guess is that you'd take it as a great compliment, even if you don't believe in the aura. What matters is the opinion the elders have formed of you, an opinion they've expressed as the highest compliment in their worldview.

Likewise, when the pope says atheists can go to heaven (and 49% of Catholics agree with him), or when 26% of Evangelicals or 46% of Mainline

Protestants say the same, most people, including atheists, can recognize this as the ultimate compliment a Christian can give and accept it graciously.

The Bottom Line: Seeing Religious Believers More Clearly

When most people consider the secular/religious mixed marriage, they think of the religious partner in traditional, doctrinal terms and on that basis declare such a marriage a terrible idea. But knowing that more than 40% of religious Americans think atheists go to heaven, that even larger portions agree more with secular positions on social issues than with the doctrines of their own churches, and that the vast majority of Americans now grow up, go to school, and live and work with people of many worldviews makes it easier to understand why these marriages are so often successful and happy.

3

Meet the Nonbelievers

Picture an atheist. If you're like most Americans, you're picturing a middle-aged white guy complaining angrily about religion. Even if you are an atheist yourself, one who is neither white nor a guy nor angry, you still might picture that, and think of yourself as an exception.

In fact, *most* atheists don't fit this stereotype, just as most Christians are not like Fred Phelps or Pat Robertson. The previous chapter unpacked that religious stereotype. This chapter does the same for nonbelievers, introducing them as they much more commonly are. By the end of the chapter it should be less unthinkable that a nonbeliever could be in a loving and supportive marriage with a religious believer.

This chapter introduces some specific types of nonbelievers. Here are a few of the more general terms:

→ ***Atheist.*** *A person who is of the opinion that no supernatural god or gods exist.*

→ ***Agnostic.*** *One who doesn't claim to know whether a god or gods exist, and often also thinks that it's unknowable.*

→ ***Freethinker.*** *Someone who holds opinions based on independent reasoning without the undue influence of authority, doctrine, or tradition.*

→ *Humanist.* Someone who believes that our highest concern should be caring for each other, and this world, and this life. Some prefer *"secular humanist"* to make it clear that no religious belief is involved.

Just as a religious believer can be religious and Christian and theistic and Lutheran, a nonbeliever can embrace several or all of the terms listed. I am of the strong opinion that God does not exist, I don't think anyone can know for sure, I try to form my opinions without relying on authority or tradition, and I think that caring for each other in this world and this life is the most important thing we can do. So I am an atheist, and an agnostic, and a freethinker, and a humanist.

The opinions we form about other people, especially groups with whom we have little personal contact, are largely shaped by the "news paradox" I described in Chapter 1. Many people think of nonbelievers as hostile and unpleasant because they see atheists only when they are hostile and unpleasant. Conflict drives the news, so atheists are mostly in the news when they are fighting against a cross on public land or a prayer at a city council meeting. If the only time you see atheists is when they are angry about religion, it's natural to think of atheists as cranky people who spend all of their time and energy opposing religion—and therefore as unlikely to marry a religious person.

Some nonbelievers fit that description perfectly, but most do not—something confirmed by recent research that we'll get to shortly. And just as religious believers often overestimate the intolerance and scriptural literalism in their own ranks, it turns out nonbelievers do very much the same thing, taking the more extreme, angry, uncompromising public advocates of atheism to be representative of their own group—and as a result having a pretty low opinion of their own group.

A Crisis of Collective Self-Esteem

The groundbreaking Faith Matters Survey of 2006[1] provides terrific insight into attitudes between belief groups. Researchers Robert Putnam and David Campbell developed a "feeling thermometer" to measure how "warm" various religious perspectives feel toward each other. The results are fascinating. People of almost every perspective tend to have warm feelings toward

Mainline Protestants and Jews, while almost every perspective is cool toward Muslims and Buddhists. Mormons like everybody else, but almost everybody else dislikes Mormons. Almost everyone likes Catholics more than Catholics like them back. And on it goes.

The survey also shows how the members of each group feel about their *own* group. Mormons have the highest self-image (a warmth rating of 87 out of 100), while those who identify as "not religious" have the lowest self-image (59). In fact, the nonreligious rate themselves lower than either Jews or Mormons rate them—64 and 61, respectively.

It isn't hard to guess the reason. Most nonbelievers don't identify with the more combative and confrontational public face of religious disbelief. Like believers distancing themselves from religious intolerance, these non-believers often resent being lumped in with the more combative voices and want to distance themselves from them.

What they often fail to realize is that they, not the high-profile spokes-people, represent the norm for nonbelief. The nice guys, the coexisters, the average Joes and Josies are the vast majority of the nonreligious.

It was hard to confirm such a thing until recently. Although religious believers have been studied from every angle, nonbelievers as a distinct group have been mostly ignored by researchers. When they are included in survey categories, atheists and agnostics are usually lumped into a vast category called the "Nones"—those who when asked what their religion is say, "None."

The "Nones" category is almost meaningless. A lot of people who claim no specific label—most, in fact—still hold many traditional religious beliefs. A good friend of mine believes in God, believes that salvation is attainable only through a personal relationship with Jesus Christ, prays daily, and has painted Psalm texts scrolling around the border of her living room ceiling—but describes herself as nonreligious, and therefore counts as a "None."

A belief category that includes both me and my praying, Psalm-scrolling friend isn't going to add much to our understanding of the texture and variety of actual nonbelief.

Fortunately, as the profile and number of nonbelievers have grown, researchers have begun to paint a more complete picture of that specific category. And it turns out that nonbelievers on average are less extreme and more diverse than almost anyone thought—even the nonbelievers themselves.

The Variety of Nonbelievers

After decades clinging to the fringes of the cultural tapestry, atheists and agnostics have swooned to see the "Nones" category that includes them growing by leaps and bounds—from 8% in 1990 to 19.6% in 2012.[2] One in five Americans claim no religious affiliation.

But Dr. Christopher Silver and Thomas Coleman, researchers at the University of Tennessee, Chattanooga, knew that a category lumping believers and nonbelievers together is a double-edged sword. It gives nonbelievers membership in the fastest-growing piece of the cultural pie, but it also makes it harder to say anything meaningful about nonbelief in America.

Talking about the "Nones" is a bit like talking about "African culture"— as if an Egyptian businesswoman, an Aka villager, and a South African footballer have any real commonality beyond their shared humanity and the continent on which they're standing.

So Silver and Coleman created a study to drill down into religious disbelief in America, to get beyond both the cartoon of the angry atheist and the vague mush of the "Nones" to a better understanding of the true variety of nonbelievers. Their results provide one of the bright, gleaming keys to understanding why marriages between believers and nonbelievers so often succeed, as well as why they sometimes fail.

Silver and Coleman knew from their own experiences with atheists and agnostics that they are not all alike. Their 2013 study, which surveyed more than 1,100 nonbelievers, provided the best description to date of just how that variety plays out.

"The *only* thing all of our participants had in common was that they do not believe in a God," said Silver. "It's what they do or don't do with that nonbelief—how it functions and exists in their lives—that ranges on an extremely wide spectrum."[3]

In the end, Silver and Coleman identified six basic types of nonbelievers:[4]

1. The Academic

Try to learn something about everything and everything about something.

— Thomas Henry Huxley, agnostic biologist[5]

Intellectual activities like reading, discussion, and healthy debate are at the heart (or brain) of the Academic Atheist's self-image. They prefer to associate with others who have the same intellectual approach to life, even if their opinions are different, as long as they are well informed. They often engage with others, both online and in person, around topics of mutual interest, including skepticism and freethought.

Academics made up 37.6% of the nonbelievers in the study—more than one in three.

2. The Activist

Cautious, careful people, always casting about to preserve their reputation and social standing, never can bring about reform. Those who are really in earnest must be willing to be anything or nothing in the world's estimation.

—Susan B. Anthony, activist agnostic[6]

Activist Atheist/Agnostics aren't content with simply holding a nonbelief position, and they don't just want to explore ideas intellectually. They want to change the world. It's not just atheist-related issues they're interested in. They are engaged in the struggle for civil rights (including feminism and LGBT rights), environmental concerns, animal rights, and other prominent social issues. In the words of the researchers, Activist Atheist/Agnostics "are not idle; they effectuate their interests and beliefs." They are often willing to ally themselves with other movements with whom they share a common interest.

Nearly one in four nonbelievers in the study (23%) were classified as the Activist type.

3. The Seeker-Agnostic

I err on the side of a kind of optimistic agnostic sense that there's something that put us all here—some energy or something that we are not in a position to understand.

—American filmmaker Mark Romanek[7]

Seeker-Agnostics recognize that it's hard to make confident statements about metaphysical beliefs. They see open-mindedness as a major virtue, recognize the limits of human knowledge and experience, and embrace uncertainty. They actively search for and respond to knowledge and evidence, and they don't hold a firm ideological position. Instead, they tend to search for what the researchers called the "scientifically wondrous" and for "profound confirmation of life's meaning." They accept and welcome the diversity of others.

Some Seeker-Agnostics say they miss being a believer in some way, whether the social benefits, or the emotional ones, or the connection it gave them to friends and family. Some continue to identify as religious or spiritual, even though they do not believe in God.

Seeker-Agnostics made up 7.6% of the respondents—about 1 in 13.

4. The Anti-Theist

I'm not even an atheist so much as I am an antitheist; I not only maintain that all religions are versions of the same untruth, but I hold that the influence of churches, and the effect of religious belief, is positively harmful.

—Christopher Hitchens, journalist[8]

When most people think of nonbelievers, they picture the Anti-Theist. The Anti-Theist doesn't just disbelieve religious claims but is actively, diametrically, and categorically opposed to them and to the influence they have on the world. In the words of the researchers, the Anti-Theist "proactively and aggressively" asserts his or her view, challenging religious ideology as dangerous ignorance that harms human dignity and well-being, and tends to see individuals associated with religion as "backward and socially detrimental." Some Anti-Theists are more assertive than others, but their opinions on religion are rarely a mystery to those around them. Many of the most prominent and well-known voices in modern atheism, including Christopher Hitchens, are best described as Anti-Theists.

Even though they are often seen as the "typical" atheist, Anti-Theists made up only 14.8% of the nonbelievers in the survey—one in seven.

5. The Non-Theist

[T]he rise of apatheism . . . should not be assumed to represent a lazy recumbency . . . Just the opposite: it is the product of a determined cultural effort to discipline the religious mindset, and often an equally determined personal effort to master the spiritual passions. It is not a lapse. It is an achievement.   —Jonathan Rauch, journalist[9]

What Silver and Coleman call the Non-Theist commonly goes by another name: the "apatheist," or apathetic nonbeliever. This is someone who does not believe but also doesn't care about religious belief, or organized atheism, or the raging debates between the two. As the researchers put it, "They simply do not believe, and in the same right, their absence of faith means the absence of anything religious in any form from their mental space."

"Those who self-identified as our 'Non-Theist' typology could not care less about religion or their own atheism," said Coleman. Compared to the Anti-Theist, they represent the opposite end of the spectrum of engagement. "For [the Non-Theists], apathy is the name of the game."

This was the smallest group in the study—just 4.4%.

6. The Ritual Atheist/Agnostic

I never wavered in my certainty that God did not exist. . . . [But] I recognized that my continuing resistance to theories of an afterlife or of heavenly residents was no justification for giving up on the music, buildings, prayers, rituals, feasts, shrines, pilgrimages, communal meals and illustrated manuscripts of the faiths.

—Alain de Botton, atheist philosopher[10]

The Ritual Atheist/Agnostic doesn't believe in God or an afterlife but finds some rituals or other traditions, even those associated with religion, to be beautiful or useful. It might be something rooted in Eastern religions, like yoga or meditation, but just as often they find beauty and meaning in the traditions of their own culture or family. An atheist who was raised Anglican and still loves the incense and pageantry of the High Church liturgy, despite abandoning the beliefs behind them, is a Ritual Atheist.

Though sometimes thought of as "spiritual but not religious," the Ritual Atheist/Agnostic is usually quick to clarify that he or she holds no supernatural or spiritual beliefs at all. Even if the rituals and teachings are found emotionally moving and meaningful, they are still seen as having an entirely natural, human point of origin.

Ritual Atheist/Agnostics comprised 12.5% of respondents—one in eight.

Now here's where it gets really interesting. After figuring out who was who and how many were of each type, Silver and Coleman ran the subjects through some well-known psychological tests:

→ **The Ryff Scales**, which measure things like autonomy, self-acceptance, the ability to establish quality ties with other people, and a sense of purpose

→ **The Rokeach Dogmatism Scale**, which measures the degree of a person's closed-mindedness and inflexibility

→ **The Multidimensional Anger Inventory**, which measures such things as the subject's frequency, duration, and magnitude of anger

→ **The NEO (Neuroticism-Extroversion-Openness) Inventory**, which measures . . . well, I think you can sort that one out

They then compared the results to the six types and found some fascinating correlations:

→ Ritual Atheists scored highest in "positive relations with others"— and lowest in dogmatism.

→ Activists scored highest in "openness to experience"—and lowest in narcissism (self-centeredness).

→ Academics had the lowest anger score.[11]

A nonbeliever with these qualities is more likely to make a successful marriage with a religious believer than one without these qualities.

When I asked Dr. Silver which of the nonbeliever types he thought would be most likely to do well in a secular/religious marriage, he didn't hesitate to reply. "If we had to speculate on the very best-suited type, it would be the Ritual Atheist/Agnostic. This group even reports that they value some religious teachings and may even participate in some rituals themselves. If you are a Christian, you might find an extremely easy time getting along with the RAA; in fact they might be sitting next to you in church!"[12]

Not that RAAs are the only nonbelievers likely to succeed in such a marriage. Far from it. Four of the other five types also bring clear strengths and compatibilities to a match with a religious believer, including Academics (lowest in anger) and Activists (most open to experience).

But when it comes to qualities that would make an atheist much less marriageable to a religious partner, one type corners the market: the Anti-Theist. Anti-Theists scored lowest on positive relations with others, lowest on "agreeableness," and highest in narcissism, dogmatism, and anger.

"It's safe to say that they would not tend to get along well in a marriage or relationship with a religious believer," says Silver. "But it's important to note that this Anti-Theist group makes up less than 15% of our sample. In terms of building a harmonious mixed-belief relationship, the outlook improves significantly for the other 85%."[13]

Just as with religious belief, the point of all this is not to pass judgment on any part of the spectrum of nonbelief—only to illustrate that the spectrum does exist and that it's very wide. In fact, rather than demonize Anti-Theists, the researchers make the important point that "anger and relative dogmatism . . . may be proper psychological responses" when you consider the life experiences of a given Anti-Theist—especially when it comes to religion. Silver and Coleman said that many of the Anti-Theists in their study had recently deconverted from religious belief and were often still experiencing negative effects as a result, including high tension and conflict, up to and including the loss of relationships.

"If we take on the perspective of a recent deconvert from a conservative religious tradition to atheism," said Coleman, "it may be easy to see how this small sub-segment is, and perhaps deserves to be, angry."[14]

But most nonbelievers don't have those issues. They haven't had a painful separation from religion, or in some cases any separation at all, and they haven't encountered other reasons to be especially angry at or about religion. "Our research showed over 85% of the nonbelievers sampled are more or less your 'average Joe,' " said Silver. "When it comes to being angry, argumentative, and dogmatic, they fall right in line with current societal norms."[15]

Silver concludes by noting that "there really is no 'atheist identity.' In the same way that religious people may or may not structure their lives around their belief in God, atheists may or may not structure their lives around not believing in God."[16] That doesn't mean the less centrally focused people are not "really" religious or not "really" nonreligious. But they are less likely to encounter difficult hurdles in marrying across the belief gap than those whose identity is more tightly focused on the very element that defines that gap.

Now, About That Dogmatism . . .

Sometimes an atheist who's loud and confident in his critiques of religion is accused of being "as dogmatic as any fundamentalist." The atheist will sometimes counter that he can't be dogmatic because atheism doesn't have any dogmas.

Fortunately, "dogmatic" has an actual definition—even though neither of these people seems to know what it is.

Dogma is an idea or principle that is to be accepted without question. *Dogmatism*, then, is the idea that your opinions or beliefs can't be questioned. To put it even more simply, it describes a person's unwillingness to allow that he or she might be wrong. It has nothing to do with how loud or confident you are, and it doesn't matter if the belief is formally inscribed somewhere or you're the only one on earth who holds it. All that matters is your own willingness to say, no matter how confident you are, that you *might* be wrong.

A religious person can be dogmatic if he dismisses even the remotest possibility that he could be wrong. And an atheist can be dogmatic for precisely the same reason—if she allows her confident opinions to lapse over into rock-solid, immovable certainty.

For their pioneering study of atheists in America, Bob Altemeyer and Bruce Hunsberger included a measure of dogmatic thinking called the DOG scale—20 statements that assess how rigidly a person's opinions are held.[17] Not just *religious* opinions—the DOG scale doesn't even mention religion. It's about opinions generally. Among the 20 statements are the following:

→ There are so many things we have not discovered yet, nobody should be absolutely certain his beliefs are right.

→ I am so sure I am right about the important things in life, there is no evidence that could convince me otherwise.

→ It is best to be open to all possibilities, and ready to re-evaluate all your beliefs.

→ The people who disagree with me may well turn out to be right.

→ People who disagree with me are just plain wrong, and often evil as well.

Respondents are asked to rate each statement on a scale from −4 (strongly disagree) to +4 (strongly agree). As you can see, some of the statements indicate a tendency to think dogmatically, whereas others indicate the opposite.

Someone without a dogmatic bone in her body would score 20 points, while someone who pins the dogmatic needle on every statement would register 180 points. A score of 100 would sit right on the fence. When the researchers gave the DOG scale test to a group of religious fundamentalists in Manitoba, for example, the average result was 126. That's well into dogmatic territory, though it still doesn't pin the needle.

And how did the American atheists in the study do?

Altemeyer and Hunsberger said they were "startled" when the atheists in the study came in at an average of 88. That's still on the less-dogmatic side, but not by as much as you might think.

They then followed up with a more religion-specific question: "What would be required, what would have to happen, for you to believe in the 'traditional' God? . . . Are there conceivable events, or evidence, that would lead you to believe?"

Even an atheist who has spent a lifetime examining the existing evidence and concluding that God does not exist should be able to conceive of some *new* evidence that *would* convince him to change his mind. Almost exactly half of the respondents were able to come up with something that would do, whether "universal brotherhood" or the physical, visible appearance of a supernatural being before them, or "a clear, undisputable miracle." These are nondogmatic answers. The respondents highly doubt any such thing will ever happen, but if it did, against all odds, they would change their minds.

But 51% of the respondents in the first round of the study, a group of atheists in California, said there was "absolutely nothing conceivable that could change their minds on the existence of the traditional God."

The researchers were so surprised that they actually reworded the question for the next two groups they surveyed:

> We found this level of closed-mindedness hard to believe, and suspected the wording of our question had not communicated our intention. So we reworked the item for the Alabama/Idaho sample, to make sure the informants knew we would take anything they would consider a test of the matter. Specifically, we inserted, "Is there *absolutely nothing* that could happen that would convince you? Or are there *conceivable* events—however unlikely or unprecedented—that would lead you to believe? What?" And 52% of the Alabama/Idaho atheists still said nothing would change their minds. *Nothing.*[18]

Even allowing that such events would be "unlikely or unprecedented," more than half still said no evidence would be enough. If God himself appeared before them every day for a year and performed an incontrovertible miracle—suspending the laws of physics, let's say, or causing the Cubs to win the World Series—they would remain unconvinced.

Now *that's* dogmatic!

When the researchers inverted the question for that group of fundamentalists in Manitoba, asking what would have to happen to make them *disbelieve* in the traditional God, every last one of them, 100%, said nothing imaginable could do this. But that's not too surprising—it is harder to prove a negative than a positive claim. The atheists should certainly be able to think of something that would suffice.

Altemeyer and Hunsberger offered a few guesses about why so many of the atheists in their sample would have such a high dogmatic score. Maybe the careful examination of beliefs most atheists undertake during their "deconversion" make them especially confident. Or maybe it's a reaction to the suffering and marginalization many atheists endure in majority-religious cultures. But I think they missed the most likely explanation of all:

They polled only members of organized atheist groups.

Take it from a 15-year member of organized atheist groups—we're not typical, even among atheists. And I don't mean that as a compliment. The tiny fraction of nonbelievers (about 1%) who are sufficiently motivated by their worldview to gather with others who share that view will naturally tend to think more dogmatically than the 99% of atheists who are not affiliated with atheist groups.

Social scientists know that gathering with the like-minded can do some funny things to your opinions. As Cass Sunstein describes in *Going to Extremes*, those who surround themselves with others who hold the same opinions—social, political, religious, artistic, whatever—are more likely to hold those positions inflexibly and dogmatically, and to move toward the more extreme versions of the opinions they share.[19] Obviously that's not the case for everyone in these atheist groups, because nearly half gave nondogmatic responses. But it's reasonable to assume that the general population of atheists would have a lower DOG score, just as the general population of the religious do. The Silver/Coleman typology seems to confirm that. They sampled a much broader cross section of the population, and all but the Anti-Theists had fairly low levels of dogmatic thinking.

Again, that bodes very well for the mix.

The Flipside of an Oxymoron:
Atheists Who Believe in "God"

Atheists who cheered the idea of Catholic nonbelievers in the last chapter are now invited to consider the even stranger flipside: atheist believers. In the 2007 Pew Forum Religious Landscape survey, 21% of Americans calling themselves atheists say they also believe in the existence of God or a universal spirit.[20] This seems even less possible than the Catholic nonbeliever. "Catholic" can be defined as a cultural label, after all, but the word *atheist* translates literally to "without god."

But no matter how much I'd like to insist that a given word means X, forever and always, language is slippery and variable. I could insist that a Unitarian Universalist has to believe in one non-Trinitarian God ("Unitarian") and that everyone goes to heaven ("Universalist") because that's what those words mean. But this would deny the fact that many or even most Unitarian Universalists today don't believe in God or heaven at all—and all the dictionary waving in the world can't convince them that they do.

Clearly the believing atheists in the Pew study have a different understanding of the word *atheist* than I do. But on closer examination, it makes a bit more sense. About three-fourths of those atheists say they believe in a "universal spirit," something that isn't necessarily the same as a god. That's why "God" is in quotes in the heading to this section.

But it doesn't explain everything. Even when you eliminate those universal spiritists, you're still left with 6% of atheists saying they believe in a personal god. I don't understand this myself, but you'll notice they didn't ask for my permission, and they don't need it. No matter how a God-believing atheist violates my own sense of the possible, there they are, blurring the neat categorical boundaries with their messy reality.

Neat and clean categories make it easier to talk, but sometimes they can make it harder to understand what's really going on. It's much better to pay attention to the full spectrum of belief and disbelief than to force people into boxes that may not reflect where they really are—especially in a book like this one.

The Bottom Line: Seeing Nonbelievers More Clearly

The common assumption about the secular/religious marriage is that it's a bad idea, a crossing of the streams that's going to end badly. But just as the real picture of religious believers is encouraging for the mix, the more you understand the wide variety of nonbelievers, the more you see why they often form successful marriages with believers.

If most nonbelievers think that religion poisons everything it touches and that all religious believers are deluded fools, marriage between believers and nonbelievers would be a bad idea. But if most nonbelievers have a more nuanced opinion of religion and religious believers—feeling that some religious expressions are better than others; that at least some religious beliefs are respectable, even if they disagree with them; that you can be both religious and intelligent; that there might be beauty and utility in some religious traditions and rituals; and (perhaps most important of all) that they could conceivably be wrong in their own conclusions—then the conditions are present for a successful relationship between religious and nonreligious partners, especially when the religious partner shows the same promising, tolerant signs.

→ → →

Let's be clear: Some mixed-belief marriages can be or can become unmitigated disasters. In fact, you are going to meet a number of couples in Part Two who simply could not make their marriages work, often for the reasons described in the next chapter. A mixed-belief marriage will probably require extensive work and communication to succeed—*just as any marriage would*—and that is the point. Contrary to the naysayers' assertions, mixed-belief marriages have just as much chance of succeeding as any other union between two independent people. And that is cause for celebration.

What Helps,
and What Doesn't

As I noted in the last chapter, some secular/religious mixed marriages go smoothly, while others are painful and difficult, or even go down in flames. When you look closely at hundreds of these marriages, certain patterns begin to emerge—the things that help these marriages succeed, and the things that don't.

It was tempting to create a Dr. Phil–type quiz for this, but any kind of sliding scale would be misleadingly simple. Instead, I'll describe the relative importance of each item and let you decide how much it applies to you, if at all.

Nine Unhelpful Things
Let's start with the bad news: nine things that can make a secular/religious relationship difficult. They aren't always terminal by any means, but couples with one or more of these situations will need to draw on other strengths to offset these challenges.

1. A couple shared a worldview when they married, and then one partner changed.

Though never enough by itself, this is one of the most consistent risk markers in the secular/religious marriage. The partner who remains the same often feels that an unspoken (or sometimes even spoken) agreement has been violated, one on which the very choice to marry is often predicated. The correlation between this factor and the tension markers in the McGowan-Sikes survey are very high. (See Chapters 7, 10, and 11 for couples in this situation.)

2. Both partners identify intensely with their (different) worldviews.

If both partners are fairly moderate in the intensity of their worldview and its centrality to their personal identity, problems are few and far between. Even if one is intensely engaged, the opportunity for compromise is still available. But when one partner is intensely religious and the other is intensely secular, the issues multiply, and the opportunity for compromise diminishes. This by itself is not always a problem, but if the intensity is accompanied by dogmatism or a strong desire to convert, the strain on the relationship can be intense.

3. One or both partners are relatively dogmatic in their thinking.

Dogmatism is not the same as intensity, and it has nothing to do with how loud or confident you are. It describes a person's unwillingness to allow that he or she *might* be wrong. A person can be highly committed to a worldview, whether religious or nonreligious, and still retain some flexibility of thinking and a willingness to admit that he or she might be wrong. One dogmatic thinker in a marriage can be challenging. Two partners who are dogmatic on opposite ends—that's deadly. (Not sure about this one? Take the DOG Scale quiz in Chapter 17.)

4. One or both partners have a strong desire to convert the other partner.

It's never a great idea to enter a relationship with the assumption or expectation that the other person will change. Because religious identity is less likely to change than most habits, and because it's tied so tightly to personal identity, a persistent expressed desire to convert one's partner causes resentment and alienation to build over time. In the McGowan-Sikes survey, a strong desire by one or both partners to convert the other correlated strongly with tension and conflict in the relationship. (For couples including at least one partner with a strong desire to convert the other, see Chapters 7 and 11.)

5. The nonreligious partner is an antitheist.

An antitheist in a relationship with a traditionally religious person—a *theist*, in other words—is obviously bringing some unhelpful baggage through the door. It's like a vegetarian marrying someone who is not merely a nonvegetarian but declares himself to be antivegetarian, directly opposed to all things vegetarian, dedicated to its eradication. Whether antitheism is a justified position is a separate question. But there's little question that it is a flag for problems in the secular/religious marriage. (See the University of Tennessee typology of nonbelievers in Chapter 3.)

6. The religious partner identifies with a significantly conservative, dogmatic, or fundamentalist denomination.

You can't draw lines between denominations or religions and assume that all adherents on one side of the line share any given attitude, practice, or belief. Many lines run straight down the middle of a given denomination, with conservatives on one side and progressives on the other. But a few denominations show an especially high correlation with tension and conflict in the secular/religious marriage. Mormonism, Jehovah's Witnesses, Pentecostalism, and conservative Evangelical Protestants are among those with the highest levels of conflict and divorce in secular/religious matches, much of which takes the form of pressure or shunning by extended family. (More on the differences between denominations and intensities and on the damaging effects of external disapproval on relationships in Chapters 2 and 18, respectively.)

7. The marriage already includes other high-risk factors.

If a relationship already includes one or more of the classic risk factors, religious differences can exacerbate the effect. Risks with a high correlation to conflict and divorce include:

→ Significant age difference between partners

→ Young age at marriage (under 25, especially under 21)

→ Parents' history of divorce

→ Premarital cohabitation

→ If one partner smokes and the other does not

→ If one or both partners have a drinking problem

→ History of previous divorce

→ Mismatched desire to have children, or more children

→ Low overall life satisfaction/marital satisfaction

→ Communication in general that is often disrespectful or contemptuous

(These factors are discussed in more detail in Chapters 17 and 20. Most of the couples in Chapters 5–12 have one or more of these risk factors.)

8. The couple experiences significant disapproval from extended family and/or the community.

A recent Harvard study found that strong disapproval from the outside puts serious stress on the relationship and even on the health of the individuals.[1] "The more people felt like their family and friends and society didn't approve of and support their relationship, the worse their health was," said Justin Lehmiller, lead researcher on the study. And if the source of the tension is the religious difference between the partners, such disapproval can greatly increase existing tensions between them. (More on extended family, as well as on good and bad extended-family reactions for couples in Chapters 5, 6, 12, and 18.)

9. There is disagreement over religious identity, boundaries, and practices for the children.

Many issues that lie dormant for a secular/religious couple prior to having kids come roaring to the surface once that Rubicon is crossed. It's all well and good to say each partner can hold the beliefs he or she chooses, but what about the kids? Do they have a religious identity? Are they free to select their own in the long run? Do they go to Sunday school or religious services? Will they be baptized, confirmed, bar mitzvahed? Are any questions or opinions off limits? Secular/religious couples who do not come to agreement on these questions as early as possible—preferably before the kids are born—are in for some very strong shock waves, especially if one or both partners have a strong worldview identity. (More in Chapter 19.)

Ten Helpful Things

Some of the helpful characteristics are just the unhelpful ones in reverse, but some are independent of that list. Here are 10 best practices for secular/religious couples:

1. Never try to convert or deconvert your partner. In matters of belief, support and encourage his or her autonomy.

Accept your differences. If your partner wants to question or challenge his or her own opinions and wants a sounding board, he or she knows where to find you. You can discuss, debate, and challenge each other's ideas, but if you want a mixed-belief relationship to work, let your partner know that in the end you respect his or her right to self-determination. (More in Chapter 17.)

2. Talk about your differences of belief as early as possible in the relationship.

Relationships should be entered into with all cards on the table. Sharing a difference in belief with a partner or potential partner as early as you can demonstrates honesty and respect. You don't have to reveal your entire personal history on the first date, but when things start getting serious—and certainly before engagement, marriage, kids—it's best to discuss the difference openly. (More in Chapter 13.)

3. Work out agreements for all shared practices, including churchgoing, parenting, and family religious identity, by defining your negotiables and nonnegotiables.

Each partner will have a long list of preferences related to religious or nonreligious practice, but not everything is nonnegotiable. Decide what you can't live without and what you can, and then compare lists for points of conflict. (More in Chapter 17.)

4. Focus on shared values more than different beliefs.

Yes, the difference in beliefs is there, and yes, it often matters, but couples can choose where to place their focus and emphasis. Values impact daily life more than most beliefs, and moderate and liberal believers and nonbelievers share more values with each other than either does with the more extreme representatives of their worldview. (Take the Shared Values Quiz in Chapter 13.)

5. Make personal respect nonnegotiable, even as you question and challenge each other's ideas.

This is closely related to item 1 but worth mentioning separately. Ideas and opinions must earn respect, but respect for each other as people is a nonnegotiable requirement of a relationship. (More in Chapter 17.)

6. Engage in and learn about each other's worldviews.

Make the effort to learn more about your partner's worldview. It's a gesture of personal respect and a great way to get to know each other. (More in Chapters 2 and 3.)

7. Remember that the opinions of believers are not always the same as the doctrines of their churches, and the opinions of nonbelievers are not always the same as those of prominent atheists.

The secular/religious marriage is not the marriage of the Holy Bible and *The God Delusion*. Most religious people aren't Old Testament literalists, and most nonreligious people don't think religion poisons everything. Take the time to find out whether and how your partner's beliefs differ from the stereotype. (More in Chapters 2 and 3.)

8. Raise children with the freedom to choose their own religious or nonreligious identity. Expose them to many traditions, beliefs, and practices.

If parents have two different worldviews, there is one clear best practice for the kids: Keep them unlabeled, and then preserve space around them so they can come to their own conclusions in the long run. Provide knowledge and experience to fuel that process, and let them know you will never withhold your love and support, no matter what decision they make. (More in Chapter 19.)

9. Support and protect each other from mistreatment or disrespect, especially by those who share your worldview, including extended family.

If your partner is being maligned, pressured, or ostracized by family or community members because of his or her beliefs, a mixed-belief partner is in a unique position to come to his or her defense. Never miss an opportunity to do so. (More in Chapter 18.)

10. Spread the word!

If you are married to someone across the gap between religious belief and nonbelief, you're in a unique position to dispel negative stereotypes about your partner's worldview. The religious partner can be a moderating voice with real-world experience when the church ladies start suggesting that all atheists are immoral, and the nonreligious partner can do the same when those in the local atheist group start suggesting that all religious people are unintelligent. You know better, so find the courage to speak up.

PART TWO

Meet the Mix

5

The Turning Points
That Make It Work
Tom and Danielle

The suburbs north of Atlanta have gone through a profound change in recent years. An influx of new residents from around the country and around the world during the economic boom of the 1990s swelled the population of the county by more than 25%. What had been a reliably white conservative Southern Baptist area transformed into a religious and cultural mosaic unimaginable a generation before.

Danielle was born there and grew up in the area in the 1970s and 1980s, the last decades of that earlier Atlanta. Her family was "definitely Southern Baptist," she says now, but "didn't go to church that much" when she was young—mostly Easter and Christmas.

When she was in middle school, Danielle's parents divorced and her sister became chronically ill, requiring months-long hospitalizations at Scottish Rite Children's Hospital. "One of the nurses started taking my sister to church," Danielle recalls, "and pretty soon we all started going with her."

The church was First Baptist Atlanta, a theologically conservative congregation under the pastorate of Rev. Dr. Charles Stanley. FBA was in its first decade of a massive expansion that would result in a membership of more than 16,000 and a global multimedia ministry with materials in more than 100 languages.

"We went for a few years, and it was not a good experience. Very strict Southern Baptist. They kicked a friend of ours out of the Sunday school for flirting with boys on a ski trip. Never even talked to her, just kicked her out. Around the same time, my sister and I began asking complicated questions in the Sunday school class. We weren't trying to be disruptive; we were just very curious. I guess we didn't follow the correct path of just listening and agreeing, because we were all asked to not come back to class. It left a very bad taste in my mouth, and I stopped going to church entirely about the time I graduated high school. I still believed—I just had a problem with the closed-door feeling of churches. To this day I do not like to exclude anyone."

She went on to attend the University of Georgia and never stopped identifying as a Christian.

On the face of it, Tom had a more religious background than Danielle. "I was raised in a liberal Catholic family, baptized, went to Sunday school, confirmed, had my First Communion, the works," he says. After his family moved to Miami, he voluntarily attended a Catholic high school for boys— "in part because some hot girls I knew thought the guys who went there were hot! What a great idea—go to an all-boys school to get girls. Eighth-grade decision making at its finest!" he says with a laugh.

Tom's family didn't attend church often. "Mostly Christmas and Easter type of stuff," he recalls, echoing Danielle. "But I did go to Sunday school. And in high school, my mom encouraged me to go to a Catholic youth program. She wanted me to socialize more and knew how to sell it: 'Oh, you'll meet friends and girls.' I went willingly for a while, then eventually quit because it was boring, not really my scene."

That's not to say he wasn't a religious believer. "I was almost always a skeptic from a very young age about things in general, even in elementary school. But I was always a believer, and very much so in high school," he recalls. "I wore the cross, I felt the spirit. I went on a religious retreat and had a profound religious experience. Hey, those things work!" he says, laughing.

It was while taking a course in Old Testament history at Duke University that Tom started calling himself an agnostic. "I was probably even an atheist at the time, but I didn't understand the distinction. The word has that baggage, you know." He assumed he was the only doubter in the family. Years later he learned otherwise. "As an adult, I learned that my father is basically an atheist and was all along. He doesn't embrace the label, but he doesn't believe. Mom is basically a Catholic agnostic—still prays sometimes, still goes to church sometimes. If things are rough, she'll go to church because it calms her. She is still technically religious, but with a big element of doubt. When I asked why I was raised Catholic despite their own doubts, they said they did that to give me morals."

Tom became part of the influx of outsiders to the north Atlanta area during the 1990s boom, moving in to work in the local division of his family's business. Not long after his arrival in 1997, he and Danielle met while playing pool in an Atlanta nightclub.

"My friend and I were working at a department store after graduating college," Danielle says. "Sometimes we would go to this place next door after work to eat and have a drink. We always ended up meeting guys there but never anyone that I was very interested in. I really enjoyed playing pool, and we were playing a game with two guys we had just met. I noticed Tom at the table next to ours. I thought to myself, 'Why can't I ever meet anyone like that?' He was tall, good-looking, and clean-cut. My friend drank more than she should have and ended up going over to his table and was very forward with them."

"That's a polite way to put it!" Tom says. "Her friend walked up to me, pressed her body against me, and said, 'Are we solids or stripes?' This is not my thing *at all*. So I flashed this sheepish, helpless look at Dani. It's the first look I ever gave her. She smiled. Right away I was plotting for her instead. Way more my type. Not so forward for one thing, but also . . . well, she was attractive, but also had this wholesome look. She looked like a good, decent, genuine person. I thought, 'I have to hand this one off to my roommate so I can start talking to this other girl.'"

"Tom and I started to talk, and I found that we instantly had a common interest in college basketball and baseball—even though he liked the teams that were rivals to mine!"

They all ended up at Steak 'n Shake, where Tom mustered the courage to ask her out. "I was not a player at all, but somehow I had a stroke of brilliance. I had just moved to Atlanta six weeks earlier, so I started with the 'new-in-town' questions. I asked what her favorite restaurant was in the area, and she named this place called Dante's Down the Hatch. So I said, 'Sounds like a great place. Hey, would you like to go there with me sometime?'"

"We instantly hit it off," says Danielle. "We had a long phone conversation before our first date. Anyone who knows me knows that I hate to talk on the phone and it is usually short. But our conversation flowed so smoothly, I couldn't get off the phone."

"I did have some disqualifiers when I was dating," Tom says, "but it never had to do with religion. If a girl liked country music, or she didn't think *The Simpsons* was funny—well, that was automatic wipeout criteria."

"So after dinner on our first date, you took me to a comedy club to make sure I would laugh," Danielle says.

"I did, yes! A sense of humor is important to me, so part of our first date was a kind of test. I took her to a comedy club to be sure she wasn't easily offended and to see if she laughed at different types of humor. Part of that goes to the open-minded skepticism thing, not just about religion but about things in general. If somebody wasn't open-minded enough to laugh, or was too easily offended, she was out. I knew I didn't want that. It wasn't about religion. Christians were fun; I knew tons of Christians. I still thought my parents were Catholic! I thought religion was false, I completely rejected the Bible and the rest, but I didn't have a big issue with people who felt otherwise."

"We actually had a lot of overlap there," Danielle adds. "I still don't take the literal meaning of the Bible, and I still don't believe in dogma. I have issues with a lot of organized religions, and I did at the time. So we had plenty of common ground even then."

They discovered this common ground through conversations early in their relationship. "Tom didn't call himself an atheist when I met him," Danielle remembers. "He called himself agnostic." Not that it would have mattered much to her. She says she had few preconceptions about atheism. "My beliefs had always been really personal, and I didn't know anybody who was an out atheist, so I don't think I even knew what to expect. Same with agnostics. I just figured, 'Okay.'"

Tom nods. "She never gave me a hard time about it at all. She was always just like, 'Okay, that's nice,'" he says.

It was during the first few years of their marriage that Tom gradually adopted atheism as his preferred label. Danielle remained Christian. There were a few tense periods as Tom struggled to accept Danielle's continuing belief, but they both felt at every stage that their common ground was strong.

"If people are struggling to find that common ground, get past beliefs to talk about values. Do you think rape is bad? Stealing? Murdering? Seems silly at first, but it makes you realize that your beliefs don't matter as much as those values. We both believe in family, fairness, and honesty, and we have a strong sense of right and wrong," Tom says. "Our values are very much aligned."

"It's true," Danielle says. "It helps that we have the same values, regardless of what we believe. You've always been a good person," she says to Tom. "I don't get my values from religion. I still believe, but I left the church because so many people did bad things in the name of God."

Their relationship hit a rough patch when Tom became more intensely engaged with his worldview. "He joined a local atheist group when we lived in Miami," Danielle recalls, "and that's when I knew he shifted from agnostic to atheist. Most of the tension came from him talking about it more. He started questioning me more about why I believed and giving me a hard time about it. He kept saying it was going to end up tearing our marriage apart, that I was going to end up divorcing him, that I wasn't going to be able to take it if he didn't believe in God. This just went on and on and on for a while."

"Except I wouldn't say the talk of divorce was that often," Tom says. "I recall religion being a consistent issue for a year or two. Maybe three. But I don't recall that much talk about divorce. I remember like two dinners where we got really stressed."

"Yeah. There were two."

"It wasn't like we were constantly saying 'Ooh, our relationship is in trouble.' To me, our relationship was strong the whole time. But there were two nights it got really tense and almost turned into a fight."

"Every detailed discussion during this time, anything that went beyond everyday stuff about the kids and what was going on, always ended up being about religion. And . . . well, I just don't talk about religion that much. But there was a time I said I wanted to go to a Bible study on Wednesday mornings after I took the kids to school. He said if I had time to go to Bible study on Wednesday morning, then I had time to get a job and start working."

Tom shifts uncomfortably, then covers his eyes with one hand. "Sorry." Danielle chuckles.

"Do you agree that it only got heated a couple of times, that for the most part it was just a consistent conversation that . . . may have been a little tense?" Tom asks.

"There was consistent conversation, and there were more than a few times it got heated."

"Okay."

"It was definitely stressful, and it was because he couldn't understand why I believed. It always came back to him saying, 'I don't know if I can respect people who believe, and you believe, and I don't know if I can . . . respect that.' It was tough."

"I don't think our relationship was ever really in trouble . . . do you?"

Danielle pauses. It's a long pause. "I don't know, because it was in your hands at that point. You were the one that had the problem with it."

"I was definitely trying to . . . come to terms . . . with it," he says slowly. "I will freely admit that Danielle was always more accepting of my lack of religiosity than I was of her religiosity once I started really digging in. You read some of the New Atheist material, and it's pretty aggressive and condemning. And a lot of it is excellent too. It really does do a great job of debunking religion, hitting the hard points . . . but I had to work out in my own head how I was going to treat religious people, as opposed to religious ideas—how accepting I was going to be of those ideas. And Danielle was the one who bore the brunt of that because she was the person closest to me."

"I remember one of the changing moments for you. You went to the Orange Bowl with your friend and his father, who were both very religious. And you came home and said, 'You know what? I know that they are extremely religious and believe in all of the dogma, but they are good people and I still want to be friends with them.'"

"Good call, way to remember that," he says. "They are really religious, I mean doing prison ministry religious. But you're right, I wanted to remain friends with him, but I wasn't sure we could remain friends because I also wasn't sure whether he could accept me. See, there's partly this fear of being rejected myself, and partly having trouble understanding why people would believe."

Tom turns to Danielle. "I would tell you some of the things I'd read about and had learned and was realizing, and I had trouble comprehending how anyone could hear those things and still believe. Really? You know that the Gospels were written 70 to 100 years after Jesus lived, by people in another country, who didn't even speak the same language and had never even been to the Holy Land, and you *still* believe?" Tom clutches his head. "Aaaagghh!" He laughs; Danielle smiles slightly.

"But we're golden now," he adds.

"Yep."

"We talk about religion, but I never really question your beliefs. Every once in a blue moon it'll come up out of interest, but for me, it was important to figure out what she believed and what she didn't. It was important for me to realize we still shared the same values as opposed to beliefs. Our religious beliefs were different, but our values were aligned."

(More of Tom and Danielle's story appears in Chapters 14, 16, and 19—look for the dotted arrows with the couple's names.)

6

Bridging Multiple Gaps
Scott and Dhanya

Bethal is a small South African farming town of about 8,000 in the middle of the open Highveld between Johannesburg and the Swazi border. Like all South African towns and cities, Bethal was zoned by race during the apartheid era, with each of four racial groups consigned to its own residential and business districts. It was into Bethal's small but thriving Gujarati Indian community of the 1970s that Dhanya was born.

Her parents were observant Hindus who followed the customs and rituals their parents instilled in them. "I've adopted many of these myself," says Dhanya. "We celebrate many of the religious festivals and always look to the Gujarati calendar when choosing dates for events or functions, choosing a name for a newborn, or traveling. We always had a small shrine at home and each member of the family prayed there once or twice a day. I still do this today."

She attended a Hindu Sunday school from age 7 to 17. "We sang different religious songs, and were taught about the different scriptures. There were also dances and religious plays that traveled from one Hindu community to another through the province."

Half a world away, Scott was growing up in something of a religious minority himself, the son of moderate Episcopalians in the Southern Baptist stronghold of Chattanooga, Tennessee. Though still racially segregated like most of the U.S. South in the 1980s, Chattanooga was Southern Baptist through and through—just white Southern Baptist on the north and west of the city, black Southern Baptist on the south and east.

He wasn't aware how low-key his own religious upbringing was until his best friend, whose family was Baptist, tried to "save" him when they were seven. "I didn't even know what that meant for a long time," he says, "but he clearly did. In my family, God didn't come up all that often. We prayed before dinner, but religion was not often talked about."

Not so at the conservative Christian secondary academy that Scott attended, whose motto was and is, "Man's chief end is to glorify God and to enjoy Him forever." Given the setting, Scott says he is "surprised in retrospect" that he was part of a core group of six friends there from very different backgrounds. "We were three Indians, one Thai, and two Caucasians, and a mix of religions—Hindu, Muslim, and Christian. We enjoyed talking about intellectual things, but rarely about religion. So I didn't learn that much about their religious views."

He attended the same Episcopal church from birth to high school graduation. "I can't say I was your ideal parishioner. I went with the family, I participated in the youth group, and I even served as an acolyte. But most of my religion-related memories were having these internal conversations with the crucified Christ on the cross hanging above the altar: just your casual how-ya-doing kind of stuff." But it was comfortable and familiar, with the same priest the entire time he attended. This kind of religion didn't bother him.

But the Evangelical brand was another matter, and a New Year's Eve Southern gospel concert cemented Scott's disdain for that kind of religion. "This was not the black choir singing 'Amazing Grace.' It was pure white Southern Baptist praise-Jesus-or-you're-going-to-hell country singin'," he recalls.

"One realization that made an impact on me that I still remember is this: I didn't want to believe that my non-Christian friends, thinking mainly about my high school friends, would 'go to hell.' I feel like this may have been the first time such a thought occurred to me. I came to the conclusion that I could not accept the idea that my friends who were very good people would be punished for their differing beliefs in some afterlife. And if I couldn't accept that, then I couldn't accept any religion that promoted that."

Scott majored in computer science and computer engineering in college. "I attended an Episcopalian service a few times in college, but it was not like the church of my youth. It was around this time that I began to think about my worldview and settled on agnosticism as a name for it. I didn't really actively stop believing stuff, but I became less interested in it and didn't go to church anymore."

After graduating from her secondary school, Dhanya studied veterinary science, first at the University of Pretoria, then at Universiteit Utrecht in the Netherlands, working on research to develop diagnostic procedures for tuberculosis in elephants and rhinoceroses. She eventually returned to Pretoria to teach at the university, occasionally popping up to the Netherlands for three months at a time to connect with the research team at Universiteit Utrecht.

In January 2008, after a few years working for a computer engineering firm, Scott decided to pursue a PhD and entered a program at—you guessed it—Universiteit Utrecht.

One Saturday near the end of February, he headed out to meet an international student group to tour a monastery and brewery just over the Belgian border. "I lived in a tall apartment complex on campus. I came out of the elevator and had stopped to tie my shoes when a very cute Indian girl came out of the elevator and left the building. I walked to the city bus stop . . ."

"And there I was!"

"And there she was. We both got on the same bus, then off at Utrecht Central Station. I started walking through the station to the other side where the group bus was parked. I think I passed her on the way because I was walking quickly, hoping I wouldn't be too late."

"Yes, he did pass me. I noticed he was walking in the same direction, and I got the feeling that he may be going to the same place as me. I was right—I saw him waiting at the bus that was to take us to Belgium."

"I smiled as she approached and asked jokingly if she was following me."

"I said, 'Yes, I'm following you.' "

"When we got off the bus, we had the option to take either a Flemish tour or an English tour," Scott says. "The cute girl was going on the Flemish tour, so I decided to go too, even though I didn't know any Flemish."

"We spoke to each other a bit during the tour, then talked much more on the bus back to the campus and exchanged email addresses," says Dhanya. "I didn't really expect to hear from him again but I did, many times."

They began seeing each other in the following weeks, then decided to continue their relationship after she returned to South Africa.

"I had already had a long-distance relationship before and thought I would not want to have another. But there was something about this girl that convinced me to try it, even though the distance was even longer and the differences between us were even greater."

"And he convinced me to try it, too."

Dhanya's parents were another matter. "They were not happy about it. They both said it would be better if I met a Gujarati boy. I said I understood where they were coming from, but asked for them to first meet Scott before they made any conclusions about him and the relationship. They agreed, but not with enthusiasm. My mum felt that since we come from completely different backgrounds and cultures, that this relationship was just not a good idea."

Scott's mother had said very much the same thing—not about Dhanya, but years earlier. "When I was in high school I asked what she would think if I married somebody of a different religion. I even hypothetically suggested Hinduism, for some strange reason. She said, in her very diplomatic way, that she would be concerned that we might have more difficulty than if we both held the same beliefs. It wasn't much more than that."

Whatever concern she had disappeared when she met Dhanya. "They both love her," says Scott. "They're even more excited to see her than me when we visit."

Once they got to know Scott personally, Dhanya's parents also came around. "When we called to tell them that Scott proposed to me and I said yes, I was rather anxious and nervous to make that call. But my dad responded by saying, 'We were waiting for this news for a long time, congratulations!' Everyone in both of our families was very happy to hear the news. Since then, their relationship has grown, and they love and care for him a lot. That makes me very happy."

Dhanya and Scott were married in Bethal's Hindu Community Hall in a traditional Gujarati ceremony (discussed further in Chapter 14).

Neither Scott nor Dhanya consider their religious differences much of an issue. "Honestly, when Scott told me he was agnostic, I had no idea what that meant," Dhanya says. "I don't think I had heard that word before, something that described this thought process. I thought it was pretty cool."

A few months before the wedding, Scott began to prefer the general term *nonreligious*. "I don't practice religion and I don't reject religion. I might be a secular humanist, but I haven't learned enough about it and myself to come to that conclusion. I don't consider myself an atheist because I am not dogmatically opposed to theist beliefs. I felt like *nonreligious* was the most correct description of my thinking now."

Both Scott and Dhanya describe their discussions about religion as low-key and respectful, though they admit to occasionally stepping on each other's toes.

"I try to be understanding about other people's beliefs, something I learned from my mom," Scott says. "But there are times when I ask an admittedly pointed question. Dhanya often doesn't know why she does some of the things she does, and she doesn't like to admit that easily. So when I ask why, she may get flustered. Earlier in our relationship, she felt that I was being critical of her, and this caused a number of tense calls over the years. Eventually, she mostly came to accept that I'm just very curious and trying to understand."

"I have never really questioned my beliefs, but there are times where I also have questions about some of the things we practice as they don't always make sense to me," Dhanya says. "And when I ask my parents, they don't always know the answers, either."

Neither Scott nor Dhanya harbors any real desire to convert the other, which helps keep tension low. "I think Scott would adopt a religion if there is convincing science-based evidence backing it," she says, "but I'm neutral on whether he should."

"I don't know if I want to see her become nonreligious, but I do sometimes wish she would look at things with a more critical eye," Scott says. "Early in our relationship, I learned about her affinity for some pseudoscientific things. We have had a few tense moments around those, and I've learned to not be so direct and brash in my dismissal of what I see as quack medicine and superstition. I'm more concerned about educating her out of those things than religion. I try to guide her to look for rational answers without forcing anything. As for religion, we're mostly at peace with what we do. I let her follow her customs and don't worry about it. They don't generally seem to affect her rationality, which makes me happy."

"I feel this is one of the reasons our marriage is happy and stable," Dhanya says. "We respect and try to understand each other's backgrounds and belief systems without pushing too hard. One of the things I admire about my husband is that he always makes an effort to understand why we do certain things and how we do them, although I don't always have the answers."

(Scott and Dhanya's story continues in Chapters 14 and 17—look for the dotted arrows with the couple's names.)

7

An Earthquake in the Center of a Marriage
Hope and David

Growing up, Hope belonged to a fundamentalist Reformed Baptist church in small-town Georgia. "It felt just like a family. Everyone loved each other so warmly, and the sense of belonging was intense. My family was always one of the first there on Sunday and last to leave. It's very comforting, as long as you stay on the inside." Her parents taught Sunday school and her father was a deacon.

David grew up in a Baptist family one county over, but under very different conditions. His parents divorced when he was three, and his mother struggled to raise her three children as she coped with severe clinical depression. "We wouldn't always know where our next meal was coming from," David says, "but the church ladies would bring the leftovers from the Wednesday church dinner to my family. There were many Christmases where my family wouldn't have had any presents under the tree except for the kindness of the church."

Eventually his mother's depression overwhelmed her, and David and his brother and sister became wards of the state, living in separate group homes. It was during this time, at age eight, under the influence of a loving couple who supervised the home, that David said the Sinner's Prayer and was baptized.

By his late teens, David and his siblings were back with their mother. They attended a Reformed Baptist church, and by age 19, David had become a respected leader and teacher.

It was there that he met a Sunday school teacher named Hope.

"He was the first person to ask me really deep questions about what I believed, not just to compare beliefs but so that he could get to know me better as a person. He was the most serious, intense person I'd ever met, but loving and gentle and easy to talk to. He asked good questions and was a great listener. I'm shy and quiet, so meeting someone who was willing to take the time to get to really know me blew me away."

She was drawn to the intensity of his faith and his certainty about his own path—he was going to be a pastor. "I believed in him with every fiber of my being, and so did most of the people who knew him. Our shared faith was the entirety of my attraction to him. I loved listening to him talk about God, I loved to hear him teach the Bible. I knew he was going to be part of something significant in the church."

David saw something special in Hope. "I knew she would be the perfect wife for me—smart and beautiful, serious minded, and very kind. Since my own home life was such a mess, I needed to marry someone who came from a functional home if my future kids were to have a fighting chance at life. And our shared faith was always a huge part of our relationship, right from the start."

He proposed on her 17th birthday. They were married in January 2001 and immediately began working toward a life in ministry but struggled to find a church home. "We fought about it a lot," she says. "I'd be drawn to one church because of the people, he would be drawn to another one because of its values. We never really settled anywhere." David applied for several ministry positions, each one a dead end. "During this time, my faith became stronger. I was beginning to truly experience what it means to 'have a relationship with God' and could feel God's love for me. I felt God actually speaking to me through the Bible. I have more of an intuitive personality so this comes easily to me. David's personality is more intellectual. His experience of his faith always seemed to be more cerebral and mine was always more emotional."

By 2003, Hope and David found a church home at last, just as their second child arrived. David led a successful small group for young families and was on track to becoming an elder, but they left the church over doctrinal differences. He continued to apply for pastorates with small churches without success. Their third child arrived, and their fourth.

In late 2007, David heard a debate between theologian Alister McGrath and atheist biologist Richard Dawkins and felt McGrath had fared poorly. "I asked myself how I would have liked him to answer instead and how Dawkins may have responded. I was disappointed in how unconvincing my own answers were, even to me. I tried to get outside of the evangelistic assumptions and suddenly saw how devastating the unbeliever's questions were to an honest person. For the first time, I saw how everything hinged on those assumptions—whether Jesus was who he said he was and whether the Bible was what I believed it to be."

For the next few weeks, David explored his doubts intensely. "I spent every available minute listening to debates and reading, trying to find satisfactory answers to my questions. I was seeing more and more how the Gospel didn't measure up to rigorous questioning, and the answers from the Christian community were only believable if you presupposed the inspiration of the Bible and its inerrancy. I remember giving myself permission to go through an entire day as an atheist—no prayers and trying to find natural explanations for those things I would normally have thanked God for. Surely, I thought, God would forgive an honest quest for truth. At the end of the day, I realized that the day wasn't much different. I wasn't struck by lightning. It surprised me how much more sense it made of the world and the wonder that it provoked in me.

"The very next day, I said to myself, 'I think I'm an atheist.' I knew that this could cost me my family so I didn't say anything to my wife at first."

He didn't need to. Hope began to put the pieces together herself. "I saw a whole stack of books in his office on atheism, and he was watching Richard Dawkins debates on YouTube. Once in a while he invited me to watch them with him. But when they were over, he'd be really quiet and not arguing the Christian side as I expected. It felt like there was one inevitable outcome."

One night, Hope said to David, "I need to ask you something. I will be okay no matter what you say, but I need to know what you are thinking regarding Christianity."

"I had to tell her that I now thought of myself as an atheist," David says. "She was shocked and asked me why. I told her about my concerns over the historicity of Jesus and the unreliability of the Bible due to contradictions and scientifically proven falsehoods. She actually started reading a bit at first and seemed to be coming along with me, but accepted the first pat answers she found."

"It was huge to hear him say he didn't believe in any of it anymore. Huge. Our shared faith was totally central to everything that we were as a family."

Soon afterward, he announced his change of beliefs in an email to family and friends. Some of the responses were supportive. Many were not.

"It felt like all of our friends and most of our family immediately turned their backs on him," Hope recalls. "There were a lot of long Facebook debates. One of our best friends sent a long handwritten letter pleading with him to return to his faith and warning him that if he didn't he'd go to hell. It wasn't exactly loving."

Hope was dealing with her own emotions as well. "I was devastated. I cried and cried. I woke up and cried as I fixed breakfast for my kids. I cried as I rocked my baby and tried to wrap my mind around what had happened. The first time we tried to have sex after he deconverted, I ran out of the room sobbing. I remember thinking that it would have been easier to deal with his death than his deconversion. I had never even had a close non-Christian friend and had never known an atheist—and now I was married to one."

> *I remember thinking that it would have been easier to deal with his death than his deconversion. I had never even had a close non-Christian friend and had never known an atheist— and now I was married to one.*

David's emotions were a complicated mix of anger and elation at his newfound freedom. "I was angry with the teachers who I trusted when they told me that the Bible was backed up by history rather than researching to see if that was true. I was angry with myself for having believed so easily and without questioning for so long. At the same time, I had a newfound curiosity about the world and an inner freedom that I hadn't felt before."

Hope felt her own faith shaken. "Suddenly I was questioning everything I believed and wondering why *I* believe what I do. Was it just because I was raised in a Christian home? It didn't feel that way. My faith was the center of my life. My relationship with God felt too real to me to even really consider turning my back on it. I felt betrayed. I felt angry. We argued about religion a lot for the first couple of years. It was hard for me to separate myself from my religion, so if David attacked what he saw to be as something illogical or inconsistent in my beliefs, I felt personally attacked and would often respond emotionally, or I'd feel like David was trying to convert me or pressure me."

Shortly after David's deconversion, Hope's family was convulsed by an unthinkable tragedy—her younger brother took his own life. Hope became depressed as she tried to work through her feelings. Had it happened six months earlier, David would have responded in traditional Christian fashion, with assurances that her brother was in heaven with God, and that God was using the situation to bring more people to faith. But that was no longer an option. "I tried to be there for her, but I couldn't give her the lies that everyone else was giving her for her comfort. To me it was just tragic, and I hated how the preachers were using this terrible time with threats of hell and lies packaged as answers to people who wanted to know why this had happened."

It was all too much for Hope. "Truthfully, we were not entirely happy before my husband deconverted. His change exacerbated every preexisting weakness in our marriage."

She decided at last that she would take the children and leave. "There was so much tension and lack of intimacy after he deconverted, I just wanted to separate. We could not agree on how to discipline our children, how to teach them, or even when they should attend church with me."

David learned of her plans by reading an entry in her journal. He was stunned. "She hadn't mentioned it to me at all. I took the next day off work and we were able to talk things through, but for a while I was fearful every day when I left for work that I would come home and they all would be gone."

"We tried counseling, but it was a disaster," Hope says. "It freaked me out to feel like we were not making any progress and like David didn't even understand what was wrong with our marriage or accept responsibility for his part of our problems. I felt like there was no cooperation and not enough mutual respect. I constantly felt like I was too angry to love. I was terrified and I felt totally alone. None of my friends at church had a clue what I was going through or how to support me. They moved on with their lives, but I had all of these shattered dreams. I just wanted to run. I honestly thought that maybe it would be easier for us if we didn't live together."

In the end, after much time and discussion, they decided to stick it out. "I wish I could say it was easy to make up my mind to love David and then move forward with that decision, but it was not. I realized that we weren't likely to end our marriage in a peaceful or friendly way, in part because of David's traumatic childhood, so I decided to stay. Five years later, I'm really glad I did."

David is glad she didn't leave, though he continues to feel deeply frustrated. "I can't say we've really worked through things. It's more like we've roped off territory and have agreed not to enter each other's space. We don't talk about religion. We don't really talk about much at all of substance. I was actually hoping at first that we could make this change together. For me, I feel like the woman I married for her rigorous intellect and independent mind has valued her beliefs over me. Rather than giving it an honest investigation, she has decided that she doesn't want to look any further. I feel hurt and disrespected by her lack of interest in the substance of our differences and reasons for them. She seems completely unwilling to accept that she might be wrong or that there might be intelligent reasons for or against her position. She is religious because that's what makes her feel good and seems unaffected by not knowing if it's true." He does acknowledge the difficulty she would face. "I can't imagine how hard it must be for her to reconsider the teachings that she has been told since birth. I just would have hoped that our relationship was worth at least an honest attempt at understanding."

Hope wishes David would reconvert just as much as David wishes Hope would deconvert. "I hope that he returns to God someday. I want him to experience the same joy in God and love and peace I experience. But if I could look ahead to the future and know with 100% certainty that David will never turn back to God, I wouldn't change a thing. It took me a long time to get to this place, a very long time, but I love my husband and we have a happy life together."

She agrees with David that challenges remain. "Five years later, we still have a lot to work out. We still struggle at times. But we're learning how to make compromises that are respectful to each other. We're loyal, devoted partners now, and I don't think we will ever divorce. But if we ever did . . ." She pauses. "If we did, our religious difference would probably be the reason."

When I ask Hope what has helped her most during this time, she doesn't pause. "Trusting God, surrendering to His will for my life, allowing His spirit to heal every hurt, to help me love when I feel empty or bitter—

He has done an amazing work of healing my heart and helping me learn to love unconditionally. Unconditional love is the biggest, most important thing I've learned in this journey. Real love doesn't act lovingly because of what I hope to get from the other person. Real love doesn't act lovingly only when the other person is behaving the way I want them to. Real love chooses to stay open. Always. In the disappointment, in the hurt, in the moments of disagreement, I try to always stay open to love. I try to show love even when I feel unloved, and I receive my husband's love even when I could choose to be angry or bitter."

"I love my wife so much," David says. "I feel the loss of our shared faith keenly and despise the distance that's between us now because of our religious difference. I know the kind of relationship we're capable of because we've been there, and I mourn the loss of that relationship every single day. To avoid conflict, we don't share our deepest thoughts with each other anymore."

"When we started this journey," Hope says, "the biggest question I had was if it was possible to have a happy mixed-religion marriage. Six years into this I would say yes, it is possible. It is hard, but marriage is hard. Our struggles are different from some other people's, but not a lot more difficult than most other couples.'"

She also acknowledges that her own views have changed somewhat. "You don't realize it, but in the type of narrow-minded church I grew up in, you are told what to think about God and what to believe about the Bible. You are handed your opinion about secular culture and other religions. It doesn't feel like it—it's just that everyone around you has the same opinion about pretty much everything, so you just embrace it. Since David left that world, he's become much more liberal in his views on . . . well, just about everything. I have too, though not as much. A lot of my friends act like I'm crazy, especially about abortion issues and gay rights. But I think more or less it's a shift for good. At the end of the day, having my nice little Christian bubble popped has been a good thing. I wish more Christians could see the way they look to outsiders like I have with my non-Christian husband."

(There is more on Hope and David's relationship in Chapters 15–17 and 19—look for the dotted arrows with the couple's names.)

8

The Difference
a Child Makes

Arlene and Nate

Ask Arlene for her fondest memories of church and she'll go straight to the black Southern Baptist church she attended in 1968 when she was all of five years old. "This wasn't the creepy, freaky, Westboro Church kind of Baptist," she says. "It was the kind with great gospel music, fried chicken on Sunday, and uplifting messages about God. I loved it."

The church was in Glendale, California, a city on the north end of the sprawling Los Angeles area. Rising north of Glendale are the San Gabriel Mountains, dividing the L.A. basin from the high desert beyond. And rising on the lower slopes of the San Gabriels in the 1960s, just below the Angeles National Forest, was a small line of suburban towns—quiet, picturesque, with a population that was mostly upper middle class and white.

Her family moved to La Crescenta, one of those suburbs, at which point Arlene discovered what she calls "the horrifying truth that we were actually white. You'd think I'd have noticed this when I was the only white girl in a black church, but my whiteness didn't register for some reason until all of the faces around me became white. I was totally shocked."

She also discovered yet another kind of Baptist church. "Not only did all the black people disappear," she says, "but so did the really good music and the uplifting messages. The sermons became just that—sermons. They droned on and weren't uplifting at all, nothing like I'd grown up with. It was like the joy and the music and the happiness dried up. The meaning of the message was the same, but the delivery and the spirit just vanished."

Her parents felt the same. They wanted a lively, down-to-earth church or nothing, and in 1960s La Crescenta, options were few. So at age six, Arlene says, "my Sunday-goin'-to-meetin' church days were over."

She spent many weekends with her grandmother, "a very sweet Christian lady" who likewise couldn't find a church that spoke to her. Around age 13, Arlene began to question everything she'd been told, and Grandma was her sounding board. "She'd listen to me go on and on for hours about what B.S. a virgin birth was, and how did people really come back from the dead, and how could God be everywhere, and if he knows what I'm going to do then how did I really have a free spirit, and on and on and on. She'd take it all in and eventually say something like, 'That's why it's called faith, Lena.' When I was finally done, she'd simply tell me that the answers I was looking for were not in the Bible—they were in my heart. She said I would eventually find out the truth if I kept my mind keen and never stopped searching for the right things. She said I'd know them when I found them.

"I respected her for not throwing the Bible at me as the answer to all my questions. She realized that times were changing from when she was a child—she was born in 1895!—and that questioning everything was now the way of the world. My grandma was and is a wonderful Christian role model for me.

"I grew up with very strong traditional values and surrounded by people that had a strong sense of their faith. That strength of faith and their unshakable personal beliefs are what allowed open and frank conversations amongst family and friends about things they agreed on as well as deep conversations about things they did not embrace."

Fifteen hundred miles away in Kansas City, Missouri, Nate was busy growing up in a Woody Allen movie with a Catholic twist. "We had Jews, Calvinists, Lutherans, and Baptists in the larger family, but mostly it was Italian Catholics. I had a great aunt who was a mother superior at a Catholic high school for girls. Almost every evening at the dinner table was an open debate, especially when my great aunt would visit. Abortion, premarital sex, homosexuality, capital punishment, the nature of God, the infallibility of the pope, transubstantiation. That was an awesome family dynamic."

Even though debates over the details were allowed, in the end "you were still expected to walk the walk," he says. "That didn't sit right with me, and they knew it. I was the black sheep."

Born with a bad case of yellow jaundice, he had been baptized quickly, just in case. "I didn't ask for it, but apparently my mortal soul was at risk," he says. The family's Catholicism was nonnegotiable, but "it was more of an obligation than an identity or belief. Going to Mass was just what you did on Sundays. It was important to my grandparents, and my aunts, but not to me or my uncles. Some of my distant Italian family members would come to Mass, and then go out and do things that would be discussion points in the confessional the following Sunday. They didn't go to confessional a lot, but when they did they were in there for some time!"

His own doubts started very young. "I can recall sitting in Mass when I was about four or five listening to the priest yammer on about absolution, and the word that came to my mind was *bullshit*! Okay, maybe not that exact word, but that's the idea. Every time I heard about this jealous God, the God that wanted you to believe or burn, I thought that this God they pray to was egomaniacal, petulant, and self-centered. We're supposed to be master over these behaviors, but we accept them in our God? Sorry, even if I did believe, that's not a God I would subscribe to."

He was confirmed and had his First Communion at age 11. "I didn't want to do it, but to refuse would have made me a pariah in the eyes of the family. So my Confirmation was a lie and my First Communion was a lie. I despised those lies, but going through the motions was what was expected of me."

As he moved into his teens, Nate grew more resentful of what he saw as religious hypocrisy and deception. "From that I pretty much ended up hating all religions that claim to have the inside scoop on the will and nature of God. It's offensive. I'm okay with someone having a belief in God, but telling me that your belief is an indelible truth is delusional. Nobody can prove or disprove the existence of God. These were the discussions we had when I was a teen, and the frustration of trying to get believers to understand that they don't exactly corner the market on truth, that their faith was just that, a faith, was maddening to cope with."

Southern Baptists earned a special place in his disdain for religion when he was 16. "I was dating a girl whose mother was a hard-core Southern Baptist. I was openly atheist and her mother could not wrap her brain around the idea. She decided that I was the Antichrist—literally the Antichrist—and asked her minister what to do. His instructions were, 'If you want Jesus to come back, the Antichrist has to do his job. Welcome him with open arms.' It instantly went from this underling hostility to an almost surreal acceptance by her family. It was completely bizarre."

After attending the University of Southern California, Nate went to work for an L.A. law firm in 1981. It was at a birthday party for a colleague at the firm that he met Arlene.

"The first thing she ever said to me, walking up from behind me, was, 'Get the f**k out of my way. You're between me and my drink!'"

"Hey—never stand between a nice Baptist girl and her drink!" Arlene says with a laugh.

Nate grins. "I was hooked."

They started dating, and the religious difference came up immediately. "We were open about everything right from the get-go," she says. "He told me he was a recovering Catholic, and that of all religions, he respected Catholics the most, hated Baptists the most, and thought they were all equally bullshit! I told him that was fine and I'd pray for him, then we'd laugh and go do something else. But I can't say I never worried about it. He just detests the Bible-thumpin' you're-all-gonna-burn-in-hell Southern Baptists he grew up with. The whole thing with that early girlfriend's mother helped me understand where the loathing was coming from. But that's not me, so we were okay."

"I figure everybody has to believe in something, right?" Nate says. "If it's not an issue with them, then it's not an issue with me."

"So we went on having these long, interesting conversations about religion for about 12 years," Arlene says. "It was a big catalyst for my interest in apologetics [the reasoned defense of religious beliefs]. I knew that saying, ''Cause the Bible and my grandma tell me so' was not going to cut it. We both found it amazing that the other one could be so well spoken and so well educated and yet be so damned wrong! But it never got too serious during those 12 years, mostly just lighthearted ribbing, really fun."

Then their son John was born—and things got serious.

"Everything stopped being anecdotal and became very real for me then," Arlene recalls. "I was a Christian, Nate was not. I had a child with a soul. My beliefs were no longer opinions but matters of life and death."

Nate felt the change immediately. "After John was born, I felt like I'd become 'unclean' because I did not believe. We didn't discuss it much at first, but by the time we settled in Arizona, there was a clear problem."

Arlene and Nate had some heated discussions about the eventual religious identity of their son. They eventually agreed that John would be raised as a Christian, but Nate would be free to share his own opinions, and Arlene would not stifle John's questions. He would be free to explore those questions, just as she had been.

But the seed of a deeper discontent about the religious difference had been planted. "As I got older, I began to realize that I was really missing the familiarity that comes through mutual faith. I wanted to share my growing feelings with someone who didn't just listen but understood." Their interesting discussions became "icy debates," she says. "It was no longer fun. It was confrontational."

I began to realize that I was really missing the familiarity that comes through mutual faith. I wanted to share my growing feelings with someone who didn't just listen but understood. It was no longer fun. It was confrontational.

"Religion was a huge factor in our divorce," says Nate. "It wasn't the only one, but it was the deal breaker. When I served Arlene the papers, she looked at the settlement clause and said, 'Great! Let's go have lunch!' We were going to kill each other the day before, but now we were instantly best friends again."

Arlene found someone who shared her faith. Brian had been a close friend to both of them for many years. Nate's divorce from Arlene was so amicable and his friendship with Brian so close that Brian asked him to be his best man at the wedding, and Nate accepted.

Brian and Arlene were married at 5 p.m. on September 15, 2000. Just after the reception dinner, Brian collapsed and was admitted to the emergency room. He underwent surgery the next morning and died of liver failure the following day.

Arlene reeled with grief. "No one knew he was that sick. Not his doctors, not me." Nate remained her closest friend through the pain and shock of the loss, as well as through her eventual remarriage, and to this day they remain the best of friends.

"Without the pesky marriage thing hanging around our necks, our sparring religious jabs and lighthearted yet in-depth discussions have returned," she says. "So it seems that it's not religious differences that ruin good relationships—it's marriage."

(More details on Arlene and Nate's wedding, their parenting choices, and their divorce appear in Chapters 14, 15, and 19—look for the dotted arrows with the couple's names.)

9

Finding a
Meeting Place
Evan and Cate

Evan and Cate were both raised Catholic. "My faith has always given me comfort," she says. "We prayed before dinner and at bedtime, and my sister and I went to Catholic school. My parents were very involved in our small-town parish, volunteering as lectors and Eucharistic ministers. I watched them, saw what their faith brought to them, and wanted the same for myself."

Evan says his faith was more incidental. "I went to Sunday school and was even an altar boy for a while. But I never had much attachment to religion growing up, so when my parents gave me the choice to stop attending Sunday school in the eighth grade, I was more than happy to take back my Sunday mornings." By the end of high school, Evan separated from religion altogether, though he kept his views to himself.

He and Cate met and began dating in college. "I continued to follow in my parents' footsteps," Cate says. "Went to church faithfully every Sunday, volunteered as a lector and as a Eucharistic minister, just like they did. Hearing the music and saying the prayers during the routine of the Mass brought me comfort, and I enjoyed sharing my faith with others." That was something that was missing in her relationship with Evan. He went with her to Mass, but she knew his faith was more nominal, even though they rarely discussed their actual beliefs.

Cate told Evan she wanted a Catholic wedding. "He went along with what I wanted to do; then after we were married he went to church with me a few times at Easter and Christmas—then stopped. I didn't understand why, and I didn't really ask why. I also told him when the time came I wanted to baptize our children. He told me he was okay with this but said he wouldn't be there for it because it went against what he believed." It was the first clear statement of its kind. "I remember feeling sad about this," Cate says, "but I went on like anything else I did and we didn't discuss it any further."

Three boys arrived, and each was baptized without Evan in attendance.

After a few years, Cate began to struggle with depression. "Evan suggested I find something that interested me and pursue the interest. I thought I'd try turning to my faith to help me deal with my emotions and went on a Catholic women's retreat with a friend."

The focus of the retreat was a renewal of faith, and as part of the retreat experience, Evan was asked to write a letter of support to Cate. At the close of the retreat, the women's families came together to show their love and support for their renewed faith. "I was all for letting Cate know how much I loved and supported her, but I was being asked to do this in a religious context," Evan says. "I felt that I was betraying my own beliefs by supporting Cate in hers. Now I've never taken issue with Cate, or anyone else for that matter, believing in God, Allah, Zeus, the Flying Spaghetti Monster, or any other deity they wish to pray to. But I do have issue when someone takes their personal beliefs and tries to impose them on someone else." It felt to Evan like a line was being crossed in that direction—that faith was becoming a wedge between them.

"We did talk about the new tension that developed between us after the retreat," Evan recalls. Cate also began thinking more directly about her actual beliefs. "During one of our conversations, she mentioned how the priest said everyone was a sinner. This did not sit well with her because she doesn't see herself that way. She also didn't like the Catholic Church's stance on gay marriage or birth control. But she kept saying that going to church gave her peace in spite of these differences. I couldn't understand how she could find comfort in a place that she disagreed with so much."

Far from withdrawing, Cate was connecting even more deeply with her faith community, even as she recognized her serious differences with it. She says that when some of the women from the retreat started planning the following year's retreat, "I told Evan that I wanted to be part of this group. It didn't sit well with him. But I had already decided I wanted to share my story of how my beliefs differed from my husband's."

As the months of planning went by, she enjoyed herself more and more. "This was the interest Evan had been talking about!" she says. "The women of the group were believers like me, and this lifted my spirits. But at the same time, I could tell it was bothering him. I didn't understand. I had finally joined a group that I enjoyed being in. He was a member of photography and beer-brewing clubs. What difference did it make if my group had something to do with my faith?"

They began talking in more depth about the ways she differed from the church. "He told me that I needed to look in the mirror and see the real me," she recalls. "I started struggling with my Catholicism. If I don't agree with most of what Catholics believe, why do I associate with that religion? Catholics say Jesus was born of a virgin. I disagree. I believe Mary and Joseph were Jesus's parents. Catholics are pro-life. I am pro-choice."

"This barely scratches the surface of the struggle we went through," Evan says. "Cate was also having a hard time coming to terms with my lack of belief. At the lowest point, we questioned whether it was even possible for two people with such differences to have a lasting relationship. Thankfully we had the sense to seek counseling. The first thing we learned was that sometimes our differences have no influence on one another and so should be respected. The second was the importance of communication. Until we went to counseling, it was hard for us to communicate our feelings other than being angry or upset. We focused on only the negative and forgot about the things that bonded us in the first place."

Evan knew Cate was struggling with her religious identity but still needed that sense of community and belonging. One day he came across something interesting online. "While on an online atheist community, he came across a secular parenting discussion being held at a Unitarian Universalist church nearby," Cate recalls. "He was curious why a church was sponsoring a secular parenting topic. Looking into it, he discovered what Unitarian Universalism is and thought this may be something to interest both of us."

The UU website had a link that caught Cate's eye. "It was to something called the Belief-O-Matic quiz.[1] You answer questions about your beliefs and it tells you which religion suits you." The quiz is run by Beliefnet and has no affiliation with UU. Cate took the quiz, and her results were telling.

"Catholic was third or fourth down on the list. But Unitarian Universalism was at the top of my list, the best fit for my actual beliefs."

She decided to read more about UU and found the seven UU Principles around which UUism is built (see sidebar). Unlike Catholicism, which was becoming a poor fit, Cate says, "I agreed with all seven principles. I told Evan that this was something I wanted to check out. The kids enjoyed themselves and even Evan enjoyed himself . . . in a church! Who would have guessed?"

The Seven UU Principles

Because Unitarian Universalist fellowships are formed around shared values instead of shared beliefs, they often represent an effective meeting place for religious and nonreligious partners. These seven values are affirmed and promoted in UU fellowships:

1. *The inherent worth and dignity of every person;*

2. *Justice, equity and compassion in human relations;*

3. *Acceptance of one another and encouragement to spiritual growth in our congregations;*

4. *A free and responsible search for truth and meaning;*

5. *The right of conscience and the use of the democratic process within our congregations and in society at large;*

6. *The goal of world community with peace, liberty, and justice for all;*

7. *Respect for the interdependent web of all existence of which we are a part.*[2]

"We've been going for two years now," Evan says. "It doesn't fill a spiritual need for me; it does fill an intellectual one. I had a group of friends many years ago that could discuss religion, politics, or any other hot topic of the day and still remain friends. I loved it. But we moved away from each other and ended up with acquaintances and family members who were always more concerned with saying how right they were and how wrong everyone else was instead of having an actual dialogue. This made me bitter towards many viewpoints, and that bitterness certainly didn't help the problem that arose between Cate and me. In the discussion groups at the UU we can debate a topic and then push our differences aside as we move the chairs away for social hour. It's refreshing."

Evan says sharing the UU experience has helped the two of them at home as well. "Now we can disagree about something and a hug and simple 'I love you' is all that is needed to move along."

He says it also taught him something about Cate. "When she was at the Catholic Church, I couldn't understand why she would be part of something that she did not share so many beliefs with. But now I've learned that for her, the comfort she feels isn't necessarily from her beliefs but from being part of a ritual and a community that shares a common thread. And now that I'm part of this community as well, it brings me great comfort too."

Cate says her experience at the UU helped her find her personal religious identity separate from a denominational one. "Shortly after we joined, I started attending the BYOT (Build Your Own Theology) class. We met for nine months, then wrote a Credo statement. It was then that I really discovered the Cate that had been looking in the mirror. I realized that I don't have to go to church to have a relationship with my God. It is something that I had been struggling with all along but finally became okay with it."

(For more on Unitarian Universalism and other noncreedal congregations, turn to Chapter 15.)

10

A Believer and
Nonbeliever Trade Places
Anna and Gary

Religion was a big part of Anna's Illinois childhood in the 1970s, and a mostly positive one. "I was deeply committed to my faith. My dad was from this big Italian Catholic family, and Mom was raised Presbyterian." Because the Catholic Church was more insistent, Anna and her siblings were raised Catholic. "We went to a liberal church that taught us not to judge other people, since we couldn't know their circumstances. They taught that there's no conflict between science and religion, so I never saw any problem with evolution or the Big Bang, and the priest was a younger man who encouraged questions. It was a good experience."

She was also influenced by a celebrity cousin on her mother's side—a former actor and well-known current evangelist. "At first his worldview intrigued me, and he had a pretty significant influence on my beliefs. But the deeper into it I got, the less it all made sense. I was in college studying biology and history just as he started his ministry, and I started exploring more worldviews."

She was working her way through college waiting tables at a local restaurant when she was asked to train the new waiter, a cocky extrovert named Gary.

"He was nice-looking and had a great sense of humor, but he was also arrogant and a little rough around the edges. It was obvious from the beginning that he was one of those people who need to be the center of attention all the time. I had fun working with him, though. He was fun and didn't take anything too seriously, which would help the shifts pass quickly."

It wasn't long before Gary's intentions became clear. "He liked me right away, that was pretty obvious, but I wasn't interested in him. He was persistent, though. He'd actually come to the restaurant when I was working and he had a day off. I would hide or duck out the back door when he came to visit. It got to be quite the game. But he kept at it, and he grew on me. After a while, I started to look forward to seeing him at work, and eventually he talked me into a date."

Their religious differences came up right away. "I think it was because I wore a little cross around my neck, this family heirloom. I was religious, but I wore it mainly for the family connection, not because of the religious symbolism."

She never knew much about Gary's family background. His uncle was a minister, but Gary never went to church or Sunday school himself.

Gary was adamant that there is no God. "He was worried at first that I would judge him and try to convert him. But by the time we were dating, even though I was religious, I didn't see myself as Catholic or even Christian, really. I believed that all roads led to God."

Anna kept exploring those roads. "I read a lot of Taoist philosophy, and my two closest friends were Lakota. I liked the Taoist idea of life flowing like a river, and the Lakota connection to nature and the belief that all humans are connected really spoke to me. I also liked that they focused on family and friends, and you could pray to your ancestors. I wasn't ready to completely give up the idea of a supernatural force behind the universe just yet, but the idea of a more impersonal, natural force behind the universe was an appealing middle ground."

By the time of their wedding, Anna considered herself a religious pagan. Even so, she still felt the insistent pull of family Catholicism. "At first I wanted a Catholic priest to officiate. I just didn't want to upset my family. But Gary wasn't too excited about attending the classes and other things the Catholic Church makes you do before they will marry you. I'm actually glad he didn't go for it. It would have felt a bit like a lie since I hadn't been a practicing Catholic for years by that time."

In the end, they asked a justice of the peace to officiate the ceremony and included readings and blessings from Lakota, Christian, and Baha'i sources. "The non-Christian things did not go over well with some of my family," Anna recalls, "and some were upset that it wasn't in a church. But we were happy with it."

Anna says that when their first child was born, "My Catholic superstitions kicked in. I felt like I needed to have him baptized. I started church shopping again, but just couldn't commit to any church for a baptism. We tried various churches over the next four years—Lutheran, Episcopalian, UCC [United Church of Christ], First Christian, Methodist, Baptist, even a charismatic church. We couldn't ever agree on one as a family, and they all seemed fake to me, so we gave up looking. Gary and I decided that if the kids want to get baptized when they are adults, they can decide on which church."

During the same years, Gary had begun to struggle with a serious drinking problem. "His uncle is a Baptist minister and a recovering alcoholic," Anna says. "He told Gary how much the church had helped him overcome his addiction. Boom, just like that, Gary accepted Jesus as his personal savior and became a Christian. He found a small Baptist church that he liked and we started attending."

Even though she was religious as well at the time, the abrupt conversion made Anna uneasy. "I wanted to support his recovery, but I wasn't comfortable with our kids being brought up in the Baptist church. It caused a lot of arguments. He didn't understand why I was so uncomfortable. Since he never attended church in his life except for weddings and funerals, he didn't understand the damage religion can do.

"One Sunday the pastor of the church gave a sermon on how evil Catholics are. I gathered up the kids and walked out in the middle of the sermon and waited in the parking lot. When Gary came out, I explained that I didn't want our kids to learn that half of their family was going to hell because they were a different kind of Christian. He finally agreed that the kids and I didn't have to go anymore."

It was around this time that her famous cousin, the one who had been instrumental in deepening her faith, began to influence her again—this time in the opposite direction. "I started to see the damage his teachings were doing to the family," she says. "He also did more to show me the contradictions and hypocrisy in the Bible and Christian teachings than he ever did to strengthen my faith."

Her oldest son, whose birth had also drawn her back into the church, played a role in pulling her out again as well. "He was always really advanced, and when he was 10, he kept asking me questions about the start of life, the beginning of things, why are there so many religions, who made

God. . . . I gave him the same answers my parents and priests gave me as a kid, but they didn't make any sense to him, so he kept challenging them, questioning things I had never questioned or noticed. I realized they didn't make any sense to me either. That's when I finally shed my Catholic guilt and superstitions again and became fully nonreligious."

When they met, Anna was religious and Gary was an atheist. Now he was religious and she was an atheist.

That each of them now occupied a position the other had rejected was a source of tension between them. But more serious was Gary's continued struggle with alcoholism, coupled with symptoms of a deepening mental illness. He became emotionally and verbally abusive, something Anna thinks may relate to abuse he suffered himself as a child.

Last year, after 15 years of marriage, they separated.

"Our religious differences didn't play a direct part in our separation, but they did play an indirect role. When I was religious, I believed that God had joined us together for a reason. My mom's side of the family, and my dad's side also to a certain extent, didn't believe in divorce. They also believe that the wife should be submissive to the husband. That had a huge influence on me deciding to stay in my marriage as long as I did. I didn't want to disappoint my family or go against God's will. I thought the reason God had brought us together was because I was to help my husband sober up and break the cycle of dysfunction he had grown up in.

"When I became an atheist, I realized that I chose my marriage, not God, and I could choose to leave it with no supernatural consequences. I also realized that there was no grand plan behind our marriage that I didn't understand, and it was my husband's responsibility to fix himself. I also realized that I was doing my kids a huge disservice by staying in the marriage. It wasn't healthy or stable for them, me, or my husband for that matter. Once I got rid of the religious guilt, I was free to leave. My kids and I are much happier now. Hopefully, he'll also find happiness one day."

(For more of Anna and Gary's story, see Chapters 14 and 19—look for the dotted arrows with the couple's names.)

11

The Unequally
Yoked Club

Cassidy and Bill[1]

Couples who marry with the same religious identity only to have one change later are often in for a period of high tension and conflict. Sometimes they push through to a new equilibrium, and sometimes—as Cassidy McGillicuddy describes in this first-person account of her own marriage—it all falls apart for the best.

I'd been out of church for a while. I guess I was 24 or so. Bill had gone to Basic Training, having no other ideas for how to make money, and in his absence I blossomed like a flower. I joined a gym, lost some weight and got toned, bought a new wardrobe, chopped off my stringy uncut hair and got a perm, and fell back in love with makeup and all that girlie stuff I'd rejected years earlier.

Bill had just come back for two weeks over the holidays that year. When I went to the airport to fetch him, I went in a smokin' hot red velvet minidress. Bill was horrified. His modest, demure little wife had changed somewhat in his absence, and clearly was not the timid little creature she'd been when he'd left.

Control freaks aren't thrilled about stuff like that. It makes them nervous when someone discovers his or her voice like I had.

Later that night, Bill told me that he had found my drawer of makeup and thrown it all away "for me."

At first my impulse was, "Well, he's my husband, and that's how marriage works, and husbands are the head of the family, after all." But I realized that the only reason I thought that was because of Pentecostalism. I wasn't Pentecostal anymore, and I didn't have to put up with being treated like a toddler. Bill knew that I wasn't Pentecostal anymore, but clearly he thought I was just "questioning" and would be back at some point. We'd been quietly bickering about it for about six months, with the conflict never coming to a head.

> I'd always assumed that our religious difference was something we could somehow work around. Looking back, I'm just thunderstruck by how naïve, how hopelessly optimistic I'd been.

What Bill had done was the mark of someone who is losing control and doesn't like it. What he'd done, this hugely disrespectful way he'd treated me, was all due to his fear that I had left Christianity for good and that nothing he could do would get me back into that ghastly, toxic religion. He was finally figuring out that I was not just a "prodigal son" but an actual, honest-to-goodness apostate.

I got up, got my stuff out of the trash can, and advised him very coolly that he was not to do anything with my stuff again without asking first. We had one of our first big post-deconversion arguments that night, centered around his helplessness, his inability to force me back into the fold. He'd tried trickery and word games; he'd tried making me read apologetics books in the hopes that one of those authors would be able to make sense of things where he clearly hadn't been able to do so; he'd tried strong-arming me and threatening me with hell. He'd tried to play upon my sympathy for him, having to go to church alone and endure all the people there asking where I was. He'd tried to sting my pride by implying that our façade as the happy Pentecostal couple, the high school sweethearts whose engagement had been so breathlessly followed the whole time up to the wedding, was fading.

Those tactics would likely have worked on someone who was merely questioning or doubting a little. But I was completely, 100% over Christianity in any flavor or form by that point.

Up until that very moment, I'd always assumed that our religious difference was something we could somehow work around. Looking back, I'm just thunderstruck by how naïve, how hopelessly optimistic I'd been. But as I looked at him across the room, I realized that he now considered us "unequally yoked." We were now, officially in his mind, a mixed-religion marriage.

His response was not surprising: He declared that he was going to war for the soul of his "sweet Christian wife." This silliness in me was just demons at work, and he'd find the right magical spell and ritual to drive out the demons and get his submissive, docile Christian wife back. It'd be this wonderful story he'd be able to tell the folks at church and the children he was still somehow convinced we were going to have because Jesus had told him we would—how he'd rescued his wife from the jaws of Hell.

The Fundamentalist View of Promises

In the world of fundamentalist Christianity, once someone's made a promise, there is no way to renege on that promise, even if the other party to that promise, or the premise upon which that promise was made, turns out to be dead wrong and even abusive.

The promises we make at any point in our spiritual "walks" are promises that are set in stone—especially if we decide that these promises have the stamp of approval from our god himself. It's awfully hard to walk back a promise you made under the misconception that your god wanted you to do this thing. If you decide later that you'd misheard that voice, or that the voice didn't exist at all, you've got problems on a scale that nonfundamentalists can't really begin to comprehend.

I felt a degree of sympathy for him. I knew this wasn't what he'd expected. All along, he'd been holding on in the belief that I'd come to my senses somehow. All along, he'd suffered under the pain of realizing that this was not how he'd wanted his married life to look or work.

When I looked across at Bill on that fateful winter night so many years ago, I felt a degree of sympathy for him. I knew this wasn't what he'd expected. All along, he'd been praying and manipulating me to make me go back to being the wife Jesus had told him I'd be. All along, he'd been holding on in the belief that I'd come to my senses somehow—through prayer, through his action, something. All along, he'd suffered under the pain of realizing that this was not how he'd wanted his married life to look or work.

I'd pulled the rug out from under him. I'd done an unwitting bait-and-switch. He'd married a dedicated Christian woman. We'd made plans around him going into the ministry. We'd operated together, as a team, the best way we could under the antiquated and misogynistic rules of our faith. I'd been the best wife I could be and followed all the rules.

And then I'd ruined everything for him.

Of course, all I'd really done was stop playing along with what had turned out to be purely a fantasy. I'd stepped outside of the prescribed dance steps on the floor and had finally begun dancing to my own music. In most couples, changes are expected, and with communication and a healthy dose of respect and gentleness, the majority of those changes can usually be incorporated into the couple's shared life together. But in fundamentalist Christianity, with its hatred and terror of change, its death grip on the illusion of soulmate perfection, its loathing of compromise, its callous (and erroneous) insistence that a good relationship is impossible between people of differing beliefs, even fairly minor changes can destroy a couple.

My deconversion was the only authentic, honest, and fair response I could make to what I had discovered. It was the right thing to do. I certainly didn't do it to hurt anybody. I did it to save my own life and sanity.

But for what it's worth, I sorrowed for the death of that fantasy life Bill and I had both been promised so many times by our various well-meaning church leaders and mentors. I sorrowed for the pain and fear Bill must have felt. I felt the same pain and fear, though for different reasons, as I contemplated the coming days and wondered how we would deal with what had changed.

When I deconverted, Bill waved my earlier resolution to die in the traces at me, as if that was a good reason for me to reconvert. I'd made a promise to serve Jesus, so I had to serve Jesus no matter what doubts I had.

But I hadn't made a promise. I'd struck a deal. In the same way that medieval peasants struck a deal with their feudal lords to exchange service and freedom for protection and care, I had exchanged my freedom and my time for various things this deity had promised. And this deity's promises had turned out to be false—in fact, the deity very likely did not exist at all.

Thus, I did not view myself as being bound by that deal anymore. I'd signed a contract whose premises had turned out to be fraudulent.

Bill didn't see things that way.

There are a lot of reasons why Christians might go this route. Some are charitable, and some really aren't. Bill wanted me to reconvert because my reconversion was important to his image. His ability to lead others was being called into question by the up-and-ups at church. He wasn't really that worried about my soul; his reasons routinely centered around the effect my apostasy was having *on him*.

> *When we leave Christianity, our spouses are stuck in a movie without a romantic co-star and a script that no longer applies. That movie's successful wrap depended on our cooperation, and we're not cooperating anymore. Of course the other person's going to be upset. They've got a good reason to be upset.*

His attitude is reflected in the stories I hear from other ex-Christians. Of course our spouses are worried about our souls, if they're any kind of loving people at all. But the promises also speak to the other person's starring role in the movie of his or her life. When we leave Christianity, our spouses are stuck in a movie without a romantic co-star and a script that no longer applies. That movie's successful wrap depended on our cooperation, and we're not cooperating anymore. Of course the other person's going to be upset. They've got a good reason to be upset.

When someone deconverts, those old promises often come back to nip at the heels of the ex-Christian like an annoying little dog. When the ex-Christian is still married to a Christian, the partner's sense of betrayal and pain is even deeper, because some of those promises feel like they relate to the marital bond. Remember, Christians generally believe completely (and utterly without any good reason, may I add) that a marriage should—even *must*—be based upon shared faith in Jesus Christ. And they almost never see a person's spiritual walk as a two-way deal instead of a one-sided promise, nor do they generally understand that you just can't force a belief to continue to exist when you've figured out it isn't true. (You try it sometime with unicorns, Zeus, or Santa Claus.)

When one spouse deconverts, the table loses a leg. The foundation cracks. Not only is the façade fading, not only is the illusion dissipating of that happy Christian family the other spouse always thought he or she would have because he or she followed all the rules, not only is the remaining spouse's sanity and good sense coming into question for still believing something he or she knows the other thinks is nonsense now, but there's a sense of betrayal, a feeling that the promise that person made about how their relationship was going to run has been broken.

And I totally get that. I got it back then. I still get it now.

Often the ex-Christian is still reeling from the pain and betrayal of discovering that the deal wasn't struck in good faith at all on the other side, so it's hard to understand the pain of the remaining Christian spouse who is feeling quite a bit of the same pain and betrayal. It's not so much about the ex-Christian spouse as it is about the remaining Christian's sense of stung pride and disappointment.

The more he insisted that I go to church and tried to shame me about the promises he thought I'd broken, the less loved and cherished I felt. Did he not understand just how abhorrent I found that religion? Did he not grasp just how false the deal turned out to be? Did he not get how betrayed I already felt about being so very wrong about something so very important? I felt like he didn't care about me, just about the façade that I'd destroyed by deconverting.

So as coping mechanisms go, insisting on doing Christian stuff in the absence of faith and shaming me about these perceived broken promises were definitely failures.

Promises depend upon conditions. They're made in good faith with the understanding we have. When those conditions alter, when the understanding we have turns out to be false or wrong, then it's not fair to hold someone to those promises anymore. It's not loving, and it's definitely not charitable. But many Christians will do so, and they'll do it even when pressing for that "promise" to be upheld would destroy the sanity of their spouse.

I can't even make a significant other go to a movie or restaurant I know he'd hate. It just isn't in me. No matter how much I enjoyed it, I'd always know my companion loathed it and didn't want to be there. The illusion of togetherness—the happy façade of being there together—would be destroyed by knowing that he was going to that trouble just for me and wasn't enjoying himself at all. To me that's not love.

I don't want illusions and façades. I want what is real. I want what is true. I want what is genuine. I want what is loving.

Love is not about making someone do something she or he hates just because it makes you happy or comfortable. Love is about wanting to delight the other, about treating that person with grace. It's about doing stuff together that both people enjoy, not just one, instead of inflicting something the partner hates on him or her. It's about showing respect for the other person's needs and desires. And it's about getting all that stuff in return.

How very different it would have been if Bill had asked me, sincerely and not just as a springboard from which to launch a reconversion attempt, "Why don't you feel bound to this promise anymore?" In the ensuing years, you can imagine I've certainly given some thought to that question.

I think I'd have answered. We'd have communicated—probably for the first time in our entire relationship. We'd have built a new promise together based on the understanding we had now and where we saw ourselves going and what we wanted out of life.

Yeah, I know—that's a lot of honesty flying around. That's a lot of illusion-dispelling and façade-slashing and curtain-tearing. I can see why it'd scare someone to plunge into that wine-dark sea, into that lusty reverberating swamp, into that forest canopy filled as it is with strange birds making calls we've never heard before now, to set one's feet upon an unfamiliar road or to move in a direction different from that which was originally expected.

But love is worth honesty and respect.

Love is worth sharing and communication.

Love is worth respecting the other person's growth and evolving understanding.

Love is worth fighting past illusions and façades, past disappointment and hurt, to build something new and true and real.

Love is worth it.

12

Trivial Differences, Common Values
Andrew and Lewis

L ewis was born in Vancouver, British Columbia, in 1985, the only child of two nonreligious parents. He describes his mother as disinterested in religious questions—"aside from a nebulous belief in 'something out there,'" he says—"and unless it specifically comes up, she never talks about it."

His father's another matter. "He's much more antireligious in nature. But he wasn't nearly as strident then as he is now in terms of his political and religious beliefs. He was a good father."

Lewis's parents separated when he was 14, and he mostly lost touch with his father's side of the family. His mother and her family became a greater influence, including some "pretty intense Holy-Roller types," he says. "My mother's always been a bit of a black sheep of the family in terms of her nonreligious beliefs, really."

Due to his parents' nonbelief, he never attended Sunday school or church as a child. "The only exception would be when I visited my aunt and uncle in Toronto when I was around age ten or so. My cousins went to Sunday school, so I went along with them. I found it a very annoying and spiritually unrewarding experience. The primary subject of discussion of one Sunday's class was to go over movies that were current at that time, and to show how all of those movies violated the Ten Commandments. They said Simba's disobedience toward his parents in *The Lion King* breaks the commandment to honor your mother and father. I found it depressing and symptomatic of a broader problem in mainstream religion—a tendency to cling to specific instructions while ignoring the broader themes and ideas behind the spirit of the message."

He remained troubled by the exclusivity and division he saw in modern religion—"especially the notion that all humanity except a small group of saved individuals will be tormented and will suffer for all eternity, with no hope whatsoever of any mercy or salvation"—so he considered himself a nonbeliever. "Unless something changed my thinking about these doctrines, I was never going to become religious."

A few years ago, when he was in his mid-20s, something did change Lewis's thinking. "I came across a website for Tentmaker Ministries. They preach universalism—the idea that the true message in the New Testament is that all of humanity will eventually become saved, and that eternal damnation for even a single human is a myth. The God of mainstream Christianity, the God who sits idly by while most of humanity falls into eternal torment when they die, had suddenly disappeared, and was replaced by a God whom I honestly could call kind, loving, and worthy of praise. The single largest stumbling block between me and religion had been suddenly removed." Further research confirmed for Lewis that this was the correct reading of the New Testament. "It was a very easy process from that point to become religious."

He gives ironic credit for his religious awakening to his nonreligious upbringing. "I think it was a big help for my emotional and spiritual development to be in a family that didn't force me to have a particular set of beliefs. It probably would've made me less likely to be free to have religious beliefs had I been raised in a stifling environment like that. I tend to react very poorly to attempts to pressure me into agreeing with something, and have always tended to need time and space to come to my own conclusions before I can be satisfied with where my head is at."

Lewis's partner, Andrew, was born to a Christian mother and atheist father in St. Cloud, Minnesota, in 1981. His parents divorced when he was an infant, and he was mostly raised by his father. But he saw his mother often. "She is the sort of Christian who wants to *be seen* at church. She has always been more concerned with public displays of Christianity than private acts of faith." Nonetheless, Andrew says, "She tried to raise me as a Christian during the times she had custody. She even had me baptized. It didn't work, even when I was a child. Most of what I learned in Sunday school seemed absurd to me from a young age. I was the kid who was always asking awkward questions, like 'How could two of *every* animal fit on the ark?' and 'If Eve was the only woman, who did Cain and Seth marry and have kids with?' My mother eventually took me out of Sunday school—I think that's why."

His father was inclined to let Andrew work things out for himself. "He raised me agnostic, never telling me that he was completely atheistic until I was an adult," Andrew recalls. "He says that he wanted me to come to my own conclusions. He never went out of his way to counter the religious things that my mother tried to teach me unless I came to him with questions." His father had himself grown up in a religious environment, the son of a Congregational minister and a mother with a divinity degree. "But my father can't remember a time when he was ever religious, even as a child," says Andrew.

Andrew went through what he calls "a phase" in his late teens and early 20s, "trying various religious ideas on for size. I never had an iota of interest in the Abrahamic religions, but I toyed with Buddhism and neo-paganism. I wanted very much to believe in something, though I ultimately admitted to myself that I didn't believe a single damned thing of the metaphysical or spiritual ideas I was toying with. I took a lot from it, though, and as an atheist I still draw inspiration from some ideas that I encountered during that time, even if in a totally secular way."

Two years ago, around the time Lewis became a Christian believer and Andrew had reconfirmed his atheism, they met online, in a forum for fans of the cartoon *My Little Pony: Friendship Is Magic*.[1]

"I know, I know, that sounds pretty bad," Lewis says, laughing, "but we were both drawn to it because it was a high-quality, compelling production, and because it provided a jolt of much-needed optimism and happiness in a world that isn't always happy or easy to get through."

"I was living with my girlfriend, Angela, and her son at the time," Andrew says, "and we'd become fans of the show and joined the forum. My relationship with Angela was already nonfunctional when she informed me that she was Internet-dating another fellow from that forum—Lewis's then Internet-boyfriend."

"Nicholas," says Lewis. "That relationship wasn't going well either."

"So Angela got Nicholas to leave Lewis, and she left me for Nicholas, eventually moving in with him and getting married." Andrew smiles. "How's that for a soap opera?"

But it didn't end there. "Shortly after the breakup, Angela prodded me a lot to talk with Lewis, to get to know him, because she felt we would get on well. She was clearly right, because Lewis and I are now living together and are getting married next spring."

Lewis's liberal approach to his faith made the religious issue irrelevant to Andrew. "He was intelligent, funny, kind, and a kindred spirit with me. He wore down my desire to be single for a while with relentless kindness. It was a red flag when I learned that he identified as Christian, but I quickly found out that he was a progressive sort of Christian. He didn't believe that the Bible was literally true, didn't believe that the Earth is 6,000 years old, and so on. Once it was clear that I was dealing with someone who lived in the same real rational universe as I did, religion was not an issue, except as a fun conversation starter. We have the same moral framework, the same scientific worldview, so the 'religious difference' has never been much of a difference. It could be summed up with the following: I am of the opinion that the universe probably started with the Big Bang for unknown reasons. Lewis is of the opinion that the universe probably started with the Big Bang because God did it, for unknown reasons. We long ago came to the conclusion that our different opinions on the existence of God were about as relevant as if we had differences on the validity of string theory."

> *Despite the fact that I'm a Christian and Andrew is an atheist, we basically have the same answers to the fundamental questions in life. We agree that it's important to be a kind, happy, and friendly person, to be genuinely there for others with no ulterior motives, to not be a jerk to those who disagree with your religious views, and to live and let live when someone isn't hurting you. —Lewis*

Lewis agrees. "Far from being an impediment to our relationship, the differences have been a great way for both of us to challenge our thoughts and ideas in life, to become more solid in our thoughts on the world, and to become closer to each other. Far too many Christians, I feel, tend to shy away from allowing their beliefs to be challenged—though I understand why, given that many of them believe that they will literally be tormented forever if they stray from those beliefs. But it's unfortunate, as the Bible rather clearly instructs followers to allow ideas to be tested by fire and to only hold on to that which survives those tests.

"We disagree on factual matters, but largely agree on value matters, and I think that that's really a difference that many people miss in life. Far too often, it's asserted that if you hold a certain factual belief—that God exists, for example—then you must also hold a certain value judgment, like you think homosexuality is immoral. That's clearly wrong. I think that our relationship is as solid as it is largely because we've allowed each other to see that the only things on which we really disagree are those matters that have very little relevance when it comes to our actual selves and our identities as human beings."

Andrew agrees immediately. "You just can't assume someone's values from their religiosity. My grandfather the Congregationalist minister, and my grandmother with the divinity degree, both in their 80s, both obviously religious. But when I came out to them as bisexual, telling them that I was moving in with my boyfriend, neither one batted an eye. They were just happy for me, and the fact that my partner was another man was completely irrelevant to them. My mother, on the other hand. . . ." He pauses. "Well, when I came out to her as a teenager, she said my bisexuality was 'just a phase.' Recently she told me, 'I am a Christian and don't believe in same-sex marriages'—as if one clearly follows from the other."

"Clearly not," Lewis says with a laugh.

"But it wasn't all bad," Andrew continues. "She also said, 'If you do get married, I'll come and wish you the best.' That's something."

(Learn about Andrew and Lewis's wedding plans in Chapter 14—look for the dotted arrows with the couple's names.)

PART THREE

Meet
the Issues

13

Discovering
the Difference

KEY IDEAS

→ Religious differences are best discussed as early as possible in the relationship.

→ Common ground, including shared values (see Shared Values Quiz), should be emphasized.

→ Personal respect—independent of respect for ideas or beliefs—must be nonnegotiable.

→ Each partner should express his or her own comfort with the difference.

→ Partners should keep communications open and invite questions.

After years of friendship, my wife and I began dating in December 1989. Within months—okay, within minutes—I knew I would eventually propose. I was 27, she was 24.

The usual series of misfit relationships in my early 20s had helped me figure out just what I wanted in the person I would marry, and she was it. Compared to everything else she brought to the relationship, the fact that she was a Christian and I was not was a footnote. Honestly, if I'd learned she had a second head growing out of the back of her neck, I'd have bought it a little hat.

We'd been friends since she was a freshman and I was a senior at UC Berkeley, but my atheism had never come up. Six months into our dating, it still hadn't. I knew the subject had to be broached before I proposed. I'd been sitting next to her in church every Sunday, so there was no reason for her to assume I wasn't a Christian believer as well. But I knew I couldn't enter an engagement, much less a marriage, on false pretenses.

I was terrified of the possibility I'd lose her over it, but I knew it was just too big to come up years later as an "oh-by-the-way, funny-thing-about-me" revelation. If it was going to be a big deal, it needed to be a big deal right then, before we got engaged, before we got married.

I figured a fast-moving car was the right place to bring it up.

We both lived in L.A. at the time and occasionally drove to San Francisco to see her parents. On one such trip, in the middle of the Central Valley, I mustered the nerve. I don't remember the exact words I said, but at some point it was out there: *I don't believe in God, it's something I've thought about seriously for years, and it's not likely to ever change. Is that, uh . . . okay with you?*

The tires thrummed for a while. She clearly hadn't seen it coming and seemed a little shaken.

Finally she said, "Well . . . is it okay with you that I *do* believe?"

I said yes, of course. I'd known that from the beginning.

Another long pause.

"It has to be okay for me to go to church." This was not in the form of a question. I said it was okay, of course it was. And then I learned something I might never have known otherwise: I learned *why* it was so important for her to go to church. As is often the case, it had almost nothing to do with theology.

She laid out the whole story. Her stepdad, a former Baptist minister, had an ugly falling-out with his church when he left his first wife for his second. As a result, he cut all ties with the church—not just that church, but all churches, all religion—and didn't allow Becca's very religious mom or her daughters to attend. Becca vowed to herself at the time that she was bloody well going to church once she got out of that house, and that no one was ever going to keep her from it again.

It wasn't religious uniformity she needed from her eventual husband. She just needed to know that that particular bit of family history wasn't going to repeat itself. It was never about salvation for her. As much as anything, her churchgoing was an act of proxy redemption for her mom.

That was an important discovery for me. I would have been troubled to learn that Becca's religious beliefs and practices were centered on the fear of hell or even a need to please God. These are beliefs that I find not just false but dehumanizing. I don't mind if my neighbor holds those opinions. As long as he doesn't force them on others, I agree with Thomas Jefferson—it "neither picks my pocket nor breaks my leg." But if the beliefs of my intended lifelong companion fell into that fearful or obeisant category, I knew it would raise compatibility questions from *my* side of the equation.

Instead, I learned that she attended church for other reasons. In addition to family history, she went for the sense of community and human connection she felt, for the opportunity to slow down and reflect, to engage the world in a different way from the rest of the week. It was rewarding and fulfilling to her for reasons I could completely respect, even if I didn't feel those needs as much myself. And her reasons were similar to the reasons most churchgoers go to church—to feel connected, to focus on meaning and purpose, to reinforce her own identity. God was the frame in which her human values were expressed, including values I shared with her.

I also learned that although she was Baptist by birth, upbringing, and baptism, she didn't hold to several specific tenets of the Southern Baptist Conference that would have presented problems for me.[1] One doctrine would have been a particular issue if she believed it: that those who do not accept Jesus Christ as their Lord and Savior are consigned to hell. Even though I don't believe in any such thing, I was glad to hear she didn't either. A relationship in which one partner thinks the other is headed for eternal punishment after death, or is even worthy of such a thing, isn't a healthy one.

Instead, by showing a tendency toward universalism—that all people are saved, regardless of beliefs—Becca was again very much in the U.S. Christian mainstream. Of U.S. Christians, 65% believe that non-Christians can end up in heaven, and the majority of those include the nonreligious among the saved.[2] Good stuff.

By the end of the conversation, I was relieved, we knew each other a lot better, she had articulated her own values and beliefs in a way that was new even to her, and the biggest secret I had was out in the open.

And it had gone just fine.

Not that it always does. I'll never forget the thirtyish man who came up to me after a talk in North Carolina several years ago, looking like he hadn't slept in days—because, as it turned out, he hadn't. He and his wife of 10 years had both been Mormon, but his religious faith had been slipping for some time. When he told her a week earlier that he no longer believed in God, she said he was "sick and evil," then took the kids and left him the same night. He hadn't heard from her since and didn't know where his children were. Neither side of the family would answer his calls. An intense shunning wall had come down around him.

The nonreligious partner doesn't always react well, either. I've heard from many who wondered if they could continue to respect their partners when they learned they were religious. "I have to admit that I suddenly saw him differently," said one. "Instead of the confident guy I thought he was, I couldn't help seeing a gullible, fearful child."

In both cases, the partner hearing the news immediately conjured an extreme version of the other position and (naturally) recoiled in horror from it. It's a perfectly human reaction. When we don't have all the information, we fill in the gaps with the worst things possible. Remember what was written in unexplored regions around the edges of early maps? They didn't just write, "Unknown." They wrote, "Here be dragons."

We often do the same thing with unknown human traits. As a defensive measure, we assume the worst. So a religious person often hears someone is an atheist and pictures Stalin. An atheist hears someone is religious and pictures Pat Robertson. *Here be dragons.*

Sometimes the shoe fits. But much more often, as we saw in Chapters 2 and 3, two people who think they are peering across an abyss will actually share most of their values, even if they've placed those values in different frames. So the revelation that a partner or prospective partner has a different worldview is not the end of the conversation; it's the beginning. If we use it as a litmus test, a lot of wonderful relationships, including mine, would end before they began.

> *The revelation that a partner or prospective partner has a different worldview is not the end of the conversation; it's the beginning.*

That conversation needs to happen sooner rather than later. If there's one thing experts on marriage agree on, it's the importance of entering into the relationship with all cards on the table. If there's going to be an issue, it needs to happen up front, before rings and vows and a shared mortgage—not to mention shared children—complicate things.

So . . . How Does It Usually Go?

The McGowan-Sikes survey asked several questions related to the first time couples learned about the difference in their beliefs. About 18% already knew about the difference before they dated, nearly half (47%) while dating, and 3% during their engagement. So altogether, the difference was out there before the wedding for about two-thirds of the couples.

Another 29% didn't discover (or reveal) the difference in beliefs until after they were married. In some cases that's because their beliefs were the same at the time they were married, and then one changed. In others, the difference was already there, but one partner—almost always the nonbeliever—didn't reveal it until later in the marriage.

This is one of the key factors in determining how smoothly things go for these couples. According to the survey, those who enter the marriage with the difference already known have much lower levels of tension and conflict later on than couples in which one partner changed beliefs after marriage. A little more than one in five (22%) were both religious when they got married, and then one became nonreligious.

The least common scenario of all was the converse: Just 1% of couples were both nonreligious at the start, and then one partner became religious. And another 1% are currently "closeted" in their own marriages, meaning even their partner does not know they differ in beliefs.[3]

Mixed at marriage	*67%*
Both religious, one becoming nonreligious later	*22%*
Both nonreligious, one becoming religious later	*1%*
One partner still "closeted" to other partner	*1%*

So how does the conversation tend to go, the one in which a couple discovers their difference in beliefs? Just over a third of those surveyed (34%) said they were indifferent to the news. About 12% said they were intrigued or interested, 3% were excited or happy, and 1% couldn't recall how they felt.

That leaves about half of all respondents expressing negative emotions—feeling worried, sad, disappointed, fearful, angry, confused, or betrayed. Religious partners were more than three times as likely to have negative reactions as nonreligious partners. A lot of this also depends on the "late change" dynamic that I mentioned. When a couple shares a belief system at the time of their marriage, then one partner changes beliefs, it's common for the changing partner to feel guilt, while the other feels shock, grief, or even betrayal. (See examples in Chapters 7 and 11.)

It's not always as simple as a single moment of change. Matthew, who was originally Baptist, lost his faith while dating Stephanie, a Christian. He eventually "rebounded" back to his faith, as he puts it, and they were engaged and then married. But shortly thereafter, he lost his faith again and now considers himself an atheist. "I feel like I've let her down," he says, a common sentiment when a change in belief happens after marriage.

Sometimes a late change in belief results in complications beyond the couple, and the stories can be heartbreaking. "My husband gave up his life as a respected Lutheran seminarian, missionary, and missions coordinator because of my loss of faith," says Christina, an agnostic in Minnesota. "Eight years of school and a life he loved. I don't doubt him now when he says he made the right choice, that he doesn't regret it or resent me for it, but at times I am concerned that someday he will regret his choosing me over his future in ministry."

But just as often there are expressions of support or encouragement. "We were both agnostic when we married, but he followed his bliss and now considers himself religious," says Jamie of Steven, her husband of 11 years. "I'm fine with that. He's still the guy I fell in love with."

"I made the terrible mistake of not telling her."

My wife, Claire, has never been the hyperreligious kind that thanks Jesus for every parking space, but I knew her Catholic beliefs were important to her from the beginning. Even though I was an atheist by that time, I was raised Catholic, so it wasn't unfamiliar to me.

I made the terrible mistake of not telling her about my disbelief until after we were married. Our relationship grew stronger over time, which made telling her even harder. I was attending church with her weekly, crossing myself, taking communion. I stupidly took the easier road of going through the motions to avoid confrontation.

But after three years of marriage, it became too emotionally drain-
ing for me. I decided I couldn't be dishonest with her anymore. I was
so nervous. Our lives were so good and happy, and I knew that this
would put a big wrench in things. I'm nonconfrontational by nature, so
I wasn't even able to tell her face-to-face. I wrote her a letter and left
it on the couch.

Her world turned upside down. The man she thought she had shared
her faith with did not. There were questions of whether she would be
able to stay with me, and many tears.

After hours of conversation filled with pain and frustration, we both
realized that we absolutely wanted to stay together. Sure, the marriage
wasn't exactly what she had envisioned, but the rest of me was still
worth it. I agreed that I would keep an open mind and never close the
door on God if he were to try to "change my heart." She agreed to be
more accepting of my lack of belief even if I remained an atheist for good.

Life slowly returned to normal. I still attend church with her, but no
more communion or crossing myself. She still hopes that I'll "come to my
senses," but I think she is getting used to it.

If I could do it over again, I would have told her much earlier while
we were still dating and the stakes were much lower. Then again, that
might have ended our relationship, and she never would've married the
wonderful heathen that she is still in love with today.

—T.J. (atheist)

See Scott and Dhanya, *Chapter 6*

As always, the specific identity and intensity of the partners makes all the difference. Scott prefers the terms *agnostic* and *nonreligious* for himself, saying, "I don't practice religion and I don't reject religion." His wife Dhanya's Hinduism makes for a more relaxed fit with a nonreligious part- ner than many other religious identities.

"Honestly, when Scott told me he was agnostic, I had no idea what that meant," she recalls. "I don't think I had heard that word before. I asked him what it meant and realized I was not even aware that there was a word that described this kind of thought process. It was pretty cool."

"Like most Hindus, Dhanya doesn't impress her beliefs on others," Scott says. "From my experience, Hinduism is a very flexible and very personal set of religious beliefs and rituals. Hindus usually pick up their customs from their family, as opposed to the more collective church-oriented customs of Christianity."

Dhanya's customs include eating vegetarian food on Mondays and Thursdays and no beef or pork at any time, and praying every morning. Her prayer involves lighting incense and a candle and singing a few Sanskrit hymns. "It's very much a ritual and not a prayer as in asking a god for something," Scott says. "At certain times of the year, she is vegetarian for longer periods and does different sorts of prayers. When somebody is born or dies, there are other rituals to be done following the occasion."

Confirming Shared Values

Suddenly learning that your partner has a different religious perspective can be disorienting. When religious believers learn that someone is not religious, some assume that their values—including empathy, compassion, even basic morality—fall away as well. A nonbeliever who learns that someone is religious often assumes that intellectual values such as critical thinking and skepticism are suddenly missing.

> A study in Journal of Personality *found that religious similarity is consistently less important to marital satisfaction than values similarity.[4]*

But if they allow themselves to discover the difference before bolting in opposite directions, couples are much more likely to find that they agree on the relative importance of basic values.

The following quiz is designed to help couples assess the level of alignment in their values (opinions about what is good or important) regardless of their different beliefs (opinions about what is true or exists).

> *I think what keeps our marriage together after 43 years is what drew us together originally—compassion. We still share a concern for the welfare of all people, especially those who are abused or whose basic needs are not met.*
> —Joe, a secular humanist married to Ellen, a Protestant Evangelical

> *He has the same core beliefs that I have. Be kind to others, share, and show compassion. I just need the religion aspect and he does not.*
> —Lena, an Episcopalian married to Sean, an agnostic Baha'i

The Shared Values Quiz[5]

The Shared Values Quiz helps partners identify their most important values and areas of potential conflict. Values are one of many predictors of relationship success, so a high difference score does not guarantee future tension or breakup, nor does a low difference score guarantee a conflict-free relationship. It is meant as a tool for partners to communicate about what is important to each of them and identify areas of potential conflict.

Rate each of the following values on its importance to you, personally, according to the scale provided. Ask your partner to (separately) do the same. After you've completed the ratings, compare results. To calculate an index of difference in important values, subtract your partner's rating from yours for each value. If you get a negative number, simply ignore the negative and make it positive (i.e., take the absolute value of the difference between your scores). Then total your differences.

3 = Extremely important

2 = Important

1 = Slightly important

0 = Not at all important

Your rating	Partner's rating	Difference in ratings	Value
			1. Business and finances
			2. Arts, music, theatre
			3. Social life/relationships
			4. Science, rationality, pursuit of knowledge
			5. Caring for others/avoiding harm
			6. Fairness and helping people who help you
			7. Loyalty/putting your family and in-groups before others
			8. Respect for/obedience of authority
			9. Purity/respecting holy ideas and objects

Your rating	Partner's rating	Difference in ratings	Value
			10. Physical attractiveness
			11. Athleticism/health
			12. Sense of humor
			13. Creativity
			14. Spontaneity/living life in the moment

Total difference in ratings: _____

Difference scores can range from 0 to 42. Larger numbers indicate greater discrepancies between your values and your partner's. If you and your partner do not share the same values, you are likely to have very different goals and priorities, which can lead to conflict and relationship problems over time. Shared values are one sign of relationship health and success. Research has shown that the act of thinking about shared values can make people feel loved and cared for.[6] Taking a moment to focus on the values you do share can be a good way to build a relationship or mitigate conflict.

Difference score 0–14: You and your partner have remarkably similar values. If you ranked these values from least to most important, the order may differ somewhat, but you most likely have the same top three values. It's likely that even if your beliefs are different, you agree on quite a bit about what's important to you. It probably comes as no surprise to you, but it's likely that your shared values make your relationship stronger and more likely to go the distance.[7]

Difference score 15–30: You and your partner tend to agree on the importance of various values, but you may disagree about which values are the most important, or might be diametrically opposed on a small number of values. As a follow-up activity, rank the values from least to most important. This might help you identify aspects of your relationship in which you are more likely to come into conflict. Having insight into what motivates each other will aid in perspective taking during disagreements and give you a common language.[8]

Difference score 31–42: You and your partner have significant disagreement about what values are important. This can be a source of tension and conflict in your relationship.[9] Maybe you said to one another, "You need to get your priorities straight!" Having very different priorities can be a challenge. As a next step, it may be helpful for each of you to rank the 14 values from least to most important. Identify the values that you both rank relatively highly as opportunities for shared activities and a place to build from. Remember that shared values are an important sign of relationship health, but that different values are not necessarily a death knell. Communication and relationship skills will be helpful while you negotiate and discuss your values (see Chapter 11).

(Many thanks to social psychologist Dr. Brittany Shoots-Reinhard of the Ohio State University for designing the Shared Values Quiz.)

The Bottom Line

A major difference in religious beliefs needs to come out as early and as straightforwardly as possible—definitely before marriage (if the difference exists at that point), and definitely before kids. Couples who use the opportunity to reinforce common ground and to start negotiating actual practices tend to do fine—if the difference existed from the start.

Couples who shared a worldview until one partner changed often have a more difficult road. Other weaknesses in the relationship often surface. But strengths surface as well, including some that may not have been identified before. The key is to recognize and articulate that the love, respect, and common ground values that formed the foundation of the marriage are still present, even though the framework has changed for one partner.

14

Tying the Knot
Across the Gap

KEY IDEAS

→ Secular/religious weddings are sometimes straightforwardly religious, sometimes secular, and sometimes a blend.

→ Some religious wedding elements join a couple to that religious identity, and some secular readings and songs contain specific renunciations of religion. These are best avoided when one partner is religious and the other is not.

→ Other religious or secular elements can be poetic, symbolic, or meaningful without those issues. (See the section titled "The Secular-Sacred, and the Sacred-Secular.")

→ A secular wedding is not antireligious—it simply lacks specifically religious elements. (See the story about Nora and Kevin under "#2: The Secular.")

→ A third tradition is often a good source for readings, music, and symbolism.

When a marriage joins partners of two different religions—Judaism and Catholicism, let's say—the wedding can be a major flash point as traditions collide. It's often the first time the couple has to directly confront their differences, and it happens in the public eye, in a place and a ritual full of religious symbols, as well as family and cultural history.

When instead the marriage is between a nonreligious partner and a religious one, there are still issues, but the collision can be much less dramatic. Religious traditions have very specific ideas about what happens when two people marry, and it goes well beyond "something borrowed, something blue" and the Chicken Dance. There are sometimes nonnegotiable sacraments grounded in centuries of history and doctrine. During most of that history, it was safe to assume the betrothed shared a religion, and the marriage was designed to join the new couple not just to each other but to the religious community itself.

A wedding that joins a Catholic partner to a Jewish one is operating from two different rulebooks, each with different mandates for everything from words spoken to rituals observed to who officiates. Some of these aren't just different but mutually exclusive, and working it all out can be pretty tricky.

But when one partner is nonreligious, one rulebook disappears. There are still deeply felt values and preferences on both sides, but the potential for conflict on the details—"do this first, then do that"—is much lower. The couple is left to work out their own comfort level with the elements of the remaining religious rulebook while incorporating other elements to reflect the secular partner's values and identity.

There's no end to the variety of ways couples find to split the secular/religious difference. One couple in the McGowan-Sikes survey was married by a Mormon bishop, but in a secular setting. One had a ceremony in the church of the bride's parents—but in the multipurpose room, not the sanctuary. A common solution is to have two separate ceremonies: a religious service, usually in a church, and a secular ceremony, whether in a courthouse, a backyard, a home, a park, or on the beach. In some countries—most of Europe, for example, and Mexico—the civil ceremony is required and the religious ceremony is optional. In some U.S. states, the opposite is true: The *religious* service is the required one.

Some couples even go beyond two services to express their own multiple perspectives: Karl (an atheist) and Monica (Catholic at the time, now Jewish) had three ceremonies: a pagan handfasting ("that was just us," Karl says), then a justice of the peace at a courthouse, then a full Catholic wedding Mass.

According to the survey, most secular/religious couples who have a ceremony opt for one that fits much of the form and features of the traditional religious wedding. In some cases (9.2%) this is because they were both religious on their wedding day. But even for the 9 in 10 who already held different views, the usual trappings of church and clergy are common:

→ 51% were married/committed in a conventional religious setting.

→ 30% were married/committed in a nontraditional setting, such as a beach or private home.

→ 10% were married/committed in a civil setting, such as a courthouse.

→ 9% had no ceremony or are not married.

As for the person officiating (if any),

→ 70% were married by members of the clergy (59% denominational, 11% nondenominational).

→ 16% were married by a civil official (judge, justice of the peace).

→ 4% were married by a nontraditional officiant (ranging from a friend to an Elvis impersonator).

→ 2% were married by a Humanist celebrant.

→ 1% were married by a combination of religious and nonreligious officiants.

Some of the most interesting responses were the 7% who checked "Other." Some described creative, nontraditional ceremonies of the skydiving/underwater/roller-coaster type, but others were clearly an attempt to split the secular/religious difference.

Half of all respondents reported no tension at all around their wedding choices, while 28% reported low to moderate tension. Just 12% reported tension above moderate to severe.

As for overall tension, the survey supports the idea that the absence of a set rulebook on the secular side gives a marked advantage over the joining of two religions. Half of respondents reported no tension at all related to religion in their wedding, while 28% reported low to moderate tension; 10% can't recall, leaving 12% who report tension above moderate to severe.

Of all the elements of a wedding ceremony, the highest tension involved the inclusion or exclusion of certain readings or prayers.

The officiant was next; about a third of respondents said that decision produced some sparks, and 10% said the conflict was more than moderate.

The big surprise in this category was location. You might expect a lot of friction to come from whether or not the wedding was in a church. But even though two-thirds of the surveyed couples were already a secular/religious mix at the altar, nearly 70% said there was no tension at all over selecting the setting. Just 8% said they experienced more than a moderate amount of tension over it.

Once again, the absence of a second rulebook opens more possibilities for compromise.

Approaching the Altar from Different Directions

As a result of one decision made by Danielle, a Southern Baptist, and her agnostic fiancé, Tom, not a single one of their friends attended their May 2001 wedding.

Okay, it's less dramatic than it sounds. "We only invited family to the wedding," Danielle says, "and friends came to the reception. I wanted it to be small because I don't enjoy the limelight. Some of our friends were really upset that they couldn't come to the wedding."

"So *that* was our big controversy!" Tom says with a laugh. "Not anything about religion."

See **Tom and Danielle,** *Chapter 5*

That statement is surprisingly common. Though the wedding can be a flash point for mixed-belief couples, most of the respondents to the McGowan-Sikes survey said religion was not a significant source of tension in their wedding. Three-fourths said there was little or no tension over the choice of location, officiant, or music for the event, while fewer than 10% placed these tensions anywhere in the top half of a 10-point scale.

The inclusion of particular readings or prayers is a bit more tension inducing. Just over half reported some level of tension, though still just 12% put this in the top half of the tension scale.

Some of this lack of tension is explained by the fact that a third of respondents shared the same belief at their wedding. Even adjusting for this yields a surprisingly low level of religious tension for secular/religious weddings. This chapter examines the ways couples navigate the challenge, creating a meaningful, emotional ceremony that does what weddings are supposed to do: solemnize and celebrate the union of two individuals into a single shared life.

The choices they made are by no means the only way to design a wedding that joins secular and religious partners, but neither are they unusual. It's worth taking a close look at the ceremonies to see the way that many secular/religious couples tie the knot.

The Three Flavors

The purpose of a wedding may seem obvious: Two people who weren't married at the beginning end up married at the end. But other changes are happening as well, and some couples include specific rituals to underline those changes. Not just two people but two extended families, two circles of friends, two communities, even two cultures are often intersecting—and in the case of mixed-belief couples, two worldviews. Partners who share a single religious identity have the option of plugging into an established wedding ritual without thinking much about the elements unless they want to. But mixed-belief couples have not only the need but the opportunity to think about what they want their ceremony to mean. In the process, they often include some combination of religious and secular elements but go beyond the traditional, underlining these other intersections in a way that is meaningful to them.

For secular/religious couples, in addition to the elements of the ceremony—the music, the rings, vows, dresses, attendants, officiant, and all the rest—there's the question of the "flavor" of the wedding, including the balance of the religious and the secular. There are three general approaches: a ceremony that is essentially religious, one that is essentially secular, or one that attempts to balance the two.

I call these the Sacred, the Secular, and the Blend.

#1: The Sacred

No one at my wedding in 1991 would have guessed there was an atheist in the room, much less that he was the guy in tux and tails. The setting was a beautiful, historic Lutheran church in San Francisco that we had chosen because it was beautiful and historic and in San Francisco, my wife's hometown—not because it was Lutheran.

We upped the religious ante with not one but two ministers: a Methodist friend of the family and a Southern Baptist uncle of Becca's whose contribution included a sermonette with a rafter-rattling reference to Matthew 21:21, the assurance that faith can move mountains. The readings were all Christian, ranging from the indispensable "Love is patient, love is kind" passage from First Corinthians (see "The Secular-Sacred, and the Sacred-Secular") to an excerpt from *The Prophet* by the Christian mystic poet Khalil Gibran.

If we'd been married 10 years later, I might have asked that we include some secular poetry or meditations. I was no less secular in 1991, but it played a much smaller part of my personal identity at that point than it would later. At age 28, I was all about music. My degrees were in music, and I was about to begin a 15-year career as a conductor and professor of music. I'd have been more offended by bad music than by all the Psalms in the King James Bible, so it was more than enough that I had complete control over that aspect of my wedding.

The prelude music included solo piano works by Ravel, played by my brother Ron, and my own arrangement of Bach's secular cantata "Sheep May Safely Graze" for strings and two recorders. Becca came down the aisle to Bach's "Air on the G String," played by the San Francisco Conservatory String Quartet. We lit the unity candle to a prelude I wrote myself, played once again by Ron, and we left to one of the great recessionals, the Widor *Toccata*, played by the organist of Grace (Episcopal) Cathedral in San Francisco.

For those of you keeping score, we had now achieved the Protestant quadfecta: a Lutheran church, an Episcopal organist, and Methodist and Baptist ministers. I was awash in Christianity—and I didn't care a bit. Musically, I was in my own heaven, and that's who I was.

Aside from a unity candle that wouldn't light until the minister liberated the wick with a pocketknife, and his mispronunciation of my name ("I present to you, for the first time, Mr. and Mrs. Dale and Rebekah Maguvvin!"), the rest went off without a hitch—a typical late-20th-century American wedding, Mainline Protestant in every detail right down to the rings and vows and "What God hath joined." Twenty-three years later, no man has put it asunder.

See **Arlene and Nate,** *Chapter 8*

Like me, Nate was happy to oblige his Baptist fiancée with a church wedding, despite being an atheist himself. "The wedding decisions were actually a matter of mutual respect for both of us. I knew it was important for her and her family to have a church wedding, and she and her family knew that jumping through religious hoops to get married in a formal religious service was not fair to me as an atheist. We found a local Baptist minister who was engaging and embraced us, and the deal was made. I was as shocked as anybody! We worked out a ceremony that was religious enough for Arlene and not too heavily religious for me," he recalls.

But the church they chose hadn't been their first choice. They originally asked Arlene's uncle, a Baptist minister, to officiate, but his church declined because Nate was not religious. "Arlene and I also both refused to go to their required 'counseling' sessions prior to them agreeing to marry us," he says. Like many couples, they say that being ticked off by the same thing brought them closer.

See **Scott and Dhanya,** *Chapter 6*

A religious wedding requires the most flexibility on the part of the non-religious partner, of course. In the case of Scott, a nonreligious American marrying Dhanya, a Gujarati Hindu South African, there were multiple gaps to cross, including not just religion but culture, nationality, and dialect.

"Scott said he did not feel strongly about a particular ceremony and I could decide," says Dhanya. That's a sentence that could just as easily have come from a Christian or Jewish partner when the nonreligious partner doesn't have a strong inclination. "I wanted to have a Hindu wedding ceremony, and so it was."

Some drama in Dhanya's family (unrelated to their marriage) resulted in Scott and Dhanya getting little help in the complex preparations for a Gujarati wedding. Things were complicated further when the usual four days of ceremonies were compressed to three. "I wanted the pre-wedding events to start on Friday," Dhanya explains, "but this was not possible as that day on the Gujarati calendar was an inauspicious day to start or perform any big event in one's life. So after consulting with the priest, we decided to have all three pre-wedding events on Saturday, the day before the wedding. It was hectic and stressful."

Scott nods in agreement. "Usually, each side's family performs some rituals, but since my side is not Hindu, we didn't have our own ceremonies. It felt a little like I was not allowed at my own party." It was this preparation period that proved the most difficult for Scott. "Preparing for the wedding was one of the most challenging things I've had to do in my life. There's no single set of customs for Hindu marriages, and it was a huge challenge for me to learn and understand what the different aspects of our wedding were going to be. So there I was, trying to help Dhanya plan our wedding, but I wasn't getting any help from written sources, and every time we talked to somebody, they gave us information that conflicted with what someone else said."

One of the greatest frustrations for Scott had to do with the meaning and significance of things. "I have a questioning mind, and nobody could explain *why* things are done in certain ways, or why it mattered. I think their customs are things that have just been done for generations, and everybody has some intuition but not many can explain the reasons. The priest can give a bit of explanation, but it's always a fuzzy and half-answered one. It was frustrating."

> *It's good to keep in mind that the nonreligious often have a particular interest in knowing the reasons behind things they are asked to say or do. When a mixed-belief wedding is essentially religious in form and content, it can help smooth out the experience for the nonreligious partner if the religious partner explains elements of the ceremony with a religious component. In some cases, this will require the religious partner to learn the roots of traditions that have been taken for granted.*

In fairness, this probably has less to do with a given culture or religion than we might think—we're just less aware of what we accept without question in our own cultural frames. If I'd asked Becca why she was supposed to wear something old, new, borrowed, and blue at our wedding, she probably would have said, "It's tradition," which is not entirely satisfying to a questioning mind. Likewise, I'd have come up blank if someone asked me why I was putting the ring on the fourth finger of her left hand. "Because that's the ring finger, dummy" doesn't really cut it.

"I did know *some* of the reasons for things," Dhanya says, with mock defensiveness. "During the ceremony we light a fire in a *havan kund*, a steel vessel in which the fire is lit. The sacred fire, Agni, is believed to be the messenger between the Gods and humans. Agni is believed to also be the great protector from evil and is the eternal witness of the marriage. We make offerings to Agni during this part of the ceremony, and each time we make an offering to the fire we say the word *sv h* .[1] Guru [the priest] told us before we began that we must both shout the word *sv h* , and whoever shouts the loudest will rule in the household. Scott says he shouted it louder, but I think it was a tie!"

"That's one thing I learned—that a Hindu wedding can be more fun than a typical Christian wedding," Scott says. "It's not so serious. We teased each other or other people involved. Our priest was cracking jokes with us. We smiled often and laughed occasionally. There's no rehearsal, but there's no worry because the priest instructs you and mistakes don't really matter. I just followed the example of Dhanya or did what the priest said. I forgot about the audience for most of the ceremony, which was two and a half hours long. I enjoyed the wedding itself, but it took a lot of effort and mental anguish to get to that point. Of the challenges our relationship has faced, the wedding prep was a big one. But we made it through."

The value and importance of religious ritual and tradition to a religious family and community transcends theology—in fact, it often has little to do with theology. Religious practices like those in a wedding tie the individual and the moment to other individuals and moments. It's about identity and connection. And if that identity and connection are important to the religious partner, as they were to Dhanya and as they were to my wife, it's important for the nonreligious partner to recognize and honor *that* element of the ritual, even if he or she completely disregards the beliefs in which they are framed.

#2: The Secular

Kevin was a nonpracticing Catholic when he first met Nora in Houston, where they both worked as pipeline engineers. Nora says she was a "full-on atheist" then, as she is now.

"I didn't want to be with someone who was really religious," she says, "so on one of our first dates, I asked him three questions: *Do you believe everything in the Bible is true?* He said no, I don't. *Do you believe everything the pope says is right—about birth control, for example?* He said no. Then the big one: *Do you think I'm going to hell because I'm an atheist?* I didn't want him to be trying to save me all the time. He said no, he said he thinks that

God doesn't judge over one little thing or condition. He believes God judges people on who they are overall."

Four years later they were married, and the wedding was entirely secular, from the location (a boat in Galveston Bay) to the officiant (Nora's uncle, an atheist who is culturally Jewish) to the music and symbolism.

"Not everyone in his family was happy that it wasn't religious," Nora recalls. "He had one grandmother who refused to come because it wasn't in a church." But in the end there was little fuss from the family over the absence of Catholic elements.

Kevin and Nora planned the ceremony carefully with her officiant uncle, including many touches that had special significance to their families or to themselves. Nora came down the aisle to Simon and Garfunkel's "Bridge over Troubled Waters," just as her mother had done years before. "She didn't know it was coming," Nora says, smiling. "It was fun to see her jump when it started playing."

After brief remarks by Nora's uncle, the ceremony turned to a symbolic ritual called a *handfasting*, one I mentioned previously in this chapter. Originally a Scottish synonym for the wedding itself, in recent years handfasting has been revived as a literal ritual in which the hands of the couple are bound together with ribbon or cloth. Nora and Kevin chose to use two ribbons, one symbolizing friends, the other family.

Her uncle wrapped their hands and said:

> *These are the hands of your best friend, young and strong and full of love for you, that are holding yours on your wedding day, as you promise to love each other today, tomorrow, and forever.*
>
> *These are the hands that will work alongside yours, as together you build your future.*
>
> *These are the hands that will passionately love you and cherish you through the years, and with the slightest touch, will comfort you like no other.*
>
> *These are the hands that will hold you when fear or grief fills your mind.*
>
> *These are the hands that will countless times wipe the tears from your eyes; tears of sorrow, and tears of joy.*
>
> *These are the hands that will give you strength when you need it.*

And lastly, these are the hands that even when wrinkled and aged,
will still be reaching for yours, still giving you the same unspoken
tenderness with just a touch.

Connecting to Tradition

When a religious partner agrees to a fully secular wedding, there is
sometimes a sense of loss for that person, even if unspoken. The loss
often has less to do with the missed inclusion of God than the absence
of traditions and symbols that connect to family, community, culture, and
tradition. Nora's use of her mother's processional music and Anna's
choice (discussed in "#3: The Blend") to carry her grandmother's Bible
are among the countless ways tradition can be underlined. Secular
resources are increasingly available with ideas for achieving this con-
nection, including one that Kevin and Nora found useful: Secular-
Celebrations.com. Having a Humanist celebrant officiate also opens a
range of resources and possibilities for rich and meaningful secular ser-
vices. Learn more at Humanist-Society.org.

This was followed by lovely secular vows:

I, Nora (Kevin), affirm my love to you, Kevin (Nora)
And I invite you to share my life in good times and in bad
When life seems easy, and when it seems hard
When our love is simple and when it is an effort
I will cherish and respect you, care for and protect you and comfort
and encourage you
This I promise you today and for all the days of our life together

And the exchange of rings.

The ceremony was short—perhaps 20 minutes—but memorable and
meaningful, rich with symbolism and significance.

See Andrew and Lewis, *Chapter 12*

Andrew and Lewis became engaged shortly after same-sex marriage was
legalized in their home state in 2012. Like Kevin and Nora, they too plan to
have a secular wedding. "The details of our service are not set in stone yet,"

says Andrew, an atheist, "but we plan to have a short secular ceremony in the same restaurant that will host the reception. We will have an officiant with some gravitas introduce us, give a little speech, guide us in saying vows to each other, and tell us when to exchange rings and kiss. Interestingly enough, my grandfather, a former Congregationalist minister and current Quaker, has agreed to officiate the completely secular ceremony. He's a good man. Like many Quakers, he doesn't feel that we have to share his religion. He just wants us to be good people and be happy."

"Even though I'm religious, my universalism means there is little purpose in pushing my religion into other people's faces," says Lewis. "The core of my religious beliefs are that a good Christian ought to strive to embody Christ in everything he does, in actions rather than just words. So I try to effectively preach the gospel, so to speak, by simply being the sort of person that I believe Jesus would want me to be, not by trying to pressure people into it. If anyone asks about my beliefs, I'm more than happy to discuss them, but I consider the specifics secondary to the commandment that all people ought to love one another to the fullest extent possible, and to show them God through that love."

#3: The Blend

Tom and Danielle's wedding showed more evidence of give-and-take between the religious and the secular. They worked together to create a ceremony that would represent them both, and the result is worth a close look.

Danielle wanted a minister to perform the ceremony. Tom asked that he be nondenominational, and Danielle agreed. "We planned the whole ceremony with him," she says. "We wanted it to be very short. I don't like the limelight, for one thing. And we cut out a lot of the overly religious tones so it could be both of ours."

"I honestly don't remember how much religious content was left in," says Tom.

See Tom and Danielle, *Chapter 5*

After a quick look at their wedding video—and it was quick, about 20 minutes in all—I could see for myself how much care and flexibility had gone into it. Take the music, for example—the same "Air on the G String" (secular) that had been my wife's processional was the attendants' processional this time, and "Jesu, Joy of Man's Desiring" (religious) was Danielle's processional.

The (nondenominational) pastor gave a Gaelic greeting (*céad míle fáilte,* "a hundred thousand welcomes"—see "Tapping a Third Tradition"), then began his introduction: "You are entering into a union that is both sacred and serious. It is sacred because marriage is established by God himself"—a clear reference to the religious side. But he moved on to underline the seriousness of the human commitment they were undertaking, and the faith in each other that it showed.

The pastor read the same passage from Gibran's *The Prophet* that had been in my wedding:

> *You were born together, and together you shall be forevermore.*
> *You shall be together when the white wings of death scatter your days.*
> *Ay, you shall be together even in the silent memory of God.*
> *But let there be spaces in your togetherness,*
> *And let the winds of the heavens dance between you.*
> *Love one another, but make not a bond of love:*
> *Let it rather be a moving sea between the shores of your souls.*
> *Fill each other's cup but drink not from one cup.*
> *Give one another of your bread but eat not from the same loaf.*
> *Sing and dance together and be joyous, but let each one of you be alone,*
> *Even as the strings of a lute are alone though they quiver with the same music.*[2]

A nice combination of religious and secular ideas there.

Next came one of the most specifically religious elements in Tom and Danielle's service—a wedding prayer adapted from the United Church of Christ. Look closely and you'll see a secular/religious couple compromising to honor and accommodate each other. Here's the original version:

> *O Father, our hearts are filled with great happiness on this our wedding day. We come before You at the altar of love, pledging our lives and our hearts to one another. Grant that, with Your help, we may be true and loving, living together in such a way as to never bring shame*

and heartbreak into our marriage. Temper us with kindness and understanding and rid us of all pretense and jealousy. Help us to be sweethearts, helpmates, friends, and lovers, that together we may meet the cares and problems of life more bravely. And as time takes away our youthful charm, may we find contentment in the greater joys of rich companionship. May our home truly be a place of love and harmony where Your Spirit is ever present. Bless us on our wedding day, our Father, and walk with us through all our life together. Amen.

Now look closely at the way Tom and Danielle adapted it:

Father in heaven, our hearts are filled with great happiness on this our wedding day. We come before the altar of love, pledging our lives and our hearts to each other. We pray that we may be ever true and loving to one another and avoid all pretense or envy, that we together may meet the cares and problems of life more bravely. And may our home be a place of love and harmony. Walk beside us Father we pray, in all our life together. Amen.

The original prayer includes so many religious references that the non-religious partner may feel overwhelmed by it. Tom and Danielle worked with their minister to create a version that was still entirely religious, but not overwhelming. It still begins and ends with clear references to God, but in between:

"We come before You at the altar of love" is now "We come before the altar of love."

"Grant that, with Your help, we may be true and loving" becomes "We pray that we may be ever true and loving."

"May our home truly be a place of love and harmony where Your Spirit is ever present" is now "May our home be a place of love and harmony."

Obviously a wedding between two Christians can and should include any and all references to God. But when one partner is nonreligious, it is considerate to soften the religious content without removing it.

We had a Baha'i marriage, which is simultaneously very religious, meaning it has a specific set of things that have to happen, and also totally nontraditional. You can get married wherever, and there is no officiant. You marry yourselves.

—Lena, an Episcopalian, about her wedding to Sean, an agnostic Baha'i

The vows were the traditional ones from the 17th-century Book of Common Prayer: "Tom, will you have this woman to be your wife, to live together in the holy covenant of marriage? Will you love her, comfort her, honor and keep her, in sickness and in health, and forsaking all others, be faithful to her as long as you both shall live? If so answer, 'I will.'"

Then it was time for the lighting of the unity candle, a modern ritual in which the couple use two small tapers to light a single larger candle, signifying the joining of two lives and families. The tapers themselves are usually lit by members of the two families—in this case, the mothers of the couple, a nice connection of the two families.

After a soloist sang "Let It Be Me" by the Everly Brothers (secular), the minister read what must surely be the single most popular element of modern weddings, and for good reason—the unparalleled ode to love in First Corinthians:

> If I speak with the tongues of men and of angels, but do not have love, I have become a noisy gong or a clanging cymbal. If I have the gift of prophecy, and know all mysteries and all knowledge; and if I have all faith, so as to remove mountains, but do not have love, I am nothing. And if I give all my possessions to feed the poor, and if I surrender my body to be burned, but do not have love, it profits me nothing. Love is patient, love is kind and is not jealous; love does not brag and is not arrogant, does not act unbecomingly; it does not seek its own, is not provoked, does not take into account a wrong suffered, does not rejoice in unrighteousness, but rejoices with the truth; it bears all things, believes all things, hopes all things, endures all things. Love never fails.[3]

In addition to being beautiful and wedding appropriate, this passage is a perfect example of the "secular-sacred"—a religious message that works just as well for the secular heart. (See "The Secular-Sacred, and the Sacred-Secular.")

They concluded with the exchange of rings, followed by a passage from *Conversations with God* by Neale Donald Walsch:

> A circle is a symbol of the Sun, and the Earth, and the Universe. It is a symbol of holiness, and of perfection and peace. It is also the

symbol of the eternality of spiritual truth, love and life—that which has no beginning and no end. And in this moment, [Tom and Danielle] choose for it to also be a symbol of unity, but not of possession; of joining, but not of restricting; of encirclement, but not of entrapment. For love cannot be possessed, nor can it be restricted. For your souls are eternally free.[4]

And the presentation of the couple.

No one present at Tom and Danielle's wedding could have reasonably claimed that God was excluded from the ceremony. At the same time, meaningful secular rituals and pieces of music were included, and none of the religious content required Tom to pledge fealty, belief, or belonging that he didn't wish to pledge.

> *I'm an atheist, raised Jewish. My wife was raised Catholic. We dealt well with our differences. We mixed traditions at our wedding, lighting unity candles and smashing a glass. We even had a bagpiper playing 'Hava Nagila,' which got a good laugh from everyone.* —Joseph

Anna (a Catholic who later became an atheist) and Gary (an atheist who later became a Baptist) had a justice of the peace officiate at their wedding. "I carried my grandmother's Bible down the aisle with my bouquet," says Anna. "It's a family tradition, so I wanted to do that for her. We walked down the aisle to the traditional 'Wedding March,' and the recessional was Schroeder's theme song from the *Peanuts* cartoons." Other aspects of the ceremony honored the diverse members of her wedding party. "I wanted them all to participate because they were some of the people closest to me, the ones who I respected, who influenced me, and who I looked up to and turned to for advice. It was important that they be able to participate in a way that reflected who they are, as well as who we were as a couple at the time. My maid of honor recited a Lakota wedding prayer; one of my other bridesmaids, who is Baha'i, gave a Baha'i reading; and my brother read a Christian prayer before we sat down to dinner. We also incorporated a few Italian traditions. It was quite an eclectic ceremony."

See Anna and Gary, *Chapter 10*

Their setting was also unique, a banquet hall in a Wild West town. "I have a degree in history and my main focus of study was the frontier expansion of the U.S. and the conflicts with Plains tribes. So we thought it would be fun to have the ceremony with a bit of a cowboys and Indians theme." Just as my own wedding choices reflected my identity as a musician, Anna's reflected hers as a historian.

Not everyone in Anna's Catholic family was pleased with the choices. "My dad's side of the family was concerned because it wasn't in the Catholic Church. And my more conservative and fundamentalist family members were concerned because we had readings from so many different religious backgrounds." There was some tension, but no boycotts or major difficulties.

Who Blocks the Altar? A Quick Denominational Tour

Most religions no longer require both partners to be of the same flock. But a few denominations continue to maintain barriers of different kinds for mixed-belief couples, and many of these affect the wedding itself.

When it comes to intermarriage, Orthodox Judaism is perhaps the most restrictive faith, refusing to accept mixed-belief marriages as valid or legitimate in any way, citing the clear Talmudic prohibition. An Orthodox Jew marrying outside of the faith is generally cut off from the Orthodox community entirely. For centuries, rabbis not only would refuse to officiate a mixed wedding but would declare such marriages entirely invalid. Orthodox and Conservative rabbis are even prohibited from attending mixed weddings.

But Orthodox and Conservative Jews are in the minority among Jews in the United States—10% and 18%, respectively.[5] The majority of Reform and Reconstructionist rabbis and all Humanistic rabbis (in other words, most U.S. rabbis) are now willing to recognize and officiate mixed marriages, including marriages to nonbelievers. Fifty-eight percent of all married U.S. Jews and seventy-eight percent of married Progressive Jews have non-Jewish partners, including many who are entirely nonreligious.[6]

The next three denominations in terms of restrictions are Catholicism, Jehovah's Witnesses, and Mormonism. But unlike Orthodox Judaism, all three do permit their members to marry outside of the faith—though all strongly discourage the practice.

When a Catholic and a person unbaptized in any Christian faith wish to marry, special permission from the local bishop known as a "dispensation from disparity of cult" is required. Such a marriage will not be considered sacramental, but often it can take place in a Catholic church if the diocese permits it, though a Nuptial Mass is out of the question. Holding a Catholic wedding outside of a Catholic church also requires a separate permission called a "dispensation from canonical form."

Many Catholics are unconcerned about the official approval of the church, or in some cases resentful of the flurry of permissions and dispensations required to marry a non-Catholic. If the Catholic partner falls into either category, of course, wedding plans are easier.

More than a third of married Jehovah's Witnesses are married to non-Witnesses, and 15% to partners who are entirely unaffiliated. This is in part because so many become Witnesses as adults, often after marrying and belonging to another religion.[7] Witnesses may marry non-Witnesses in civil ceremonies, but not in the Kingdom Hall, the worship center of Jehovah's Witnesses. Ceremonies are still expected to follow strict guidelines of behavior and avoidance of rituals or symbols with "pagan" roots.

Mormons are among the most endogamous religious groups, meaning they tend strongly to marry other Mormons (83%). Only 5% of married Mormons have religiously unaffiliated partners.[8] This is largely explained by the Mormon doctrine of "celestial marriage," the idea that marriage joins two people not just until death, but eternally. Members are permitted to marry in civil ceremonies, but "sealing"—the process that binds two people for all time—can take place only in a Mormon temple between two baptized Mormons. Unless spousal conversion down the road is in the plans—never a healthy thing to count on—the Mormon who marries a nonreligious partner in a civil setting is consciously giving up on eternal marriage.

Aside from Old Order Amish and Mennonites, few Protestant denominations have doctrinal obstacles to mixed-belief weddings. That doesn't mean they always welcome them, and some individual churches or clergy may refuse to officiate or allow the use of the church building. (For one such example, see Arlene and Nate's story in this chapter.)

Ninety percent of married American Hindus have Hindu partners, the highest level of endogamy (in-group marriage) among major U.S. religions.[9] But unlike the other endogamous groups, there's no doctrine at the root of it. Hindus enjoy absolute freedom of belief and practice, including the freedom to associate fully with people of other religions.[10] And several Hindu traditions are entirely atheistic, which also makes consorting with the nonbeliever a nonissue. When Hindus do marry out, any conflicts tend to be cultural rather than religious—at least from the Hindu side. And because Hindu weddings are built more around traditional practices than specific theological beliefs, it's easier to weave them into a secular service than it is for many other traditions.

Conservative Islam permits Muslim men to marry Muslim, Jewish, or Christian women, though Muslim women may wed only Muslim men. There's no doctrinal allowance for a spouse who is nonreligious, so as in Judaism, no conservative Muslim cleric is likely to officiate a wedding in which one of the partners is nonreligious. But a cleric in one of the progressive Islamic movements—again, much like in Judaism—is more likely to do so.

The Secular-Sacred, and the Sacred-Secular

Why is First Corinthians 13 such a reliable staple of modern weddings? It's a gorgeous, poetic passage about love, of course. But it also isn't limited to a single point of view. It's from the Bible, and therefore religious, but the text itself doesn't put love in an exclusively religious frame. Religious and nonreligious hearts alike are receptive to the idea that life without love is hollow ("a clanging cymbal"), that it is patient, kind, and slow to anger, never envious or boastful, and always forgiving—especially as the couples stand at the altar. It originates in a sacred source but is just as meaningful to secular ears. It doesn't refute God but also doesn't mention him. It mentions faith, but only to underline the fact (twice) that it is less important than love. It's a perfect example of the "secular-sacred," something that can fulfill both a secular and a sacred purpose without alienating either one.

The passage mentioned from *The Prophet* ("Let there be spaces in your togetherness / And let the winds of the heavens dance between you") is another example, written by a Christian philosopher, but including only light allusions to religion, and containing a message about retaining your own identity even as you join in marriage, an idea that resonates just as easily with the nonreligious.

The Vedas, the Qur'an, the texts of the Buddhavacana, and biblical passages from such books as Proverbs and Ecclesiastes include many other examples of sacred texts that work well in a secular context.

There's also a growing body of moving and humane literature from writers who are not just secular but atheists and humanists themselves. A moving passage from *Unweaving the Rainbow* by atheist biologist Richard Dawkins that begins, "We are going to die, and that makes us the lucky ones" has become a staple in nonreligious ceremonies of all kinds.

Humanist philosopher A. C. Grayling's *The Good Book: A Humanist Bible* imagines what the Bible might have looked like if, instead of drawing on Mediterranean religious texts, it had drawn on the rich variety of secular philosophy from around the ancient world. The result is not a dry anthology, but the same kind of narrative stream commonly found in religious texts, and a wonderful source of inspirational readings.

Grayling's *Meditations for the Humanist* and André Comte-Sponville's *The Little Book of Atheist Spirituality* are two more sources of poetic and meaningful passages that are grounded in nontheistic values without denigrating religion—perfect examples of what might be called the "sacred-secular."

Tapping a Third Tradition

One inspired response to the challenge of a mixed-belief wedding is the inclusion of symbols, rituals, or readings from a tradition to which neither partner belongs. It's an effective way of underlining the basic human values to which they both subscribe without grounding them exclusively in one perspective or the other.

Common examples include:

→ **The Buddha's sermon at Rajagaha, verses 19–20**[11] ("Do not deceive, do not despise each other anywhere. Do not be angry nor bear secret resentments; for as a mother will risk her life and watches over her child, so boundless be your love to all, so tender, kind and mild," etc.)

→ **The "Apache Wedding Prayer"**[12] ("Now you will feel no rain, for each of you will be shelter for the other. Now you will feel no cold, for each of you will be warmth to the other. Now there will be no loneliness, for each of you will be companion to the other," etc.)

→ **The I Ching**[13] ("When two people are at one in their inmost hearts, they shatter even the strength of iron or bronze. And when two people understand each other in their inmost hearts, their words are sweet and strong, like the fragrance of orchids," etc.)

→ **The Ritual Song of Krishna and Radha**[14] ("Let the earth of my body be mixed with the earth my beloved walks on. Let the fire of my body be the light in the mirror that reflects his face. Let the water of my body combine with the water of the lotus pool he bathes in. Let the breath of my body be air soothing his exhausted limbs. Let me be calm sky over my beloved," etc.)

Though this kind of cross-cultural borrowing is not for everyone (and some are downright hostile to it),[15] many others find it a unique and poetic way to underline their connection to a larger human identity beyond either of their own traditions.

The Bottom Line

At its best, a marriage joins unique individuals without erasing their individuality. A wedding ideally celebrates both the individuals and the union.

When partners share a religion, the new union will usually take on that same religious identity. But when they differ in their perspective, the marriage itself becomes as unique as the partners. No two will be quite alike, which is why the secular/religious wedding runs such an incredible gamut.

If one partner identifies more strongly with his or her worldview than the other, the ceremony will often lean in the direction of the stronger identity. My wife's Christian identity was more important to her than my atheist identity was to me in 1991, so our wedding was straightforwardly religious, and I was represented not by my worldview but by something that mattered more to me: music. Scott's nonreligious identity was moderate and Dhanya's Hindu identity was strong, so they had a Hindu wedding. Nora's atheism was more central to her than Kevin's Catholicism was to him, so their wedding was secular. And when both identify very strongly with their different worldviews, two (or more) separate ceremonies are often the solution.

Communicate openly, think outside the traditional box, and work together to create a ceremony that honors both the union and the very different individuals in it. The act of creative compromise is terrific practice and an outstanding metaphor for the lifelong secular/religious partnership you are creating together.

15

Church, Prayer, Holidays, and More

KEY IDEAS

→ Churchgoing often has less to do with theology than with meaningful connection to others.

→ Churchgoing includes elements that for many believers are uniquely beneficial.

→ Noncreedal congregations offer a unique alternative for mixed couples seeking a shared experience.

→ Because religious and secular expressions of most major holidays have coexisted for generations, holidays are not often a major issue for secular/religious couples.

→ Shared practices such as prayer or grace can often be adapted to reflect shared values rather than a single belief.

What happens entirely in my head, including my thoughts and beliefs, is nobody's business but my own. But when I put thoughts or beliefs into action, I have to consider the impact on others, especially those whose thoughts and beliefs differ from my own. This chapter looks at a few of the most significant shared experiences secular/religious couples have, and how they find compromises without compromising their essential values.

Going to Church

After the knot is tied, and before kids arrive (if any do), one issue rises to the top as a common source of tension or uncertainty for the secular/religious mix. It's not a belief but a practice: the act of attending religious services.

If you want to figure out the churchgoing norm for these couples, best of luck—there really isn't one. When we asked whether one, both, or neither partner regularly attends religious services, these were the results:

→ Both partners currently attend religious services of some type together: 8%.

→ One attends regularly and the other never has (since marriage): 15%.

→ Both attended in the past, but now just one partner does: 14%.

→ Both attended in the past, but now neither does: 13%.

→ One attended in the past, but now neither does: 9%.

→ Partners split to attend different types of services: 1%.

→ Neither used to attend, but now one does: 1%.

→ Some other configuration: 9%.

→ Neither partner has attended services regularly since they were married: 29%.[1]

In all, about a third of secular/religious couples report that at least one of them is currently a regular attender of religious services, meaning about two-thirds do not include even one regular churchgoer. This seems at first to confirm a common worry in many books on mixed-belief marriage—that marrying outside of the faith pulls the religious partner away from the church. But the best survey data indicate that the attendance habits of those religious partners is not far off the mark for the general U.S. population. Only 36% of Americans overall claim regular religious attendance.[2] So a religious believer with a nonreligious partner isn't much less likely to attend church than the average American.

It's no surprise that the churches being attended are mostly the ones in which one or both partners were raised: about 20% Catholic, 9% Baptist, 7% Methodist, 6% Mormon, 5% Lutheran, and so on. But one denomination had a much higher percentage than you'd expect from this pattern: Unitarian Universalism (UU).

Seven percent say one or both of them attend UU services with some regularity, even though just 1% of respondents were raised UU, and only about 2% identify formally as UUs now. This speaks to the unique place in American religion held by UUism, a denomination built around shared values and principles rather than shared beliefs. Since that's a pitch-perfect description of the foundation for the secular/religious marriage, UU fellowships are often a perfect place for couples who share values but not necessarily beliefs to meet in the middle. (For more on UU, see the section titled "The Noncreedal Solution," as well as Evan and Cate's story in Chapter 9.)

Seven percent of individuals in secular/religious marriages say one or both of them attend UU services with some regularity, even though just 1% of respondents were raised UU, and only about 2% identify formally as UUs now.

A lot depends on the past experience the nonreligious partner has had with church. Some see church as a place of manipulation, ignorance, and fear. Others are fascinated by the window it gives into the human mind and heart. Still others have no strong feelings one way or another. Many feel a sense of loss when they think of church, even a little envy, while others feel nothing but relief at leaving church and religion behind.

I fit mostly in the "fascinated" category myself, thanks in part to a background in anthropology. My and Becca's experience as a couple fell into the 13% survey result—both partners once attended, and now neither does.

When Becca first learned I was an atheist, she made it known that she would still be attending church. She never insisted that I join her, but it was clear that she would prefer sharing that experience with me each week. This wasn't a problem for me, nor was it new. I attended the United Church of Christ growing up, then a Unitarian fellowship as a teenager. Over the course of 25 years I'd attended churches in seven other denominations and even held a music ministry position shortly after college, though I was an atheist the whole time. My college major was anthropology, and I've always seen religion as a great source of insights into the human mind and heart. I always listened to sermons with a Bible in my lap to see the context and would leaf to any verse that was mentioned. Attending those nine denominations gave me a broader and deeper religious literacy than I could have had through study alone.

For the first year we were dating, Becca and I went to Bel Air Presbyterian Church in California. The church was pastored by the charismatic Rev. Donn Moomaw, a College Football Hall of Fame football-player-turned-minister who gave the invocation and benediction at both Reagan inaugurals. (We twice had the surreal experience of sitting directly behind the Reagans in the service, or as I remember it, behind their hair.)

Years later after we married and moved to Minnesota, we ended up at Wooddale Church, a large Baptist-aligned church on the outskirts of Minneapolis. The senior minister at the time was Leith Anderson, and we both found most of his sermons intelligent, insightful, even relatively progressive.

But his associate ministers, who often had five-minute bits in the service, were another thing entirely. Their messages were often intolerant and narrow-minded. We often found ourselves united in irritation on the way home by something we'd heard from them. (That's a common bonding experience for many secular/religious couples, by the way, especially when both partners are progressive.)

But even Anderson's messages sometimes grated on me, and after six years, the experience of attending what was essentially a Baptist megachurch began to wear me out. My angry venting about the service became the reliable soundtrack of every car ride home, and Becca became gradually quieter during those rides. I was processing the content, while she attended for the experience of spiritual reflection. I began to feel that my weekly postgame rant was diminishing her experience. It wasn't fair to her. But I also felt it wasn't fair for me to be made fist-clenchingly angry once a week.

I didn't know what to do.

Push finally came to shove one Sunday in 1999 when Anderson preached on Second Corinthians 6:14–15: "Do not be yoked together with unbelievers. For what do righteousness and wickedness have in common? Or what fellowship can light have with darkness? . . . What does a believer have in common with an unbeliever?" His message, adapted from this passage in his 1994 book, *Winning the Values War in a Changing Culture*, was clear:

[This passage] does not forbid friendships with non-Christians, but it does say that there cannot be a soul-bond with an unbeliever. There is an inherent danger for a Christian marrying, becoming a business partner with, or even a best friend with a non-Christian. . . . Christians should beware of entering into fellowship relationships with non-Christians. The higher principle that applies in every relationship is to be sure to "not share in the sins of others" (1 Timothy 5:22). . . . The most important basis for fellowship is a common denominator of Jesus Christ.[3]

He did mention briefly this passage in First Corinthians (7:12–14) that seems to say the opposite:

If any brother has a wife who is not a believer and she is willing to live with him, he must not divorce her. And if a woman has a husband who is not a believer and he is willing to live with her, she must not divorce him. For the unbelieving husband has been sanctified through his wife, and the unbelieving wife has been sanctified through her believing husband.

The last thing I heard before my ears filled with my pounding pulse was his explanation of the seeming contradiction: Don't marry an unbeliever by any means. But if your faithful spouse loses faith, stay married so you can strive to bring him or her back to Christ.

That was it for me. I could hardly see straight for the rest of the service. As much as I wanted to support Becca, I couldn't attend a church where a biblical passage equating me with wickedness and darkness was cited approvingly, and the most progressive and intelligent minister on the staff said quite clearly that my wife made a mistake in marrying me.

In the car on the way home, I told Becca I was done with church.

"I was devastated," she said later. She continued to attend on her own for a couple of years. As I learned when I first told her I was an atheist (see Chapter 13), churchgoing for her was as much an act of repairing some bad family history as anything, but she had hoped we would go together.

Eventually we found a middle ground at the First Unitarian Society in Minneapolis. It's a noncreedal congregation, meaning they gather not around a shared set of beliefs (creed) but shared values. We both attended for two years, then eventually, without fanfare, joined the two-thirds of secular/religious couples in which neither partner attends services, creedal or noncreedal. (See "The Noncreedal Solution" in this chapter and "The Seven UU Principles" in Chapter 9.)

Churchgoing and Happiness

The claim is often made that churchgoing leads to higher marital satisfaction. But that claim runs into one awkward fact: The divorce rate of Christian Evangelicals, among the most churchgoing of all Christians, is 34%—the highest of all major U.S. religious groups. Baptists are in second place, at 29%. Atheists—obviously the least churchgoing—are tied with Lutherans and Catholics for the *lowest* divorce rate, at 21%. The survey that revealed these divorce rates was conducted not by an atheist, but by George Barna, a prominent Christian Evangelical researcher.[4]

Of course not all unhappy marriages end in divorce, and author Naomi Schaefer Riley quotes some relevant figures measuring the *difference* in church attendance between spouses and checking that against marital satisfaction. Satisfaction is highest if both attend the same amount (a satisfaction rate of 8.25 out of 10), and lower if one partner attends a lot more often than the other. The difference isn't large, but it's there.

Here's where it gets interesting: If one partner attends church regularly and the other doesn't, it has little impact on the happiness of the one who stays home. But the churchgoer is another story. Marital satisfaction is a *full point lower* for the churchgoer than the nonchurchgoer—7.2 versus 8.2. To put it in plain terms, if your partner goes to church on a regular basis and you don't, he or she is probably less satisfied with the marriage than you are.

It's easy to see why. The churchgoer sits alone, surrounded by couples sharing the experience—a weekly reminder of something she doesn't share with her partner.

"It's hard to not have common religious or sacred experiences anymore," says Julie, a Mormon whose husband left the church several years ago. "Before we used to attend the Mormon temple together and talk about our sacred experiences. Now he no longer values those sacred experiences, which were defining moments of our marriage for me, and we no longer have many sacred experiences together. We do still have our love, and intimacy has a sacred feel to it at times, but I have felt there is a hole in our relationship."

For Arlene, that hole eventually grew to consume her marriage to Nate. "I started going to church regularly again when [our son] John was about six.

I knew Nate would sit through it if I asked him to, but I respected his feeling and never pushed the issue. But the questions about 'Where's Nate?' began to grow, so Nate would make an appearance once in a while. He would be polite, but obviously not engaged when deeper conversation would take place." Finally the charade got to be too much for her. "I just told everyone at church that Nate was an atheist. While people prayed for him and all that, he was still more than welcome at every event. He started coming more often and finally felt comfortable not having to pretend. That was great for everyone else, but I still really wanted a partner who shared my beliefs."

See Arlene and Nate, *Chapter 8*

Filling that hole is a particular challenge for couples whose relationship was founded on that shared core from the beginning. Recognizing the need is the first step.

"I have to admit I wasn't getting it for a long time," says Rick, a secular humanist whose wife is Catholic. "Elena would come home after Mass and say, 'I just wish you were still there with me,' and I'd say, 'Believe me, you really don't want me there.' I thought she wanted me to 'get religion,' but eventually I realized that wasn't it at all. She was having this rewarding emotional experience every week, and she wanted to share it with me. I couldn't do Mass every week for my own reasons, but I started thinking about what we could do together."

Eventually they found a common experience they could share. "We got into a meditation routine together, and it clicked. I actually look forward to being together on a different level." He even gained insight into the gap she feels from the empty space next to her at Mass. "She was out of town one week and I meditated alone, and I totally missed her being there. It just wasn't the same. So the next week I went with her to Mass, and I've gone a few times since then. I can't manage it every week, but I know she really appreciates the times I do, and it makes a difference in my own head to know why I'm there."

He's far from alone in this. Many nonreligious people find it possible to accompany their religious partners to services once they reframe the experience—even services as visibly participatory as a Catholic Mass. "My wife is more of a traditional Mexican Catholic than anything," says Joseph, an atheist in Northern California. "She doesn't think much of the typical

Catholic beliefs and puts lots of emphasis on the ceremonial aspects of the religion, like taking communion and attending church every week. I was originally apprehensive about attending Mass with her. It was always boring for me, and I struggled with the participation that was expected of me. 'Should I kneel? Should I bow my head during prayer?' Over time I realized that my wife couldn't care less if I participate or believe—she just wants my company while she attends Mass. I thought about how nice it is when my wife and children are with me when we are doing something I'm interested in, and she simply tags along with a smile on her face." Sitting beside her in Mass once a week has become a way for him to return her patient companionship.

"Now during Mass I smile and shake hands and converse with my fellow humans. If the topic comes up and I can elaborate on my own personal beliefs, it's always met with a bit of surprise, but it's never escalated into a heated debate like I used to think it would. People are typically fairly accepting and respectful of other's beliefs . . . and I learned that during Mass."

> *People are typically fairly accepting and respectful of other's beliefs . . . and I learned that during Mass.*

Social scientists wouldn't be surprised to hear that a churchgoer's experience of church has more to do with those around him than with God or theology. A 2010 Harvard/University of Wisconsin study confirmed that churchgoers are generally happier than nonchurchgoers.[5] But they dug deeper and found something fascinating:

→ Churchgoers with close friends in the congregation are happiest.

→ Nonchurchgoers are next.

→ Churchgoers without close friends in the congregation are last— lower in life satisfaction than those who stay home on Sunday.

If you attend church regularly and have at least 10 good friends in the congregation, your life satisfaction on average will be almost *double* that of churchgoers with no close friends there. The researchers say that no other factor—not individual prayer, not strength of belief, not reported feelings of God's love or presence—accounted for the overall difference in happiness. "[Life satisfaction of churchgoers] is almost entirely about the social aspect of religion rather than the theological or spiritual aspect," says lead researcher Chaeyoon Lim. "People are more satisfied with their lives when they go to church because they build a social network within their congregation."[6]

And though some couples (like Rick and Elena) find other shared experiences fulfilling, that isn't always the case. Connecting in the context of a religious community is often uniquely fulfilling. "We think it has to do with the fact that you meet a group of close friends on a regular basis and participate in certain activities that are meaningful to the group," says Lim. "At the same time, they share a certain social identity. . . . The sense of belonging seems to be the key to the relationship between church attendance and life satisfaction."[7]

Couples looking for a meaningful alternative to attending church together should keep in mind that churchgoing isn't always something that can be replaced by a bridge club or taking long walks together. For many people, though not all, church provides a unique blend of social connection, regularity, meaningful activity, and belonging that can be hard to replace.

The Noncreedal Solution

Most congregations are built around the assumption of a shared creed or set of beliefs about the world. In most cases, these will include a belief in one or more gods and a number of related doctrines. In a few, such as the Sunday Assembly or Church of Freethought in several U.S. cities, congregants are assumed to specifically *not* believe in a god or gods. In either case, half of a secular/religious couple may feel a less than perfect fit.

Couples in that situation who nonetheless would like a shared congregational experience should consider one of the noncreedal options—congregations built not around shared beliefs but shared values. The most widely available option is Unitarian Universalism, a fascinating religious denomination formed when the two most liberal denominations of the mid-20th century—Unitarians, who believed God is one entity, not three, and Universalists, who believed that everyone is saved—merged. The two denominations had been on the front lines of social justice for a century before they merged, agitating for the abolition of slavery, getting arrested on picket lines for women's voting rights, protesting wars, and feeding the hungry—the kinds of things nondogmatic churches do really well. Both continued to get harsh treatment from mainstream Christianity. Finally, in 1961, the two merged to become Unitarian Universalism (or UU).

Since that time, UUs have developed an interesting and courageous experiment: a religious denomination built around something other than beliefs. UU is creedless. That doesn't mean people sitting in the UU pews don't have beliefs, just that their community is built around something else: shared values and principles like the worth and dignity of every person, justice and compassion, and a free search for truth and meaning. Many UU members are religious believers, and many are nonbelievers, which is why so many secular/religious couples find it a perfect meeting place for their shared values.

Not all find what they need at a UU fellowship. Some atheists say UU feels too much like church, and some believers say it doesn't feel enough like church. They both have other options individually, though shared experience is harder to find. One former Methodist who now attends a UU fellowship said she can't get her atheist husband to attend. "I just miss the time spent together and the fact that nothing has stepped in to fill its place," she says.

But for mixed couples willing to compromise a bit to have that shared experience, UU is worth looking into.

See Evan and Cate, *Chapter 9*

"We tried liberal Protestant churches, and almost joined one until I learned I would be prevented from attending my children's baptisms," says Evan, an atheist. "However, we have been attending a UU church recently. I am enthusiastic, but sometimes Cate [a Catholic] feels there isn't enough Jesus. I tend to feel like UU embraces both Catholic (her) and nonreligious (me), so UU is a perfect middle ground. I have learned how comforting it is to be part of a community."

> *When I was young, I often got in trouble with Sunday school teachers in the Mormon church because I asked difficult questions. By the time I was in high school, I knew I couldn't be a Mormon. Later I discovered that one of my great-great uncles had been disowned by the family, probably for being gay, and he became one of the founders of the UU congregation that I later joined. I found his name in the membership book, which gave me a strong feeling of connection.* —Lisa

Families with Jewish identity on one or both sides can look into Humanistic Judaism, a noncreedal, God-optional expression of Jewish culture and values. Founded in 1963 by Rabbi Sherwin Wine, Humanistic Judaism currently has more than 40,000 members embracing their Jewish identity without theistic requirements. As noted in Chapter 2, it's not a heresy but one of the five officially recognized branches of Judaism today.

If you're lucky enough to live in a city with an Ethical Culture Society, well, I'm jealous. Founded in New York City over a century ago by social reformer Felix Adler, the Ethical Culture movement is a network of multi-generational, God-optional communities built around the motto "Deed before creed." Most of the Societies are in the northeastern United States, but several others are scattered across the country in Texas, Virginia, North Carolina, Illinois, Missouri, Oregon, and California. If UU is "too religious" in tone for the nonreligious partner, consider the Ethical Society—still congregational, but born as a philosophical social reform movement, not a traditional religious denomination.

Saving Grace

Prayer, meditation, and other solo expressions of belief shouldn't require any negotiation between partners. But when one partner wants the other to join in the activity, a little communication and compromise is in order to be sure both partners are comfortable.

See **Hope and David,** *Chapter 7*

A common example and good illustration is the practice of saying grace before a family meal. Not long after David deconverted, he asked Hope to consider making a change to their family tradition of saying grace. Not to discard it—he knew it was important to Hope. But given his own change of beliefs from Christian to atheist, he wanted to find a way to preserve the practice in a way that wouldn't exclude or marginalize him.

"It was a difficult step to make at first," Hope admits. "Saying a prayer at meals is a big part of Christian culture. But David was wonderful about how he approached me. He was really gentle, he shared his point of view and asked me to think about it, then he gave me a couple days to get back to him about it."

Even so, she says, "The conversation was really painful for me. I didn't want to let it go. But I realized a mealtime blessing is more of a culture thing, not so much a biblical command or an essential element of my faith.

Unlike some other things, at the end of the day, I felt like this was not a hill to die on. We went through a few weeks of not saying anything at all, which was awkward for both of us. So I suggested we find or write a less religious blessing as a compromise. We both hunted around and sent each other some ideas by email. In the end, I'm happy with our compromise: 'For the meal we are about to eat, for those who made it possible, and for those with whom we are about to share it—we are thankful.' "

Meeting on the Secular Side

Only about one in four survey respondents have ever attended atheist and humanist meetings or events with any regularity, and just one in six currently does:

→ Neither has attended any such meeting regularly since their marriage: 72%.

→ One attends regularly, but the other never has: 12%.

→ Both attend together, at least occasionally: 3%.

→ Formerly one did, but now neither does: 3%.

→ Formerly both did, but now neither does: 2%.

→ Formerly neither did, but now one does: 1%.

→ Formerly both did, but now only one does: <1%.

As recently as 5–10 years ago, most atheist or humanist groups gathered once a month for a talk by a guest speaker who usually spoke on topics related to science or the debunking of religion, with an occasional book club in the mix. This semi-academic format has a limited appeal, especially for families, many younger people, and anyone looking for the social or community engagement aspects that religious congregations offer.

Just as many churches woke from their sermon-heavy formats a generation ago, a sea change has swept through the atheist/humanist movement, transforming many freethought groups from single-focus lecture societies to vibrant communities whose programming in a given month may include social events, community volunteering, food and clothing drives, support for members in need, and of course the occasional talk or book club meeting.

"We found a local freethought group on Meetup about eight or nine years ago, went twice, and never went back," says Rachel, a California agnostic whose partner is a Reform Jew. "[My partner] didn't mind the religious critiques in the talks, we just both found it incredibly boring. Almost everybody in the group was an older white man. I'm a Latina in my 30s. The talks were preaching to the choir. I couldn't wait to get out. But last year I saw an article in the local paper about the group doing some volunteering and decided to check it out again. I could not believe it was the same group! People of all ages, men and women and kids, and I wasn't the only person of color. They have picnics, they volunteer twice a month. They have child care! I dragged him back in, and we never left."

Holidays

You might think that holidays would present a major issue for secular/religious couples, but in fact it's rarely a big deal. Not one couple I surveyed or interviewed mentioned the holidays as a point of contention. Part of the reason is the "one rulebook" advantage mentioned in Chapter 14. Partners from two established religions often bring two conflicting rulebooks to the table for holidays. But nonreligious partners don't have a single set of essential rituals for any given holiday, so there's less collision and more room for mixing and experimenting.

It also helps that most major religious holidays, like Easter and Christmas, have developed secular parallels, and that the secular and sacred have coexisted quite well for many generations. When I was young, our Christmas decorations included Santa, a tree, lights, stockings, . . . and a manger scene. Our music included "O Holy Night" and "Jingle Bell Rock." I never quite knew how they fit together, but I knew what they all meant, and I loved it all. Like most kids, I just accepted it as the way Christmas is.

So it continues today, with a mishmash of symbols and traditions that all signify the warmth, love, and fellowship of that holiday season. That some of the same symbols and traditions have religious meaning to others is something I can easily respect as long as that meaning is not forced on me. In turn, I would never think of forcing a secular interpretation on someone else, despite the manufactured "War on Christmas" nonsense. Many mixed-belief couples attend Christmas services in addition to secular celebrations. Few find the mix difficult to achieve.

The same applies for other holidays with religious roots, like Easter, Thanksgiving, and Valentine's Day. All can be deeply meaningful and important to believer and nonbeliever alike without the need to agree on the meaning or purpose of symbols and rituals associated with each.

Then there are holidays with natural roots, including the vernal and autumnal equinoxes. Because Earth spins on a tilted axis, the days grow longer and the nights shorter for half of the year, then reverse for the other half. Deep poetry exists in feeling the swing of that planetary pendulum, and religious and nonreligious people alike can and do celebrate those moments as well.

The Bottom Line

If they don't mind pursuing their paths separately, secular/religious couples should have little difficulty doing so. But those who are looking for shared experience and practices—attending church or a freethought group, engaging in prayer or meditation together, or celebrating holidays—have many options that can be meaningful to both partners. Know what you want and need (and which is which), be willing to reasonably accommodate what your partner wants and needs, and communicate openly and honestly about it.

16

Who Are You?

KEY IDEAS

→ For many people, a worldview label has at least as much to do with the sense of self and connection to other people as it does with beliefs.

→ The arrival of children often intensifies the sense of identity and the need to connect to a community, especially for the religious partner.

→ For many religious people, religious identity is a uniquely powerful form of identity.

→ The need to belong and connect is sometimes less intense for the non-religious. One common exception that presents challenges for mixed couples is when the nonreligious identity is defined by antipathy or resentment toward religion.

The province of Québec has always been the most Catholic part of Canada. It was 83% Catholic in the mid-20th century and considered the most religious province in belief and practice.

But the 1960s brought a secularization known as "the Quiet Revolution," and by the early 2000s, Québec had become the *least* religious province in belief and practice. Regular church attendance dropped down around 10%, and only 22% of Quebécois said they considered themselves religious. Yet 83% still call themselves Catholic, even though most no longer believe in God or practice the religion.[1]

Catholicism in Québec has more to do with who you are than what you believe. The French-speaking Catholic minority in Canada is surrounded by English-speaking Protestants, and their Catholicism is tied tightly to their French identity, to which they are fiercely loyal. To stop identifying as a Catholic is to disappear into the English-Protestant mainstream. So even if someone has stopped believing in every last aspect of Catholic theology and never sets foot in Sunday Mass, he or she will still proudly tell a pollster, "I am a Catholic."

That may make the average person's head spin a bit, but it doesn't surprise social scientists. As noted in Chapter 15, a 2010 Harvard/University of Wisconsin study found that things such as identity, belonging, and social connections to other people play a more important part in attracting religious adherents and fulfilling their needs than theological beliefs.[2]

Religious Belonging

Religious and nonreligious people both tend to think of religion in terms of beliefs. In fact, there is reason to believe we overestimate the importance of the beliefs to religious people and greatly *underestimate* the importance of identity and belonging.

I've heard scores of nonreligious partners in mixed marriages describe the same frustrating situation: They bring their best, shiniest arguments against a religious partner's beliefs only to have the partner shrug or say, "I know it's not rational, but I still believe." Both often fail to recognize that identity and belonging can be the real values that cement the individual to his or her religion—neither of which responds to argument. When a religious person refers to being part of "something greater than myself," for example, that greater thing is very often the community of the religion itself.

"Realizing that her religious beliefs had more to do with loyalty to her family than loyalty to God was one of the breakthrough moments in our marriage," said one lifelong agnostic about his wife of 11 years. "We had a whole new way to talk about it that was less frustrating."

Nonreligious identity can provide the same intense feeling of identity, especially among those who were once intensely connected to a religion. It's often noted in the freethought community that those who were fanatically devoted to a fundamentalist religion before losing their faith often end up becoming the most fanatically devoted, antitheistic atheists.

Not everyone feels the pull of identity and belonging equally. Some religious people aren't especially social, and many nonreligious people tend toward solitude and introversion. I'm certainly not a social person. I'm happier with a book or with a few close friends and a bottle of wine than I ever am in a large group.

My wife is another story. Becca loves the social and longs to be connected to other people. She's energized by crowds and can talk and laugh at a party for hours, long after I've completely lost my marbles and started sorting the hors d'oeuvres by color. That difference in our "social thirst" and desire to connect with others kept me from seeing how important that part of her religion, the sense of belonging, was for her all those years. We rarely argued about beliefs, but when we did, I was frustrated by her shrugs. What I didn't realize is that she was saying, "I don't really care about all that. It's who I *am*." She remembers her mom seeing her off to school each day, saying, "Remember, you're a Christian young lady." Along with the implied message to be good, it gave her a sense of belonging.

For whatever reason, this was never something I felt the need for—with the exception of one point in my life I'll get to shortly. The whole thing puzzled and even frustrated me, especially the shrugs and deflections of friends when I'd ask about their beliefs. I failed to realize that the beliefs were not the issue. Then a few years ago, one friend gave me the breakthrough I needed to understand this part of it, the part my arguments couldn't reach.

I've known Daniel since college. He is Jewish, but his religious identity wasn't important to him when we first met in college in the 1980s. It was only later, especially once he became a father, that his Jewishness suddenly became the center of his identity. When I shared on my Facebook page an article by a sociologist describing the many different things people get out of religion, Daniel commented: "I think the author of this article missed a big one: Identity."

> *The arrival of children often results in a more intense engagement in religious identity by the religious partner. (See Chapters 8, 9, and 19.)*

There it was again, that thing I didn't really understand. Why the particular need for religious identity? Don't we all belong to families, communities, nations, ethnic groups, and a hundred other things that give us a sense of identity? What's distinctive about religious identity? What itch does it satisfy that other kinds of identity do not?

Daniel is one of the smartest, most decent people I know. He was a voting rights attorney for the Justice Department at that time, a superhero job in my eyes, and has now continued changing the world through a major public interest nonprofit. If anyone could explain the distinctive draw of religious identity, the part that other identities fail to fulfill for so many people, it would be Daniel. I asked for his thoughts later on, and his reply was the clearest explanation of religious identity I had ever heard.

"There are several kinds of personal identity," he said, "but I think they fall into three categories: where and who you've come from, where and who you are now, and where and who you want to be in the future. The identities you choose can only serve the last two. They can't tell you where you've come from."

We'd both had the experience of choosing a community when we were in college—the same one, in fact: the Cal Marching Band at UC Berkeley. We were both on our own for the first time, and we'd each felt the alienation and loneliness of being one student among 32,000. Then we joined that organization of 160 students with a century of tradition, a common purpose, even its own values and principles. It became our tribe, our identity. Sometimes when I'd walk across campus, I'd start to feel lost in the sea of humanity; then I'd see another bandsman, and suddenly I had an identity, a tribal connection. After we graduated, Cal itself became that touch point. When I meet a Cal graduate, anywhere in the world, I feel an instant kinship. And if I meet a Cal Bandsman, it's downright electric.

So why doesn't this tribe, and any number of others, do the trick for Daniel? What's special about Jewishness?

"Religion is different," he said. "I have found value in thinking of myself as a link in a chain, a link that's important to keep building, so my son can be another link after me. My people have been around as a unique identified group for 4,000 years, despite being targeted for genocide and eradication more times than any people on earth. That alone creates value for me. I am tied to history, and I hope my son and his children will have that same feeling of being part of a people, an identity, greater than themselves. I'm connected to people I've never even known, but who observed many of the same traditions that I do now, who had to suffer through more than I can comprehend to make sure I could be born who I am. I honor them and their memory by proudly sharing that same identity years after their deaths. I feel that grounding strengthens me."

So it was that sense of belonging that led him to God?

"*God*? Oh no, I don't think I believe in God," he said with a laugh. "But whether you believe in God or not, we as a people, and all the cultural things that even irreligious Jews love—our food, our community, our contribution to the arts, our sense of humor, our music—none of that would exist had we not shared a common bond of God, faith, and observance, which formed the traditions that held us together."

I was getting it.

"I can go anywhere in the world where there are Jews and find something familiar and people who will accept me as a brother. That's something no other identity of mine can afford. Think about how a Catholic might be greeted in a Russian Orthodox church, or a Shi'ite Muslim in Mecca. Israel views me as a citizen in exile, and secular Jews in Argentina and Russia and France and South Africa honor our common heritage. It's something I think most secular Jews don't credit enough—that the religion must be given credit for making them who they are."

The permanence of the connection is one of the strongest appeals to him. "I may move from the United States, and I and my future generations will cease to be American, just as I'm no longer from Russia and Poland, even though my family originally was. [My son] Joshua may go to Stanford, and no matter how hard I retain my Cal allegiance, my grandkids will have no connection to Berkeley. But I will teach my son to value his Jewish identity in whatever way he chooses to maximize the chances that his children and future generations feel a connection to me, even if they don't know me, and to their fellow brethren, whose ancestors shared the same bond I share with my fellow Jews.

"If push came to shove, and someone asked me, 'Who are you?' my first answer would have to be, 'I am a Jew.'"

→ → →

Judaism and the Catholics of Québec are unique in some ways, but the same thing applies to almost every religious identity to varying degrees. When you say "Baptist" to someone born and raised in a loving Baptist family, that person won't just hear a set of claims about God, Jesus, and what's required to achieve eternal life. "Baptist" also often brings to mind a connected community, a loving family, a lineage, the names and faces of people who have loved and cared for him or her, and the acts of kindness and generosity he or she has witnessed in its name. It is the frame in which values both spoken and unspoken have been placed all of his or her life. And though the nonreligious mind might immediately go to a list of unpleasant Baptist values, it's the more basic human values, the ones common to most worldviews but framed for each person in his or her own, that provide the deep and heartfelt connection to a given religious identity.

Belonging for Nonbelievers

Though it's not always the case, nonreligious people are often less drawn to ideas such as "belonging" and "community" than the religious. Those who were formerly religious were often able to walk away from the church precisely because they didn't have the community "itch" that the church scratches so well.

Those nonreligious people who do have that itch can find community and connection to others in many other ways. It can be a shared interest—hiking or volunteering or making music—or a simple matter of geography, like those people who live in the same neighborhood, or fans of the home football team, or one's ethnic or cultural background. It can revolve around stated values, such as the Seven Principles of Unitarian Universalism, or it can simply be the connection and support of a close, caring family. Any one of these may or may not fulfill a felt need for community for a given person. It's often a matter of trial and error.

Connection to others in the nonreligious community can be especially important for those (like David, discussed shortly) who have only recently transitioned out of religion. It can be a very lonely, isolated feeling at first. But connection to like-minded others is easier than ever for the nonreligious. Atheist and humanist groups exist in virtually every city and town in America, and Meetup.com offers one of the best ways to find them.

Because the freethought community grew up along with the Internet, a lot of the connection and community for atheists and humanists takes place online, including websites like Atheist Nexus and Freethought Blogs. Recent efforts like the Sunday Assembly movement and several "Churches of Freethought" are working hard to create meaningful weekly congregations for nontheists who need and want that physical community.

The Opposition Factor

One of the risks for couples finding separate communities is that religious and nonreligious groups sometimes define themselves in direct opposition to each other. Religious messaging frequently warns against the horrors of disbelief ("The fool says in his heart, 'There is no God.'... There is none that doeth good"),[3] whereas many atheist groups include members with strong resentments against religion, often stemming from a painful separation from their faith or family shunning, and can spend an inordinate amount of time and energy discussing, critiquing, opposing, and even ridiculing religion.

See Tom and Danielle, Chapter 5

"We did run into this problem socially," says Danielle, a Baptist married to Tom, an atheist. "He's active in local atheist and humanist groups, and we've made a lot of friends through them. But sometimes it's challenging for me because from certain people I will hear so many religious jokes, and so many knocks on God, and so many antireligious conversations... it just gets very frustrating. But a lot of the other people there are our friends, so I still want to go, and I still have a good time."

"I don't like those conversations very much either, to be honest," says Tom, speaking for many other atheists. "I'm an atheist activist as a career. When I go to hang out, I don't want to talk about atheism anymore! It bores me. Okay, I don't believe in God, and neither do you. I don't need to talk about it anymore—I'm done." This points to a common evolution in nontheistic identity. "A lot of people who've been there for a few years have already gotten to that point, and it's often the newer people who need to get through that still."

As I mentioned in Chapter 3, Cass Sunstein describes this dynamic very well in his book *Going to Extremes*. Those who surround themselves too completely with others who share their opinions tend to have those opinions challenged too seldom. Amid all the nodding heads, they often move toward uncritical extremes of the opinions they share. In a secular/religious couple, that can increase tension and conflict at home.

Of course many groups on both sides rise above the pettiness, preferring to positively express their own worldview instead of denigrating another. Religious and nonreligious partners are uniquely positioned to counter the extremes in their own groups, adding a dose of firsthand experience when the conversation turns to stereotyping the "other side."

Engaging in separate communities can cause some mixed-belief couples to struggle to find a shared connection, something that's especially hard on those who once shared beliefs. "Some of our greatest struggles as a mixed-religion marriage are forming community," says Hope. "Mostly David has his friends and I have mine. His friends are mostly from his freethought group on Facebook and mine are mostly from church. I went to his atheist group once, and would have gone more often but it was easier for him to go by himself. Now he doesn't go that often either."

See **Hope and David,** *Chapter 7*

It's common for such couples or individual partners to describe a period of searching before something clicks into place as a fulfilling answer to the need for community and identity. As noted in the previous chapter, many couples find noncreedal congregations like Unitarian fellowships, Ethical Societies, or Humanistic Jewish congregations to be an effective solution. Others find groups based on shared social, political, or volunteer interests, while still others are happy to connect with separate communities while maintaining their own connection as a couple within the family unit. (For more on this option, see the section in Chapter 15 titled "The Noncreedal Solution," as well as Evan and Cate's story in Chapter 9.)

The Bottom Line

It's a good idea for a nonreligious person with a religious partner to recognize that religious belonging can be genuinely different from other identities and uniquely fulfilling for some people, and that it isn't necessarily tied to theological claims. I've had many atheists and humanists in mixed marriages tell me that realizing their partners were getting something else out of their religious identity and practice—that it wasn't all about heaven and hell, God and Jesus, after all—made them much more understanding and less frustrated in the relationship.

Religious partners may notice the same desire for connection with like-minded others in their nonreligious partners, especially those who have recently transitioned out of religion. Atheist and humanist groups, online communities, and even "atheist churches" are meeting that need in various ways and at various levels.

17

Communication and Respect

KEY IDEAS

→ Each partner should make a serious effort to learn about the other's worldview.

→ Some differences matter (much) more than others; each partner should define his or her own negotiables and nonnegotiables.

→ Respect for individuals is nonnegotiable; respect for ideas is not.

→ Dogmatic thinking by either partner is the greatest obstacle to communication and compromise.

→ Research indicates that mixed-belief couples often exhibit particular strength in communicating to work out differences.

→ Contrary to conventional wisdom, avoiding sensitive topics is not always a bad idea.

→ One of the greatest sources of tension and conflict for a mixed-belief couple is the strong desire of one or both partners to convert the other.

When bluegrass banjo legend Pete Wernick and his wife, Joan, were first married, neither was religious. He had been raised Jewish, and she was a former Catholic. But eight years later when their son, Will, was born, Joan felt the familiar pull back to Catholicism. Pete remained a secular humanist.

They were both concerned about the new divide in their worldviews. But they were so serious about making their marriage strong and enduring that they sought out counseling before major problems arose.

"The first and best exercise was affirming our common ground," says Pete. "We shared a deep love for each other and more than 12 years of good history. We both wanted to live good lives, follow reasonable morals, be kind and thoughtful, and so on. We both wanted to be with and give a lot of love to our son, to see him grow up well in a two-parent household."[1]

If you know any conventional wisdom about relationships, you know what the counselor put front and center: communication. And with an issue as potentially divisive as religion, it's even more important for a couple to communicate clearly and well.

Pete and Joan each laid out points of conflict, realizing that some mattered much more than others. "We decided disagreement wasn't a problem if it didn't affect a decision about behavior. Most religious disagreements don't directly affect what we do, but concern which abstractions we take as fact. I found I could sometimes consider her 'outrageous' beliefs something like her having interests, hobbies, or politics that I didn't empathize with. The challenge is greater regarding the different *behaviors* called for by differing religious beliefs, like praying, or attending different services or meetings. But in general these can go on independently, leaving lots of opportunity for common ground."[2]

Think of it as sorting negotiables from nonnegotiables, and communicating clearly about which is which.

Sorting Negotiables and Nonnegotiables
In Chapter 15, Hope described grappling with the family tradition of saying a Christian grace before meals after her husband became an atheist. In the end, she decided that this was a negotiable aspect of her religious practice, grounded more in Christian culture than biblical mandate, and she and her husband settled on a blessing that was still meaningful but less exclusive to one perspective.

It's a perfect example of a key best practice in the secular/religious mixed marriage: identifying which practices are negotiable and which are nonnegotiable and communicating the difference clearly.

A religious believer may identify churchgoing as nonnegotiable for himself or herself, but attendance by a nonreligious partner as negotiable— even if it's strongly preferred. A crucifix on the wall might be nonnegotiable; *which* wall it's on might be negotiable.

A nonbeliever might identify the right of the children to choose their own religious identity as nonnegotiable while seeing certain religious practices in the home, such as prayer and churchgoing, as negotiable. Observing kosher or halal dietary restrictions might be negotiable while observing orthodox restrictions on sexual practice might not.

As long as a couple's nonnegotiables don't conflict, plenty of room exists for reasonable compromise. The more open and clear this process is, and the more evenhanded—with each partner showing a clear willingness to compromise—the better for the relationship.

As for Pete and Joan, sorting negotiables from nonnegotiables was key. "We agreed to avoid picking on each other's beliefs, especially around Will. We agreed that to maintain harmony, anything provocative such as art, symbols, or statements of religious belief or disbelief would not be displayed in common areas of the house such as the living room, dining room, or our bedroom. No books or movies addressing religious themes or issues. Our two individual rooms were and still are exempted."

Pete and Joan started with a clear foundation of love and respect, as well as a mutual determination to make things work. It's hard to go wrong when that foundation is in place—and hard to go right when it isn't.

See Tom and Danielle, *Chapter 5*

Tom and Danielle achieved a breakthrough in communication when Tom realized some of their differences of opinion mattered more to him than others, and some were more sensitive to her than others. "I'd say, 'Do you think the Gospels were written by people who knew Jesus?' *No.* 'Do you think Jesus walked on water?' *Maybe he did, but I don't think so,* she'd say. 'What about revelation?' *No, that's ridiculous.* We could go through all of this very skeptical stuff and be totally calm, totally rational, until we hit certain questions: 'Does God exist?' *Yes.* 'Why do you believe that?' *I don't know.* And when I'd start probing, you'd see the defense mechanisms coming out. Walls would start going up. The tone would change, the body language would change. . . . Other questions like, 'Was

Jesus the son of God?' *Yes.* 'Did he rise from the dead?' *Yes.* 'Why do you believe that?' *I don't know.*"

"I understand there's no logical reason to believe in it," Danielle says. "That's why I don't feel the need to push it on anybody else."

> "I began to realize that I was okay with the places where she still had these beliefs. They didn't hurt me, they didn't hurt the world around us, they didn't hurt our kids. So I didn't want to push on her sensitive psychological spots anymore. I didn't need to."

"So I eventually came to realize that there were these certain points when she would shift from logical to defensive," Tom says. "And I began to realize that I was okay with the places where she still had these beliefs. I realized they were illogical, but . . . I didn't want to push on them anymore. They didn't hurt me, they didn't hurt the world around us, they didn't hurt our kids. So I didn't want to push on her sensitive psychological spots anymore. I didn't need to. That took a long time to get to. But I didn't want to keep pushing and making her uncomfortable."

Separating Types of Respect

Both of these couples were only able to build a successful foundation for communication once they sorted out the difficult concept of respect.

Respect is usually defined as "a feeling of admiration or esteem" toward a person or idea. At least four levels of respect are in play in mixed-belief relationships:

1. Respect for the person

2. Respect for an idea or opinion

3. Respect for the right of a person to hold an idea or opinion

4. Respect for a person's intentions in holding an idea or opinion

People are inherently deserving of respect as human beings, and granting that respect is a nonnegotiable condition of relationships and communication. No one can be faulted for shutting you out if you declare disrespect for his or her very personhood.

But ideas and opinions are different. It would be dishonest for me to claim that I respect all ideas and opinions, or that all of my opinions are automatically deserving of respect. If I tell you that you are going to die tomorrow, you'll want to know (preferably today) how I came to that conclusion. If I say that I saw it happen in a dream, you'll probably breathe a sigh of relief. You are unlikely to say you "respect" that opinion. You may respect me as a person, my intention, and my right to hold the opinion, but you would be justified in withholding your respect for the opinion itself when it's reached by a process you think is entirely invalid.

I know people who reject astrology but have confidence in psychology as a means of understanding the people around them. I know others who reject psychology but have confidence in astrology as a means of that same understanding. They can try to convince each other of the validity of their respective approaches, but until they do the hard work of examining their different approaches to knowledge, neither can assume the other *respects* the ideas themselves. And that's okay.

The same is true of religious and nonreligious people, their ideas, and their opinions. In many cases there's no conflict—both religious and nonreligious people often form their opinions using the same methods and approaches. When that's the case, they can respect each other's ideas, even when they strongly disagree. But if they differ strongly in the *ways* they come to their conclusions, respect for each other's ideas is naturally harder to come by. A religious person who considers scriptural authority infallible and human reason unreliable is unlikely to respect the opinions of a nonreligious person who relies on the scientific method and rejects scripture as irrelevant—and vice versa. It's especially important to give yourself permission to withhold respect for an idea when you consider it to be not only false but harmful to others. It's the beginning of a conversation.

But couples with radically different ideas often feel that they must declare respect for each other's opinions. Sometimes that's easy to do. But when it isn't, all is not lost. Granting your partner clear personal respect, acknowledging his or her right to hold independent opinions, and recognizing good intentions lays the needed foundation for the relationship itself.

Personal respect can't be assumed—it must be attended to and reinforced, especially if belief is a major part of a person's identity. As one Christian partner put it, "My husband does not respect religion and does not understand that repeated disrespect of one's religion can cross the line into disrespecting the individual who holds the belief."

Contempt: The Biggest Warning Sign

The Four Horsemen of the Apocalypse are said to precede the end of the world. University of Washington psychologist John Gottman identifies what he calls the Four Horsemen of the Apocalypse that can predict the end of a relationship.

The first three—defensiveness, stonewalling, and criticism—need attention, but are all survivable, Gottman says. But the fourth—contempt—is the single most important sign that the marriage is in serious trouble.[3]

Contempt is criticism that suggests the other partner is inferior and the criticizer is superior. It's often signaled by tone of voice, body language, or facial expressions. Even rolling your eyes can signal contempt.

But if mutual personal respect is made clear and continually reinforced, ideas can often collide without serious risk to the relationship, as long as both partners keep the difference in mind. No matter how closely we hold them, our ideas, opinions, and beliefs are ultimately separate from ourselves.

Dogmatic Thinking

Nothing presents a greater obstacle to communication than the inability to admit that you just *might* be wrong.

The word *dogma* refers to a body of knowledge or claims, usually established by an authority, that is to be accepted without question. Because communication is about give-and-take, dogmatic thinking, which prevents any possibility of compromise or change, is the death of meaningful communication.

Not all religious beliefs are held dogmatically. That varies by the denomination, the belief, and the person. But some beliefs are indeed held dogmatically, meaning they are presented as truths beyond the possibility of challenge or disconfirmation. And it's not confined to religion: A landmark study published in 2006 showed that some atheists hold their beliefs dogmatically too.[4]

The researchers provided atheists with 20 statements (quoted in the lists below) and asked their level of agreement with each.[5] The goal was to determine to what degree they hold opinions dogmatically—that is, to what extent they are willing or unwilling to consider the possibility that they might be wrong. Indicating strong agreement with certain statements shows a relative lack of dogmatic thinking, such as:

→ It is best to be open to all possibilities, and ready to reevaluate all your beliefs.

→ Flexibility is a real virtue in thinking, since you may well be wrong.

→ The people who disagree with me may well turn out to be right.

However, indicating agreement with others shows a tendency toward dogmatism:

→ There are no discoveries or facts that could possibly make me change my mind about the things that matter most in life.

→ I am so sure I am right about the important things in life, there is no evidence that could convince me otherwise.

→ "Flexibility in thinking" is another name for being "confused and indecisive."

You'll notice that the nondogmatic questions all revolve around one thing—the willingness to say that you *might* be wrong—whereas the questions that indicate a dogmatic approach all involve an unwillingness to ever do so.

Some people hit the roof at the very idea that they are dogmatic: "Call it 'dogmatism' if you want," they'll say, "but my opinions are based on rock-solid fact." That may justify tremendous confidence. The problem arises when confidence lapses over into unbending certainty—the unwillingness to consider any future circumstances, no matter how unlikely, in which your opinion could prove wrong. It's the death of discourse and a serious problem in the secular/religious marriage.

Quiz: The DOG Scale[6]

The psychologist Robert Altemeyer developed a brief quiz to assess the degree of dogmatism (inflexibility and resistance to change) in a person's thinking. The more dogmatic someone's thinking, the higher the score, and the less well he or she will tend to communicate with someone of a fundamentally different perspective. The quiz presented here is adapted from the work of Altemeyer and his associate, Bruce Hunsberger.

In the left margin, use the following scale to record your reactions to each of the statements provided:

– 4—Very strong disagreement   0—Neutral or no opinion

– 3—Strong disagreement   1—Slight agreement

– 2—Moderate disagreement   2—Moderate agreement

– 1—Slight disagreement   3—Strong agreement

                                 4—Very strong agreement

STATEMENTS

____ **1.** Anyone who is honestly and truly seeking the truth will end up believing what I believe.

____ **2.** There are so many things we have not discovered yet, nobody should be absolutely certain his beliefs are right.

____ **3.** The things I believe in are so completely true, I could never doubt them.

____ **4.** I have never discovered a system of beliefs that explains everything to my satisfaction.

____ **5.** My opinions are right, and will stand the test of time.

____ **6.** It is best to be open to all possibilities, and ready to reevaluate all your beliefs.

____ **7.** My opinions and beliefs fit together perfectly to make a crystal-clear "picture" of things.

____ **8.** Flexibility is a real virtue in thinking, since you may well be wrong.

____ **9.** There are no discoveries or facts that could possibly make me change my mind about the things that matter most in life.

____ **10.** I am a long way from reaching final conclusions about the central issues in life.

____ **11.** I am absolutely certain that my ideas about the fundamental issues in life are correct.

____ **12.** The person who is absolutely certain she has the truth will probably never find it.

_____ **13.** I am so sure I am right about the important things in life, there is no evidence that could convince me otherwise.

_____ **14.** The people who disagree with me may well turn out to be right.

_____ **15.** If you are "open-minded" about the most important things in life, you will probably reach the wrong conclusions.

_____ **16.** Twenty years from now, some of my opinions about the important things in life will probably have changed.

_____ **17.** "Flexibility in thinking" is another name for being "confused and indecisive."

_____ **18.** No one knows all the essential truths about the central issues in life.

_____ **19.** People who disagree with me are just plain wrong, and often evil as well.

_____ **20.** Someday I will probably realize my present ideas about the big issues are wrong.

You can score yourself informally by noting whether you had a tendency to give higher scores to the odd numbers (relatively dogmatic) or to the even numbers (relatively nondogmatic). For a more precise grading, use the following formal rubric provided by the researchers.

FULL GRADING
Assign scores to your answers in the right margin according to these instructions. Grade odd-numbered items first according to this scale:

If you put −4 on the left, write 1 on the right.

If you put −3, write 2.

If you put −2, write 3.

If you put −1, write 4.

If you put 0, write 5.

If you put 1, write 6.

If you put 2, write 7.

If you put 3, write 8.

If you put 4, write 9.

Now grade the even-numbered items:

If you put −4 on the left, write 9 on the right.

If you put −3, write 8.

If you put −2, write 7.

If you put −1, write 6.

If you put 0, write 5.

If you put 1, write 4.

If you put 2, write 3.

If you put 3, write 2.

If you put 4, write 1.

Add the numbers in the right margin for your final score.

FINAL SCORE

20–60: Your approach to thinking and opinion formation is nondogmatic. Whether religious or nonreligious, you approach questions with maximum flexibility and openness to change. This bodes well for communication in the secular/religious marriage.

61–90: Your approach to thinking and opinion formation is moderately dogmatic, which often correlates with moderate difficulty in communication for secular/religious couples, depending in part on the other partner's score.

91–180: Your approach to thinking and opinion formation is relatively high in dogmatism, with minimum flexibility and openness to change. This often correlates with communication challenges in a mixed-belief marriage. Challenges are multiplied if both partners register as dogmatic in two different worldviews.

Challenging Context—And a Major Advantage

Communication in a secular/religious marriage often takes place in a complex context. The nonreligious partner might have emotional scars from childhood religious experiences. The religious partner might have baggage related to the suppression of religious practice. If one partner changed perspectives after marriage, there's often sadness at the loss of the relationship that had been envisioned. These and a hundred other personal issues swirl around many couples, complicating their ability to communicate around religious issues.

Here's a small glimpse of the more challenging personal stories I encountered in researching this book:

"I had eclampsia when I had my son, and we both almost died. I find it hard to have a situation where it would have been so healing for me to be able to talk about my experience in religious or spiritual terms with my spouse, but to instead feel the awkwardness you always feel when you're trying to tell a nonreligious person about your religious experience. Sometimes I find that very sad."

"Unfortunately, in many ways, I feel like as an atheist my voice is not heard, or counted, and the development of our children, and style of home life, is dictated entirely by my wife, who is an Orthodox Jew. I feel guilty for my feelings, like I am betraying her beliefs, and powerless to override her wishes."

"It's hard to not have common religious experiences anymore. Before we used to attend the Mormon temple together, and talk about our sacred experiences. Now, he no longer values those sacred experiences, which were defining moments of our marriage for me, and we no longer have many sacred experiences together. We do still have our love, and intimacy has a sacred feel to it at times, but I have felt there is a hole in our relationship."

"It is very difficult to show my wife that my rejection of her beliefs is not a rejection of her. When I speak against specific religious beliefs or the actions of some religious people, she often seems to take it personally, even when I know that had I made the same criticisms as a Christian she would agree with me. She would also break down days after a religious discussion, and cry to me, 'You're trying to take what I love away from me!' Sometimes she would say that I was taking God or hope away from her."

"I think he is missing out on the comforting nature of religious life."

"I feel like my choice to leave the Mormon church was a one-sided renegotiation of our marriage vows that changed the very definition of what our marriage is. My husband has been supportive of my choice but unwilling to really talk much about it to me. I worry that his expectations for what our marriage is are not going to be met."

"His view of himself because of his [Baptist] religion is that of someone who is not worthy, when in fact, he is one of the most incredible men I have ever known. It saddens me that he thinks I will be tortured for all eternity for not believing. I feel a sense of guilt for causing him worry, even if I think his worry is not logical."

"I am concerned that Mormonism is the true church of Christ and that the requirements of Mormonism are necessary for salvation, and that our child will not fulfill those requirements. I fear that our relationship with our extended family will go downhill, and that our child will suffer as a result. I'm fearful that our differences in belief will cause us to be separated in this life or the afterlife. I really wish he would stop trying to convert me to his worldview. I'm not really interested."

"I respect my partner's beliefs but feel badly that she does not go to church because I will not attend."

As hard as these issues can be, some intriguing research indicates that the same challenges can confer a benefit on mixed-belief couples in "dyadic consensus"—the ability of a couple to come to agreement on issues that are important to the functioning of the relationship.

Multiple studies suggest[7] that couples in a mixed-belief marriage often communicate more effectively about important issues in the relationship than those in same-belief relationships—not just religious issues, but the full range of issues that come up in any relationship, including the following:

→ Family finances

→ Recreation

→ Friends

→ Philosophy of life

→ Dealing with parents and in-laws

→ Goals and priorities

→ Amount of time spent together

→ Division of household tasks

→ Career decisions

And why would mixed-belief couples communicate better? Because they *have* to. Couples with the same religious perspective can often ride on the assumption of shared values and practices for years before hitting a snag, at which point the conflict-resolution muscle in the relationship may be weak from lack of use. But couples who are mixed-belief have to negotiate multiple issues right out of the gate. Direct communication becomes the norm, and they develop communication skills that serve them well for a wide range of issues, from religion to finances to parenting.

> *Couples who are mixed-belief have to negotiate multiple issues right out of the gate. Direct communication becomes the norm, and they develop communication skills that serve them well for a wide range of issues.*

Scott and Dhanya's relationship offers a good example of dyadic consensus that developed because it had to—not only because of the religious distance, but cultural and even physical distance as well. "Communication is our secret weapon," Scott says. "It got us through our long-distance relationship and many things since then. We may have an argument, or one of us gets upset, but afterwards we always talk about it. Always. We continue to talk about whatever the problem is until either we're tired of discussing it or we feel everything is covered. It's difficult coming from two different nations, cultures, religions, and dialects. That's why we have to work hard to resolve issues. We're not always happy or the perfect couple, but we never stop communicating. And we have to be truthful. I'm not always the most diplomatic, and Dhanya knows that."

Dhanya smiles. "It's true, he's not always diplomatic!"

"I think it's better to say something than to leave it unsaid. Sometimes she is initially sensitive about it, but she gets over it, and then we discuss it."

See Scott and Dhanya, *Chapter 6*

Much of the tension comes from Scott's probing questions about her culture and religion. "It gets a bit tense when I don't know the answers, and Scott has a lot of questions!" she says. "But it's not the questions themselves that are frustrating—it's not getting the answers easily."

But occasionally there's more to it, including times when she feels he is disrespectful. "It irritates me when he makes jokes that I think are in bad taste about some of the deities in Hinduism. When I say that he is being disrespectful, he does not see it that way. I guess I can understand when I think about it from his perspective, as he does not have the context or background to understand why the joke he made was not appropriate.

"Once I prepared food during the month of Shravan, and before we started eating I placed aside some amount of each food item on a plate which I would place at my prayer place. It was an offering to the gods and also to give thanks for the meal. Scott said something along the lines of whether the gods were going to eat the food that I offered. He was trying to be funny, and I did not think it was funny. I was annoyed."

The food offering, known as *prasad*, is offered first to the deity, then distributed among those assembled.

"I realized that the incident left a stronger impression on her than it did on me," Scott says. "For me, that was just one of those lame jokes that comes out. I joke about things that I don't understand or don't make sense to me, and the prasad didn't make sense to me. So I made a joke about it, and she was clearly annoyed. I probably thought it was an overreaction at first. Then, I realized how wrong I was later, perhaps when we talked about it before going to sleep. I probably apologized profusely. That's how things usually go."

"I did explain the purpose of what I was doing to him, which is what he wanted," Dhanya says.

This difference in perceived boundaries of appropriateness is just as common in the collision of secular and religious values sensibilities in Western culture. When asked for the shaping influences on his sense of humor, Scott points to television shows like *The Simpsons, South Park, The Daily Show,* and *The Colbert Report.* "All of these share a theme of irreverent comedy, something I have an appreciation of and a tendency for. That plus my inclination to interpret words literally lend aspects to my sense of humor that not everyone can accept or understand. For example, I have a tendency to look at things in a different and occasionally twisted way. Even though it goes against my natural tendencies, I've learned not to joke about the things she does for her religion. My humor can still be irreverent in other ways."

"I really appreciate that he has made this change," Dhanya says. "We both respect and try to understand each other's backgrounds and belief systems. One of the things I admire about my husband is that he always makes an effort to understand why we do certain things and how we do them, although I don't always have the answers."

Sometimes the conflict is harder to avoid, as it has been for Julie and Matthew. She was born and raised in a Mormon family, and he converted to Mormonism prior to their wedding. "He initially read and studied and talked a lot to me about my beliefs to strengthen his own beliefs," she said. But within two years, Matthew said he had lost respect for Mormonism and became agnostic.

Julie was devastated. "We did consider divorce a little bit. Mormonism was my life, not just my religion. He has researched the problems of Mormonism very well, but he hasn't made an effort to understand my Mormon beliefs. I have let go of many of my old beliefs, and he's excited to see that."

They talk about their religious differences "all the time," and both admit to a strong desire to convert the other—a serious source of conflict in a mixed-belief marriage (see Chapter 4). Asked to describe their conversations about religion, they choose some unsurprising adjectives—*sad, irritating, angry,* and *frustrating*. But importantly, they also include *loving* and *respectful.* "Matthew has little respect for my religion, but he respects me," Julie says, and over time, the exchanges have become much less heated. "Lately they are very respectful, but they used to be quite angry."

Part of the solution has been finding and communicating the real issues, not the seemingly obvious ones. As noted for some couples in Chapter 15, for Julie it was never about theology—it's the empty space next to her in the pew each Sunday. "The real hurt for me is not having common religious or sacred experiences anymore. Before we used to attend temple together and talk about our sacred experiences. Now, he no longer values those sacred experiences, which were defining moments of our marriage for me, and we no longer have those shared experiences. We do still have our love, and intimacy has a sacred feel to it at times, but I have felt there is a hole in our relationship."

Realizing that this was the main issue, not the abstractions of Mormon belief, was a breakthrough moment for the couple. "In two short years we have gone from yelling each time religion came up to having long, nearly tension-free conversations about religion. We're a long ways from getting divorced now. There's still a lot of love here."

The Unexpected Value of Agreeing to Disagree

Conventional wisdom has it that strong differences of opinion should be confronted directly and discussed. That's often the best advice. But an intriguing new study by San Francisco State University psychologist Dr. Sarah Holley suggests it's not always true—especially for couples who have been together for many years. Holley followed 127 couples for 13 years and found that avoiding sensitive topics by mutual agreement does not tend to increase marital stress after all, and may even have a positive effect. Couples are essentially saying, "I value our relationship more than the opportunity to win this point."[8]

Marital therapist Mark McGonigle suggests that instead of wrangling about the substance of certain contentious issues, each partner should instead try to find out why the issue is especially important to the other person—what McGonigle calls the backstory behind their "stake in the ground."[9] I gave an example of the importance of backstory in Chapter 13 when my future wife explained the real reason that churchgoing was non-negotiable for her. It had more to do with her stepfather's refusal to allow the family to attend than with specific beliefs. Understanding this allowed us to engage the question of attending together in a positive and productive way.

By no means is avoidance healthy for all topics. The key is to separate what matters from what does not. You want to agree on how best to handle religious questioning from the kids, for example. But if the question of Noah's Ark creates tension, it may not be worth the price.

See **Hope and David,** *Chapter 7*

Sometimes the avoidance is temporary, and a little time is needed before reengaging a topic. "We went through a time, maybe a year or two, where we just gave each other some space," says Hope after her husband became a nonbeliever. "We talked about work and the kids. He let me be me, I let him be him. We tried to appreciate and respect each other. We both realize that these things are not always easy to talk about, and we give each other space to process things."

Realizing that more things are negotiable than we first think is often a breakthrough in communication. "I just got to the point when I realized that I had this long list of expectations and it was like I was charging his credit account every time he didn't live up to my expectations," she adds. "I decided to shred the emotional credit card and forgive the debt. This idea freed me up tremendously. It freed me to love without thinking about what I was getting in return or how my husband was behaving. I chose to believe that regardless of how I was feeling about us at the moment, I love him, he loves me, and we are going to be okay."

> Secular/religious couples in which partners make a sincere effort to learn about the other partner's worldview, and to engage in practices related to that worldview (churchgoing, freethought meetings or events, etc.), report much lower levels of tension and conflict than couples in which one or both partners are perceived as not making that effort.[10]

The Biggest Mistake: Trying to Convert Your Partner

Of all the survey variables, one soared above the rest as a source of tension and conflict: a strong desire by one or both partners to convert the other.

A passive hope that your partner may switch teams someday is common enough and not a significant source of tension. It's when one or both partners feel and *act upon* a strong desire to convert the other—a self-reported 8, 9, or 10 on a rating scale of 1–10—that tension and conflict rise dramatically, along with the couple's own estimate of their likelihood to divorce. Such couples are much more likely to describe their discussions of religion as *irritating, tense, sad, angry, frustrating, disrespectful,* and even *emotionally or verbally violent,* than couples who describe a greater degree of acceptance of their religious differences.

> *My passive desire for him to convert to Catholicism is just because I know it would make things easier, just as my conversion to atheism would. I do wish I had someone to go to church with, but I would never try to convert him, nor expect him to try to convert me.* —Susan, Catholic

This relates to another classic bit of relationship wisdom: It's just not a good idea to enter into a relationship with the intention of changing the other person in any significant way. When the religious difference comes into being after a couple is married, there may be more *justification* for wanting a partner to change, but the fact remains that accepting the difference is one of the best things a person can do for the health and stability of the relationship.

In many cases, couples who began differently end up with the same beliefs without any prodding or pressure. A nonreligious partner may become religious or a religious partner may become nonreligious under his or her own steam. The latter happened in my own marriage about 10 years ago when Becca started thinking about her own beliefs in a new way. "I read Karen Armstrong's *In the Beginning* and I began to think about why I believed," she says. "The more I read and talked and debated, the more I realized that my belief was based on my label as a 'Christian young lady.' It had more to do with uniting with my mother against my stepfather than with actual belief."

About two years later, she decided that she was no longer a believer and now identifies as a secular humanist. But importantly, I never pushed or even encouraged her to change her mind. I neither wanted nor needed her to change anything about herself. Our differences had caused very few problems in our relationship because our actual values were so closely aligned. And even though there are some benefits to sharing a worldview, I was quickly aware that we had lost some of the diversity in our family, and that this was indeed a loss. When you're surrounded by people who share your opinions and perspective, it's easy to lapse into sloppy thinking. You tend to think and speak more carefully when you aren't confident that every head in the room will nod at your every thought. I knew I'd have to redouble my efforts in that area once Becca was no longer religious.

Our kids also lost the benefit of growing up with parents of two different religious perspectives, a hugely helpful thing for their own explorations. The possibility of indoctrinating them into a single worldview, intentionally or not, goes way down when two parents have different perspectives. I knew we'd have to be more intentional about exposing them to other voices once we lost that in-house diversity. It hasn't been difficult to do that; it just takes more effort than, "Hey, be sure to talk to Mom, too."

Getting Inside Each Other's Beliefs

Passive acceptance of religious differences is a great start. But for couples looking to push further into positive and open communication, one gesture rises above the rest: a willingness to learn about, and even participate in, a partner's worldview.

Partners who changed worldviews may already be familiar enough with the one they left. In that case, the other partner has the greater opportunity to learn about the first partner's new perspective. Couples who were different from the start often have the advantage of mutuality as both partners can extend the effort and appreciate the other doing the same.

For the nonreligious, familiarity may involve attending services or other events with a partner; reading books or websites about the history, beliefs, and practices of the religion; and getting to know others of the same perspective. Religious partners might join a partner at a humanist or atheist meeting, visit websites suggested by a partner, and check out books or videos by some of the prominent voices of atheism and humanism.

> We've mostly just talked a lot, about both of our different perspectives on life and the universe and so forth. We're always very interested in the other's view, as we both consider each other to be intelligent individuals whose opinions and thoughts in life are worth serious consideration because they're held by someone whom we respect a great deal. —Mark, an Independent Christian married to Linda, an atheist

But remember that the ultimate goal is not just to learn about the worldview generally. You want to know how your partner sees the world, which may be dramatically different from the doctrines of a church or the pronouncements of a high-profile atheist. Catholicism frowns on contraception, but the Catholic you are married to is more likely to smile on it. Christopher Hitchens may think "religion poisons everything,"[11] but the atheist who married a Methodist, like most atheists and humanists, is unlikely to go nearly that far. The solution? Talk to each other to find out what you both actually believe.

The Bottom Line

Pete and Joan's approach is the best summary of communication done right in the secular/religious marriage. "We've learned to use some primary tools of the discipline of conflict resolution," Pete says. "We find and affirm common ground and a common goal and agree to disagree on things that are opinion only. We agree not to provoke unnecessarily and have worked out other policies about behavior and compromise. Evenhandedness is a key concept—if something applies to one of us, it apples to the other. And we've learned to trust the stability of the resolution once we reach it.

"Looking back," he adds, "I see that over time we gained confidence that we could maintain our individual identities, and that we could trust our working compromise in how to expose our son to our divergent beliefs. I came to a strikingly positive, though almost preposterous realization: What we were doing amounted to *a model for world peace*! I figured if we could live together with relatively low friction on this very divisive issue, there was hope for the Israelis and Palestinians."[12]

18

Extended Family

....

KEY IDEAS

→ Most family issues arise from religious extended family.

→ No family is ever a monolith of identical beliefs and attitudes. The diversity can help defuse tension and open communication.

→ Preserving the faith and practice of the religious partner and of eventual children are the most common concerns of extended family.

→ If tension is relatively mild, concerns can often be alleviated as religious extended family get beyond stereotypes of nonbelief by getting to know the nonreligious partner.

→ If tension is moderate or worse and ongoing, it should be addressed directly with an eye not to "victory" but détente—reducing tension and building mutual confidence.

....

No couple is an island. No matter what strengths two people bring to a relationship, there's still the larger context of their extended families and their community. A supportive context gives a huge advantage to nontraditional couples of all kinds, from same-sex to interracial to interbelief.

On the other hand, a couple trying to make a nontraditional partnership work in a family or community that's hostile to the idea has an uphill battle, even if their relationship is solid. Add the stress of family or community disapproval to a marriage that already has its own problems, and sometimes it's too much for the relationship to take.

It's not news that relationships suffer when they take place in the harsh light of family or social disapproval. Romeo and Juliet managed about four days. And according to multiple studies, even real-world relationships tend to be less happy and less stable when they lack a supportive context.[1]

A recent Harvard University study went even further, suggesting that being in a relationship that others disapprove of can have direct negative impacts not just on the relationship but on the emotional and physical health of the people involved. "The more people felt like their family and friends and society didn't approve of and support their relationship, the worse their health was," said Justin Lehmiller, lead researcher of the study. "Specifically, these participants reported lower self-esteem, as well as more health symptoms like headaches, nausea, and loss of sexual interest."[2]

Fortunately, social acceptance of mixed marriages of all kinds is growing and attitudes are relaxing. As noted in Chapter 1, public opposition to interracial marriage dropped from over 90% to 15% in just two generations, and opposition to same-sex marriage has fallen from 68% to 47% since 1996. Though there are no long-term data on public opinion regarding interfaith marriage, the numbers tell the story: Since 1950, interfaith marriages have risen from 20% of new marriages to 45%.[3]

One of the more surprising results of the McGowan-Sikes survey is that only 10% of respondents identified pressure or concerns over religious issues by extended family as a source of tension or conflict in their marriage. For most, it's a minor issue or none at all. But for those still living with the disapproval of their extended family or community, the challenges are as serious and painful as ever. This chapter is for them.

Meet the Parents

→ *48% of those in secular/religious mixed marriages said the difference of belief was a "complete nonissue" for their parents at the time of their wedding.*[4]

→ *16% said parental concern was "mild to moderate."*

→ *Only 4% reported significant parental concern.*

→ *13% said parents did not (or do not) know about the difference.*

→ *19% can't recall.*[5]

Getting on the Same Page

When mixed couples experience pressure or tension from extended family over religious identity or practice, step one is always the same: Get on the same page. If a couple is unable to reach agreement on the issue, there's very little chance of coming to a productive agreement with extended family. Use the dyadic consensus superpower of mixed-belief couples (see Chapter 17) to define your negotiables and nonnegotiables, compromising as necessary to reach agreement on issues such as churchgoing and parenting so extended family pressure can be met effectively.

Where the Family Pressure Is

When it comes to the extended families of secular/religious couples, there is an occasional story of atheist in-laws being disrespectful or aggressive toward a religious son- or daughter-in-law, but the overwhelming majority of serious conflict, pressure, and tension from extended family originates on the religious side of the equation. That there are fewer atheists in that generation is one likely reason, but the absence of specific doctrines and traditions to defend against unorthodoxy is most likely the greater cause.

It's not always the religious partner's family that creates these tensions. Because most nonreligious partners have families of origin who are religious, general tensions over the partner leaving the family faith will often spill over into the marriage relationship, even resulting in alliances between the partner's religious parents and his or her religious spouse to bring the lost sheep back into the fold.

Drawing Out Family Religious Diversity

Even nonreligious people who recognize diversity among the religious fail to recognize it in their own extended families. To an atheist, everyone else can seem to have exactly the same beliefs and attitudes. It can certainly feel that way when the family gathers around the table at Thanksgiving or Christmas and all heads bow. But even in the most orthodox religious communities, complete conformity of belief is an illusion. A spectrum of belief and a range of intensity in every group and every family exists, no matter how it appears on the surface.

Recognizing this diversity is a huge step toward a healthy relationship with extended family for secular/religious couples. The two of you may embody the greatest diversity of belief in the family, but it's not the only diversity.

In a typical American religious extended family, everyone might go to church every week and show other signs of having exactly the same beliefs. The extended family might include traditionally religious grandparents and some aunts, uncles, and cousins on the same level of belief and intensity. But in every family, some are likely to have moderated views, whether or not they've expressed them out loud.

Rachel's husband, Don, is a deacon at the Southern Baptist church but wasn't especially religious until they were married. Uncle Jerry hasn't ever really thought about it, but he goes to church and bows his head at the table, so he looks as religiously orthodox as anyone. Uncle Bill learned about Buddhism in college and finds it intriguing but figures it wouldn't go over well in the family, so he's never pursued it. Cousin Lynn considers herself a devoted Baptist, but one of her best friends is Jewish and another is Mormon, and she just can't believe God would send them to hell. Cousin Kelly has read atheist author Sam Harris and thinks he's on to something. And Aunt Susan wears a T-shirt saying, "May the God of Your Choice Bless You"—not exactly a Southern Baptist sentiment.

Despite this healthy diversity of belief and intensity, it's natural when the family comes together for all members to take on the religious intensity and color of the most devout. As a result, it seems like everyone is on exactly the same page. Drawing out the true spectrum through natural conversation is one of the healthiest things any family can do to make the full spectrum feel welcome—including your mixed marriage.

Three Key Issues

Conflict and pressure from religious extended family take many forms, but three issues rise to the top:

1. Concerns that a marriage to a nonbeliever is spiritually invalid (e.g., 2 Cor 6:14), or in some denominations (e.g., Mormons) that eternal marriage is not possible

2. Concerns that the faith or practice of the believing partner will be threatened

3. Concerns about the religious identity and practice of the couple's children

Because the first issue is grounded in theological rather than practical concerns, it's the most difficult to address. If progress is made, it usually occurs over time through the "re-fencing" process described in Chapter 1. If someone dislikes or distrusts a certain group, then learns that someone they know and love is part of that group, they build a small "bump" in the mental fence separating them from the reviled group to put the loved one on their side as an exception. You might recall that the Faith Matters team named this the Aunt Susan Principle: "We all have an Aunt Susan in our lives, the sort of person who epitomizes what it means to be a saint, but whose religious background is different from our own. . . . But whatever her religious background (or lack thereof), you know that Aunt Susan is destined for heaven."[6]

Becoming the "Aunt Susan" exception to a negative stereotype is the first step, and often the most powerful one, a nonreligious person can take to reduce tension from religious extended family. It usually happens by patiently contradicting the negative stereotype over time, and actions will tend to make more of an impression than words, and watching it happen is a gratifying experience.

Occasionally it happens in small, surprising bursts. My own most vivid Aunt Susan transformation was not with a family member but an elderly neighbor who'd known and liked me for 10 years before learning I was a nonbeliever. "So you're . . . an *atheist*?" she said. I said, "Yes, I am." "But you're such a *kindhearted* person!" she replied with a stunned smile. These are powerful moments in the deconstruction of stereotypes, and when they happen, they can do wonders for reducing tension in a secular/religious mix.

The second issue (threat to the faith or practice of the believing partner) should rest as completely as possible in the hands of the believing partner. Freedom of religion is a principle so central to our culture that it's enshrined in the U.S. Bill of Rights and the Universal Declaration of Human Rights,[7] and for good reason. No nonreligious partner should interfere with the belief or practice of a partner unless that belief or practice is demonstrably harmful or abusive.[8]

That leaves concern for the kids—an issue tackled later in the chapter.

Where Do You Come From?

Backstory makes all the difference in a secular/religious mix. The religion in which someone grew up, and the intensity of that identity, is a strong predictor of whether tension and conflict will be a significant part of a secular/religious marriage.

Catholicism is front and center once again in the secular/religious mix. It's the most common identity for the religious partners and the most common denominational upbringing for both partners (22%)—followed by several Protestant denominations (see the sidebar).

Whether or not they themselves are religious now, those who come from Mainline Protestant, Reform Jewish, or Buddhist backgrounds, for example, report less tension in their marriages over religious issues than those who were raised as Jehovah's Witnesses, Orthodox Jews, or Mormons. For others, including those raised Catholic, it's the intensity of their family's religious practice that often determines how smoothly their mixed marriage is going today. This applies just as much to the nonreligious partner, and sometimes even more so. How smoothly did the separation go when he or she left the family faith? What was the denomination, and what intensity?

When asked about the general religious identity of their families of origin:

→ *30% of survey respondents said they were raised in "very religious" families.*

→ *45% said their families were "somewhat religious."*

→ *12% said their families were "somewhat nonreligious."*

→ *7% said their families were "very nonreligious."*

→ *6% said their families were a "secular/religious mix."*

So whether they themselves are now religious or not, three of four were raised in families that were religious to some degree—and most of those in the survey who were raised in nonreligious homes were outside of the United States.

When asked for the specific religious identity of their family of origin, if any:

→ *22% said Catholic.*

→ *10% said Baptist.*

→ *4–6% each said Methodist, Lutheran, Episcopalian, or Presbyterian.*

→ *5% said agnosticism.*

→ *5% said "spiritual but not religious."*

→ *4% said Mormon/LDS.*

→ *4% said atheism.*

→ *3% said Pentecostalism.*

→ *3% said Judaism.*

→ *About 1% each said Jehovah's Witnesses, Unitarian Universalist, Hinduism, Humanism, or United Church of Christ.*

→ *Less than 1% each said Islam, Christian Orthodox, or one of several other worldviews.*

One slightly surprising exception to the pattern is Lutheranism. Most with Mainline Protestant backgrounds end up managing the mix with little tension, but more than half of those raised Lutheran reported high levels of tension from extended family over religious issues. This probably speaks to the wide diversity in Lutheranism, from the fairly liberal Evangelical Lutheran Church of America to the conservative confessional Lutheranism of the Missouri and Wisconsin Synods. Though the survey did not break down responses to that subdenominational level, the results indicating high tension likely represent those more conservative traditions.

Fifty-nine percent of respondents said they were raised by two religious parents, and 11% were raised by two nonreligious parents. Fully 24% of those currently in a secular/religious mix grew up with one parent who was religious and another who was nonreligious at least part of the time.

So how did all of these parents feel about their children marrying outside of their family's religious identity? Nearly half (48%) of respondents reported that their marriage to someone of a different religious perspective was a complete nonissue for their parent(s). Sixteen percent reported mild or moderate parental concern, and only 4% reported significant parental concern. About one in eight (13%) said their parents did not (or do not) know about the difference in beliefs, and nearly a fifth (19%) said they couldn't remember whether their parents were concerned—which is probably a good indication that they were not.

These are some of the most interesting results of all. The garment-rending Tevye who disowns the child who marries outside of the flock is by no means gone from the landscape, but he's a lot less common today than in the past, and certainly less common than most of us assume.

Seeking Détente

An atheist dad once approached me at a convention, thanked me for my books on nonreligious parenting, then proceeded to show that he hadn't read them very carefully.

"My mother-in-law is hyperreligious," he said, "and she's always complaining because we don't take our kids to church, give them religious toys, and teach them to sing 'Jesus Loves Me.' I finally sat her down and said, 'Okay, look. Let's get some things straight. I am not going to apologize to you or anyone else about raising my kids without religious brainwashing. I don't know why you are so *obsessed* with this. It's no big deal that we don't go to church. In fact, if we can get the kids to the age of 18 without seeing the inside of a church, I'll consider it a great success. I don't want to hear any 'Jesus this' or 'Jesus that' around the kids. If we can agree on that, you can spend time with them."

Just a few words in, she would have lost the ability to hear him as the blood began pounding defensively in her ears. No one can really hear and think under this kind of assault. And the veiled threat at the end is a particularly nasty touch.

Now I don't know his situation. Maybe this woman had put him through 10 kinds of hell. Maybe there was no hope of achieving anything beyond that verbal flipping of the bird. But even if the former is true, the latter almost never is. There is almost always something more to be gained. But with this aggressive approach, he had slammed the door on that possibility.

He looked at me for affirmation.

"Oh . . . okay," I said hesitantly. "So . . . how's it going?"

"Well, we haven't spoken since then," he said. "But I *won*."

It was all I could do to keep from screaming, *Nooo!* By framing the issue in win-lose terms, he had misunderstood both the problem *and* the solution. What did he win—the right to raise his children as he wished? Assuming he and his partner had already reached agreement—always the first step—he was already parenting the way he wanted to. So the problem isn't that

Grandma is actively preventing them from parenting the way they want to—it's the tension and dissonance that's created by her disapproval. And he had made that, the real problem, much worse with his monologue. Reduce the tension and you most often reduce the symptoms of the tension as well.

And the best way to do that is by seeking not victory but *détente*.

Anyone who lived in the United States during the Nixon years tends to hear that French word in the German accent of Henry Kissinger. Tension was high between the United States and the Soviet Union. Détente is a process that seeks not victory but "a relaxation of tensions and building of mutual confidence." It is not a ceasefire nor a compromise, but something designed to make an actual exchange of warheads less likely. In the Cold War, détente meant (among many other things) exchanging ballet companies, art exhibits, speakers and such to show each other our human sides. In family relationships, it's about exchanging other kinds of humanizing messages.

> *My parents and I have a détente of sorts. We love and accept each other. We know we don't share religious beliefs, so we talk about other things. Do they still pray for us to come back to the church? No doubt! But I don't mind. It's just one of the ways they show love.* —Beth, former Catholic, now agnostic atheist

Many couples in similar situations don't even try to have this conversation. "There's no point," they say. "My mom is never going to change her mind." But *a change of mind isn't the goal.* Reducing tension is.

I do think it's best to sit down and address tensions about your mixed-belief parenting with any religious family member who is especially distressed by it. The key is to aim for a reduction in tension, not a "win." You're the parent. You've already "won" the right to do your thing. What you want is to scale back the tension and discomfort resulting from those choices so your kids can grow up in the best possible family situation. And you can do it without giving up anything. That's détente.

Couples who have decided to protect their children's ability to think freely and come to their own conclusions about religion should be proud and confident in that approach. But they must be careful to do so in the most effective way possible. Angry threats or insulting accusations are likely to make matters worse, not better.

It's important to reiterate that there is usually no problem at all. Many religious grandparents are entirely respectful of their children's rights to approach religion any way they wish with their own kids. Others offer nothing more challenging than the occasional grumble or plea. If you have relatives like these, be grateful. But when a grandparent or other relative threatens, harasses, or pressures you, or actively interferes with your right to raise your kids as you think best where religion is concerned, it's best to confront the issue directly by having a conversation with the relative in question.

The approach I recommend is based on a technique called Nonviolent Communication, a powerful and effective concept developed by Marshall Rosenberg[9] and others. It starts with *empathy*—making an effort to grasp and feel what the other person feels, to hear things as he or she hears them, and to frame what you have to say accordingly. It can leave people feeling heard, understood, and honored—*even if they continue to disagree*. It can lead to amazing breakthroughs by helping them to recognize that win and lose are not the only meaningful terms in dialogue.

Building a Breakthrough Conversation

Once you've decided to talk with family members to relieve tension around religious issues, keep three things in mind:

1. Relieving tension is the goal, not "winning." I can't stress this enough.

2. The couple should come to full agreement; then the partner whose family is involved should do the talking. This is true even if the nonreligious partner is the one whose family is putting on the pressure. The worst possible scenario is the guy who approached me at the convention—the atheist partner lecturing his religious mother-in-law. His partner should have been the one talking to her own mother.

3. Family members usually have the best of intentions. Pressure about your parenting choice almost always comes from a good place—a wish for the children to have the best possible upbringing. Even if you strongly disagree about what's best, recognize that their hearts are usually in the right place.

For the best result, there are four important elements to the actual conversation:

1. Honor the person. You can continue to think whatever you wish about the person's beliefs. But people deserve respect as people. Refuse to grant that and you have no basis for discourse. If nothing else, honor their intentions, which are usually good.

2. Empathize. Make a real effort to see things as the other person sees them.

3. Reassure. Some of his or her concerns can't be helped. Some can. Reduce the concerns by addressing those you can.

4. Include. This is huge. A clear gesture of inclusion can repair an immense amount of damage and bring down walls. Most people will respond to that generous gesture with a desire to not abuse it. For the rest, some reasonable limits can be placed.

Here's what the conversation might sound like:

(*Honor*) "I wanted to sit down and talk this over with you because you are important to us. I know you want what's best for the kids, and I appreciate that."

(*Empathize*) "I know your religious faith is a big part of your life. If I were in your position, I think I'd feel just the way you do—worried that this big part of who I am wouldn't be shared with my grandchildren."

(*Reassure*) "I want you to know that it *will* be shared. It's important to us that the kids learn about faith so they can make a choice for themselves. I'm confident that they will make a good one."

(*Include*) "We want you to help us teach the kids by telling them what you believe. Let's set up a time for you and me and Amanda to have a cup of hot chocolate so you can talk to her about your faith. How does that sound?"

The religious partner can reinforce the message further by showing his or her own comfort with allowing the children to explore ideas freely.

Some parents will insist that the conversation can't work because it doesn't address the real concern Grandma has expressed: that the kids will not be saved. But if the reports of scores of couples are any indication, this isn't the real concern—even if Grandma swears it is and honestly *thinks* it is. The real concern often has more to do with her connection to her grandkids.

Most deeply religious people have their religious faith woven into their personal identity. It's not just Grandma's explanatory system or moral code; it's often *who she is*. She's likely even to see it as the *best* of who she is. When her first grandchild was born, her visions of herself as a grandmother often centered on sharing the deepest and most meaningful part of her life with her grandchildren. The news that they would not be specifically raised in that faith would strike her first and foremost as the end of that vision. Worse still, she would often feel personally dishonored and shut out.

The last step in that conversation has proven uniquely powerful for many who have tried it. Doing away with the fear that a wall would separate them from their grandchildren and inviting them to share their faith has a greater ability to provide a breakthrough than anything else I've found. Details still have to be hammered out—no scaring the kids with hell, for example—but once the conversation has happened, they will be infinitely more receptive to a few simple ground rules.

Sometimes it won't work. But I've heard from so many people that this was the approach that finally achieved something positive—including many who had sworn in advance that "it'll never work with my dad"—that I recommend it with real confidence. And it's because it has worked for so many that I'm convinced this feeling of exclusion is more important than concerns about salvation.

Best of all, once the tension is relieved, an extended family with a spectrum of beliefs and attitudes can really be your kids' best resource for religious literacy.

The Bottom Line

Most mixed-belief couples today experience little conflict with extended family over their religious differences. But for those who do, it can be intense and upsetting, even leading to conflict in their own relationship.

Couples dealing with such conflict must start by getting on the same page as a couple using the skills described in Chapter 17. Serious tension should be addressed directly, ideally by the partner whose family is creating the tension. The approach should be empathetic and constructive, honoring the individuals and their intentions.

19

Kids in the Mix

KEY IDEAS

→ Agreement on family approach to religion should be reached early—preferably before having kids.

→ All opinions about metaphysical things should be expressed as opinions (e.g., "I think . . ." or "I believe . . .").

→ Identity pairing between a child and one parent and exclusion of the other should be avoided when possible.

→ Mutual respect should consciously be practiced in order to give kids a model of coexistence.

→ Children should be given space to make their own autonomous choices in the long run.

→ Children should be raised to be religiously literate.

A lot of the issues in the secular/religious marriage run through the relationship like threads. Extended family issues, churchgoing, communication—all of these ebb and flow over time as couples find their level of comfort with the mix and (hopefully) refine their relationship skills. But three moments stand out as exactly that—moments. Not themes, but key events that test and define the relationship.

One is the first discovery of the religious difference. Another is the wedding. The third, and often the most challenging, is the birth of the first child. Even when joined in marriage, two people can often agree to disagree, even about something as personal as religious beliefs. But a child manifests the relationship in an awe-inspiring way. Two people, two sets of genes, two families come together to create a single, new human life. Nineteen years after the birth of my son, I still can't get over that. It's insanely beautiful.

The child is also, for better and worse, a unique vessel for the hopes and dreams of the parents. And when one parent is religious and the other is not, those hopes and dreams may take very different forms, creating a new level of conflict.

Parenting is both a professional and personal focus of mine, so this chapter could easily grow large enough to consume the rest of the book. But each chapter is intended to open the conversation, not address and solve every problem. And when it comes to parenting from a mixed secular/religious partnership, four issues rise to the top:

1. Rituals

2. Identity

3. Churchgoing, prayer, and other practices

4. Respect, doubt, and questioning

This chapter explores these issues in the lived context of real couples.

The Circumcision Decision

On the morning of August 2, 1995, I stood in a recovery room of our local hospital, exhausted from watching my wife give birth. She was also tired for some reason—maybe from watching me watch her—and was drifting in and out of sleep.

A nurse approached me through the fog and asked if we wanted our son circumcised. Her pen was poised expectantly over a clipboard. My long silence confirmed that I hadn't thought about it one bit.

"Most people do," she said. If I had been a parent for more than an hour, I might have countered, "If most people jumped off a cliff. . . ." But I was new at this, so I just nodded. The next day, the knife fell.

Circumcision was originally a religious ceremony, a gesture of faithfulness to God. Despite its near universality now, it was not at all common outside of Jewish and Muslim practice until the 1890s, when a few religious enthusiasts, including the strange character John Harvey Kellogg, recommended circumcision as a cure for "masturbatory insanity."[1] (For girls, he recommended applying carbolic acid to the clitoris.)

Kellogg spent much of his professional effort combating the sexual impulse and helping others to do the same, claiming a plague of masturbation-related deaths in which "a victim literally dies by his own hand" and offering circumcision as a vital defense. "Neither the plague, nor war, nor small-pox, nor similar diseases, have produced results so disastrous to humanity as this pernicious habit" of masturbation, warned Dr. Alan Clarke, one of Kellogg's co-crusaders.

Given all this hyperbole by well-titled professionals, the attitudes of American parents in the 1890s turned overnight from horror at the barbarity of the "un-Christian" practice of circumcision to immediate conviction that it would save their boys from short and insane lives. It was even reimagined as a symbol of Christian fidelity and membership in the church, and a number of supposed health benefits were suggested.

But organizations including the American Academy of Pediatrics[2] and the American Academy of Family Physicians[3] have issued statements declining to recommend the practice, suggesting that any benefits are marginal at best. The practice almost ended completely in the United Kingdom after a 1949 research article noted that 16–19 infant deaths per year were attributable to complications from the procedure.[4]

Regardless of religious perspective, parents should approach the decision with all information, including the mandates of their faith (if any) and the considered opinions of the medical community. Because Becca's Christian identity did not include a circumcision mandate, our decision was not a religious one—just an unfortunate matter of going with the majority. If we had a do-over, I would decline. No invasive medical procedure should be undertaken that involves risk with few if any demonstrable benefits. It's a form of genital mutilation, after all, albeit a more familiar one.

There's also no rush. A boy can choose to go under the knife at 18 if he wishes. Considering just how unlikely that is might give parents pause.

"A Bath"... or "An Insoluble Bond"?

"I always thought of the christening in salvational terms," says Sarah, an Independent Christian married to Justin, a secular humanist. "My kids would be baptized to join their souls to Christ; that's how I always understood it. But when our daughter was born, my husband said he didn't want her baptized."

"I wanted her to make her own decision when she was older," Justin explains, "without having to deal with a choice that had been made for her."

"But I just couldn't imagine *not* having it done," says Sarah.

She talked to her pastor and learned that her church saw baptism primarily as a ritual to wash away original sin. "I was honestly taken aback. I didn't know that was the meaning. That seemed medieval to me. But I still wanted to have it done, and now I had to figure out *why* I wanted it." So she and Justin talked it through. "Eventually I realized that it wasn't even about the connection to Christ. I think that is a relationship that a person should enter into willingly, and it happens in the heart, not in a ceremony."

She tried to imagine *not* having their daughter baptized, just to see what feelings it brought up. "And the funny thing is, my first thought wasn't about Jesus. I probably shouldn't say that, but it's true. It was a simpler thing. My first thought was, 'But I was baptized, and my mother and daddy were baptized! She *has* to be baptized! It's what we do!' So it wasn't about salvation, or original sin, or connecting her to Christ. It was about connecting her to my family."

Justin's reaction to this news surprised even him. "I was suddenly okay with it, or at least more okay. I didn't like the idea of this supernatural ritual, and I really didn't like the original sin nonsense. But I was okay with her being welcomed into Sarah's family tradition that way, and even into their church. It's a nice church and a good community. Even if it meant something else to the church, I was fine knowing what it meant to Sarah and what it didn't."

"And I appreciated that," she says.

The experience Becca and I had at our megachurch was similar and different. I said I'd prefer not to have our son baptized. Becca said that was fine. "But would it be okay if we just had him dedicated instead?" she asked. "You know... for Grandma?"

It was a family thing, just as it was with Justin and Sarah. I said, "Sure, why not," or words to that effect. Doing this meant more to her than not doing it meant to me.

What I didn't know was what a dedication actually entailed in this and many other churches. It was built around a solemn parental promise, something I learned only in the moment the minister turned to us and said:

> In presenting this child for dedication, you are hereby witnessing to your own personal Christian faith. Dale and Rebekah, do you announce your faith in Jesus Christ, and show that you want to study Him, know Him, love Him, and serve Him as His disciple, and that you want your child to do the same? Do you pledge to teach your child, as soon as he is able to learn, the nature of this holy sacrament; watch over his education, that he may not be led astray; direct his feet to the sanctuary; restrain him from evil associates and habits; and bring him up in the nurture and admonition of the Lord?

Or words to that effect.

Becca squeezed my hand, hard. It was not a squeeze of joy at the moment we were witnessing in our child's life. I knew that. It was a squeeze that said, *Oh no, my love, I didn't know, I promise I didn't, and if you can find it in your heart to fib, just a little, I swear that I will never, ever ask you to do this again for any other children we may have. Amen.*

I squeezed back, and together we turned to the minister and said, "Sure, why not."

Or words to that effect.

Becca didn't like the idea of promising such a thing any more than I did. She wanted our kids to make their own decisions regarding religious identity. She had no intention of "directing his feet to the sanctuary," nor did she agree with the implication that other choices would be the same as "leading him astray."

Had we known at the time that there were other options, including more liberal and flexible Christian denominations, we might have pursued one of those instead. Or we might have considered a Unitarian child dedication, in which parents work with the minister to create the kind of service they want. It may or may not include a religious blessing, it will usually include an expression of the parents' hopes for the child, and it often includes a promise by the congregation to support and encourage the child in his or her own search for truth and spiritual enrichment. The parents are not required to be baptized, nor to pledge any particular upbringing for the child. That would have been better.

> *Our first son was baptized at the Episcopal church my wife grew up in. I was only reluctant, but now I feel more strongly against the practice. While the church is mostly friendly and liberal, it's still not completely welcoming of atheists. It also bothers me that baptism is required at all to be welcomed into the community—'All baptized Christians are welcome at our [communion] table.' We've not yet come to agreement, so our youngest remains unbaptized. I know this bothers my partner, and I'm not sure how to navigate the issue.* —Richard, secular humanist

There's also a growing tradition of meaningful humanist naming ceremonies conducted by humanist celebrants trained by the Humanist Society (http://humanist-society.org). Though Becca would become a secular humanist herself nine years later, I doubt that would have satisfied her or her family when my son was young. For us, the Unitarian ceremony would have been ideal. Live and learn.

Lena (Episcopalian) and her husband, Sean (agnostic/Baha'i), worked it out more intentionally, without the need for any fatherly fibs.

"There was a little bit of a discussion when we baptized our two boys," says Lena. "He was certainly not for it. My argument was, if there is no God, then it's just a bath—so what does it matter?"

Well . . . to be honest, it's never just a bath, even if there's no God, because baptism has always been about more than God. In most Christian denominations, the ceremony is also meant to forge a bond between church and child and even to reaffirm the faith of the parents. Even the Episcopal Church, which is far less doctrinally strict than most, calls baptism "a full initiation into Christ's body, the church," a bond that is "indissoluble."[5] And it says the ritual "is designed to deepen the Christian formation of those who will present infants and young children for baptism,"[6] and "parents promise to see that the child . . . is brought up in the Christian faith and life."[7]

So whether or not God exists, a human commitment to a particular faith is also being pledged. That's a sensible concern for many nonreligious parents, and even for many religious parents—the ones who would prefer to wait until a child can choose his or her identity.

In the end, Sean weighed these issues and agreed to the ceremony with one condition: "He didn't want to be required to say anything himself about belief in Jesus or God," says Lena. "I completely understood and was grateful that he let me baptize the boys and that he would attend. He is that kind of man and that's why I love him."

The baptism question is less serious than circumcision in one way—no sharp knives in tender places—but it's more serious in others. Questions of honesty arise, as well as the potential for one parent to feel that the child is being formally bonded to a community in a way that excludes that parent. The first step as always is to be well informed about the purpose and meaning of the ceremony, not only to the church but to the religious partner and his or her family. Whether you forgo the ceremony, or modify it, or find a different denomination, or go the distance, couples should come to agreement between themselves first, then present a unified decision and reasoning to the extended family.

"Everything became very real for me when John was born"

The marriage of Arlene (Baptist) and Nate (atheist) exemplified the impact a child can have on a secular/religious couple. For 12 years before the birth of their son John, their religious differences were mostly fodder for comic relief. "It never got too serious during those years, mostly just lighthearted ribbing, really fun," Arlene recalls. "But everything stopped being funny and became very real for me when John was born. I was a Christian, Nate was not. For Nate, the most important thing was that John grew up to be a critically thinking person who did not just believe everything he was told. But I was suddenly faced with the very real fact that I had a child with a soul. What I believed really did matter in the long run."

See Arlene and Nate, *Chapter 8*

Their discussions got heated around the question of John's religious identity. "I found myself telling a grown man that his opinions were not good for my son—and yes, John became 'my son' during these arguments. I was like a mama bear protecting her cub from the outside influences that did not agree with my conservative worldview."

Eventually they came to an agreement. "The religious identity would be mine to give John, but Nate would never lie to John about his differing views. When John was old enough to ask Nate how he felt, Nate was free to let loose. I promised to raise John with the open and loving religious spirit I had been raised with and not to stifle his questions."

Even though Arlene raised John specifically as a Baptist, her approach was spot-on for best practices in the secular/religious mix:

→ Recognize diversity of belief.

→ Point to the other parent as a positive example.

→ Affirm the child's own free choice in the long run.

"When John was about eight," she says, "a Mormon friend of his told him that only Mormons go to heaven. I told John that not everyone believed that same way. When he asked me if only Christians go to heaven, I told him that it's not in my pay grade to decide who goes where. And I told him his dad didn't believe that, which opened the door for their conversation."

Fourteen years later, John identifies as Christian, "but that's about as defining as he'll go," says Arlene. "He does not follow a church. In the end, he doesn't care who believes what. He's just like me—we love who we love because of who they are and not what they believe. His best friends are a Buddhist, a Catholic, and a crystal-rubbing humans-are-from-aliens ex-Mormon. He loves God and prays and believes but does not judge and does not limit his loved ones to those that believe like he does. It's a family tradition."

"Daddy, did you know you're gonna burn in hell?"

Tom (atheist) and Danielle (Baptist) found a similar balance for how they wanted to raise their children. But unlike Arlene and Nate, they talked through their approach to parenting years before the kids arrived. "We decided before we got married that I could take the kids to church at Christmas and Easter, but Tom didn't want them in Sunday school every week. I didn't want that either, but I wanted them to be raised at least knowing so they could make their own choice. So that was our agreement before we even had children," Danielle recalls.

"It was you get to teach them what you believe, I get to teach them what I believe, and let them make up their own mind," Tom says.

"It took all of five minutes," Danielle recalls.

Other discussions happened along the way as the kids grew up. At one point, after much searching, Danielle found a Methodist church she liked in Miami and wanted to take the kids. Tom agreed. "I took them to church and Sunday school every week," she says, "but I was very sensitive to what they were taught because I had such a bad experience [see Chapter 5]. Tom played basketball on Sundays, and he trusted me that they weren't learning the dogma and the bigoted stuff. There wasn't a problem . . . until they started the preschool at the church."

See Tom and Danielle, *Chapter 5*

● ● ● ● ● ● ● ● ● ● ● ● ● ● ● ● ● ● ●▶

"Yeah." Tom's expression darkens a bit. "Cory said two different things that made me think, 'Okay, this should stop.' One was, 'Daddy, did you know that we have to die for Jesus?' Then he came home another day and said, 'Daddy, did you know you're gonna burn in hell because you don't believe in God?' I suddenly realized he was now going to this church six days a week. We don't know if it was the teachers, the other students, who knows. But he got the message at age four that if you don't believe their way, you're going to burn in hell, and that's when I was like, boom, you're done."

"I completely agreed," says Danielle. "I didn't want the scare tactics at all, but he picked that up in the preschool. We switched to a secular school the next year. But he kept going to Sunday school."

"Dani was totally cool about it," Tom says. "She was very upset that he would get those messages, and so we both agreed that this preschool was done, and we'll see how Sunday school goes."

A few years later they moved to another city, and Danielle was once again without a church home. "We haven't gone to church here because I can't find one that I'm comfortable with," she says.

Tom nods. "It seems that they're either too liberal for you, where you don't get the church feeling, or they're too conservative and you're like, oh boy."

"Exactly. Tom supports me in taking the kids when we do find one. He said he would have them go every other Sunday with me, and then the other Sundays they would stay home and have a science lesson with him. But I can't find one that's going to teach them the more moderate beliefs."

"But then . . . what are the children?"

After revealing their religious difference to someone else, the most common question any mixed-belief couple will hear is, "But then . . . what are the children?"

Because a family's worldview identity has usually been placed on the kids at birth, the idea of raising a child with no specific worldview label—religious or irreligious—is as confusing to some people as raising a child without a name. But many secular/religious couples do exactly that—raise a child who may participate in and learn about two or more distinct worldviews without being claimed or labeled by any until he or she is old enough to choose.

Richard Dawkins notes that referring to a child as "a Catholic child" or "a Muslim child" or "an atheist child" should sound as silly to us as saying "a Marxist child" or "a Republican child."[8] These labels represent complex perspectives that they cannot yet claim to have examined and chosen freely. Until they can, there's no need to force the issue.

The freedom to choose or change one's religious identity is a gift of autonomy so universally valued that it's enshrined in Article 18 of the Universal Declaration of Human Rights: "Everyone has the right to freedom of thought, conscience and religion; this right includes freedom to change his religion or belief, and freedom, either alone or in community with others and in public or private, to manifest his religion or belief in teaching, practice, worship and observance."[9]

This does *not* mean our kids shouldn't engage in religious practices or belief. It means the exact opposite. Erecting a wall between the child and all religious experience isn't necessary or good. In fact, closing children off from these experiences can violate their autonomy just as much as restricting them to a single fragment of religious opinion. This issue is about resisting the urge to place a complex worldview label on a child before she is ready for it. She can go to church or Sunday school, read the Bible, and pray without being called a Christian, Muslim, or Jew, just as she can challenge religious ideas, debate religious friends, and read *The God Delusion* without being an atheist.

A child with one religious and one nonreligious parent is in a uniquely lucky position to do all of these things—learn religious concepts *and* challenge them, engage in religious practices *and* wonder if they are meaningful, pray *and* question whether her prayers are heard.

My own parents achieved this without even intending to. We went to a UCC (United Church of Christ) church every Sunday, but we were never asked to pledge ourselves to the denomination or even to call ourselves Christians. At the same time, we were encouraged to think and question and explore ideas. As a result, I came to my current views on my own. It's the thing I value most about my worldview—that it's really mine. Why would I deprive my kids of that feeling of authenticity?

Some kids raised this way end up choosing a religious identity; others choose a nonreligious one. In both cases, the individual receives the gift of genuine autonomy in a major life decision. And in neither case does the child have to go through the guilty turmoil of deciding whether to accept or reject a label placed on him by his loving parents.

When asked to check all statements that were true about the eventual religious or nonreligious identity of their children:

→ *63% of parents in secular/religious marriages said, "I am confident they will make a positive choice, even if it is not the same as mine."*

→ *78% said, "I will love and support my child regardless of their choice."*

→ *55% said, "I would prefer they end up identifying with my worldview."*

→ *9% said they would be "deeply disappointed" if their child chose the worldview opposite their own (religious for the nonreligious parent, or nonreligious for the religious parent).*

→ *<0.5% said, "Certain choices could lead me to end contact/ support."*

This final (unfortunate) answer was given by just 2 of more than 400 parents in the survey. Though you might assume they are religiously orthodox parents, not a single religious respondent in the survey suggested he or she might cut off contact or support from his or her child. The two who did were both nonreligious.

Disappointment is another matter. Religious parents were twice as likely to say they would be "deeply disappointed" if their child became nonreligious, compared to nonreligious partners who would be "deeply disappointed" if their child became religious.

The happy bottom line: *The clear majority of parents in both cate-gories are fine with their children making either choice, and both express confidence that those choices will be positive ones, even if different from their own.*

Secular/religious partners are in the ideal situation to facilitate this open process. Both parents can and should wear their own identities proudly, even as they point to each other for alternate points of view. When my daughter came to me at age eight and asked whether Jesus really came alive after he died, I gave my honest opinion: "I don't think he did. I think that's just a story to make us feel better about death. But talk to Mom. I know she thinks it really happened. And then you can make up your own mind and even change your mind back and forth a hundred times if you want." And Becca did the same for me, always sending the kids to hear my perspective after offering her own.

Both parents should share the experience of their perspective, then say, "Here's what I believe with all my heart, it's very important to me and I think it's true, but these are things each person has to decide for herself, and I want you to talk to people who have different beliefs so you can make up your own mind. You can change your mind a thousand times. There's no penalty for getting it wrong, and I will love you no less if you end up believing differently from me." Imagine if that was the norm! Imagine kids growing up with an invitation to engage the most profound questions freely and without fear.

Some religious leaders who are concerned about the loss of religious identity insist that children raised by parents with two different worldviews are subject to "confusion" and "alienation."[10] In fact, this is rarely the case. Children accept as normal the world with which they are presented. Someone raised in a one-religion home may see anything else as unthinkable and confusing. But children whose parents differ on religion see *that* as normal, and they tend to adapt perfectly well.

Hope had the same worries about her children being confused when her husband became an atheist. "But when I asked my oldest what it was like to have mixed-religion parents, she said, 'I don't think that having parents with different religions is that much different from having same-religion parents. I think it just changed the way we think about it.' " Her answer made Hope . . . hopeful. "Even though I might sometimes feel stressed out by our difference in religion, it feels like normal to our children. They are aware that our family is a little bit different from some other families at my church or at my husband's atheist group, but it's not different to them—it's their normal."

See Hope and David, *Chapter 7*

It isn't always easy on the parents themselves to see their kids exposed to another point of view. "Before David left the faith, we were a very committed Christian family," says Hope. "We taught our children the catechism. We watched Christian videos, sang Christian songs, and built the Christian bubble around them like 'good' Christian parents do." But since David's change, she has adopted a more balanced parenting approach—which is not always easy. "Part of my faith is teaching my children about God, but I also think it is important to be respectful of my husband and his nonbelief. I let our children know that this is my belief, other people believe different things, and they have to make up their own minds when they are older. I admit I've had a hard time learning how to achieve this balance. We've had lots of arguments over this, especially when I've crossed the line into being dogmatic or I have felt David was being disrespectful of my faith. As a Christian, it can be heartbreaking to listen to him talk to our kids about stuff like evolution and God not being real and the Bible not being true. Before he became an atheist, we had raised our kids with Bible stories and worship songs. David had been an active part in teaching them about our faith, and now he was actively teaching them something opposite. Sometimes I don't know how to handle that. But I'm learning. It's a process."

David struggles to find the balance as well. "We did have to reach some agreements. Each of us tells the kids our honest thoughts regarding religion so long as we also encourage the kids to ask the same question to the other parent and listen to their answer."

I will always love, support, and be there for my kids no matter what they believe later in life. As a Christian, all I can do is live my life and show my family what I believe. I will never, ever be upset if they believe something else. In fact, I will be happy if they are true to themselves. —Julie, Lutheran married to an agnostic

As for the religious identity of their children, Hope and David have reached agreement on one of the essential best practices: keeping kids unlabeled and free to explore beliefs and experiences before choosing their own religious identity, if any. "Before David deconverted, I mostly just assumed our children would follow us in our faith," Hope says. "But now we do not assign a spiritual identity to our children. We both tell them that they are free to make up their own minds and to change their minds as much as they want. We say that they are too young to really make an informed decision one way or another. I take them to church with me most Sundays. Sometimes the kids want to stay home with him. Sometimes I let them, and sometimes I insist they go."

"Sometimes I feel like a sell-out by letting my kids go to church so regularly," David admits. "I want them to enjoy their friends, but I hate the B.S. they are fed while there. I want to have more time with them so we can discuss my thoughts regarding religion rather than just hearing the other side at church. It is gratifying to me that they at least know that not believing is an option and that unbelievers aren't bad people, as they are sometimes told at church. I hope, as they grow older, they will develop thoughtful questions of their own and I'll be able to offer my perspective more."

Hope and David's five kids are each finding their own way, knowing their parents support them. "My oldest is 12," says Hope. "She is a daddy's girl, and right away when he announced that he didn't believe anymore, she said she did not believe in God either. This has given her some trouble on the bus and with classmates as we live in the Deep South, but she has remained steadfast in her nonbelief. Honestly, as a person of faith, my desire would be for her to one day have faith in God, and I would be disappointed if she lived her life without faith. But I love and support her no matter what."

Their second oldest is 10 and a steadfast believer. "She has always believed in God," says Hope. "I try not to put any pressure on her and try to let her know she needs to make an informed decision when she is older. This is a huge area of struggle for me," she admits, "because it goes against every Christian cultural instinct."

Hope describes their younger children as indifferent for the moment. "Our five-year-old son sometimes says he believes in God, because he likes the praise music and loves coming to church with me. And sometimes he says when he grows up he won't believe in God anymore."

In the end, both Hope and David say they are confident their kids will make positive choices, even if those choices differ from the ones their parents have made.

Religious Literacy and Churchgoing for Kids

In 2010, the Pew Research Religion and Public Life Project surveyed Americans to assess their basic religious literacy.[11] The results confirmed that Americans, faithful as we are, don't know much about religion:

→ Only 55% knew that the Golden Rule isn't one of the Ten Commandments.

→ Just 54% knew that the Koran is the holy book of Islam.

→ 45% could name all four Gospels (Matthew, Mark, Luke, John).

→ 47% knew that the Dalai Lama is Buddhist.

→ 38% knew that Vishnu and Shiva are Hindu deities.

→ Just 18% knew that Protestants, not Catholics, teach that salvation comes through faith alone.

Our knowledge is even slim when it comes to our own religions:

→ Almost half (45%) of Catholics didn't know that their church teaches that the communion bread and wine actually become the body and blood of Christ.

→ Just 47% of U.S. Protestants knew that Martin Luther founded their branch of Christianity.

If religion is mostly a matter of family inheritance, these things may not matter. But parents who want their children to make a free and informed choice—including most secular/religious couples—need to help their kids encounter a wide range of religious and nonreligious ideas and practices. To make it as inclusive as possible, think of it as worldview literacy.

Most nonreligious parents support the idea of exposing their kids to a broad range of religious ideas, which might explain why they were the most religiously knowledgeable group in the Pew survey. Those who don't might be convinced by the arguments in the sidebar titled "Why Religious Literacy Is Important."

Why Religious Literacy Is Important

1. **Knowledge of religion is vital to understanding the world.** If most people identify as religious and express themselves in religious terms to some extent, the world can be baffling without a basic understanding of religion.

2. **We don't want our kids left out of the cultural conversation.** Most political and social issues end up with religious opinions somewhere in the debate. The more you know about where those opinions come from, what they're based on, and what they mean, the better you can respond to those ideas.

3. **It helps us to make an informed decision.** The more information we have, the better our decisions tend to be. People who make a conscious choice about their worldview are more likely to end up in a positive one, whereas those who simply take what they're born into without examining it get the luck of the draw. A strong religious literacy helps a person choose well, which is better for everyone.

4. **Exposure to difference makes people less afraid of it.** The best way to get over the fear of those who are different from us is to experience that difference ourselves.

So how do we raise religiously literate kids? Having them attend church seems like an obvious answer. But as the Pew Forum study shows, a person can sit in church 52 times a year and still know very little about that religion and almost nothing about any others. Knowledge of other religions is an essential part of religious literacy. Experiencing just one denomination is like studying haiku and thinking you know poetry.

Helping our kids to become religiously literate also doesn't require long lectures or reading volumes of religious history or scripture. There is an easier and more fun approach. It's done by:

→ Encouraging them to notice religion in everyday life, in the culture and in the news

→ Cultivating their curiosity about it

→ Following that curiosity into knowledge

→ Connecting the dots to create a full picture of religion

Religion is in the news, from the stem cell debate to terrorism to global warming to nonviolent activism. It's in movies, in books, and on television. Politicians end their speeches with "God bless America." Norse gods are represented in the days of the week, Roman gods in the months and planets. Even the idea of the seven-day week is rooted in Jewish and Babylonian creation stories. Holidays were originally holy days. Countless figures of speech, from "a drop in the bucket" to "a wolf in sheep's clothing," have biblical origins. Nike shoes, Midas Mufflers, a road atlas, the Olympics, and the first U.S. space programs all borrow names from Greek mythology. All of this is religious influence.

Religious literacy is about thousands of small, everyday moments and caring enough to weave them together. Step one is noticing the saturation. Step two is finding it interesting, which is easier for kids when no one is insisting that they must accept it to be a good person. It's just knowledge, and it helps our understanding of who and what we are.

Keep it broad. Read myths and stories from many traditions. Watch movies with religious themes, such as *Little Buddha, Kirikou and the Sorceress, Bruce Almighty, Fiddler on the Roof, Jason and the Argonauts, Gandhi, Seven Years in Tibet, Schindler's List,* and *The Ledge.* This list alone touches six different belief systems, including atheism—five more than you'll get in a typical Sunday school. Drop in on a Hindu temple or a Sikh gurdwara. And chat with believers. Ask what they believe and why, and then share your own thoughts.

Over Half of the Survey Couples' Kids Attend Services or Sunday School

About 30% of the children of secular/religious couples surveyed attend religious services or Sunday school regularly, and 23% do so occasionally.

About one in six (16%) attended in the past but do not attend now. Roughly one in three (32%) have never attended.[12]

The denominations most commonly attended by children of secular/religious couples were as follows:

→ *18% Catholic*

→ *11% Baptist*

→ *8% each Unitarian Universalist and Latter-Day Saints*

→ *7% each Independent Christian, Evangelical, Methodist*

→ *5% each Lutheran, Episcopalian*

As you do all this, bit by bit, thread by thread, a more complete picture of religion as a human endeavor begins to form. It's fascinating, no matter what your perspective.

Regular churchgoing or Sunday school attendance in a single denomination isn't essential to religious literacy, but it can be a valuable way for kids to experience religious belonging in depth—as long as both parents are vigilant about fear-based messaging (see "Keeping the 'Hell' Away from Your Kids" on page 231).

See Anna and Gary, *Chapter 10*

"Our kids never did get baptized, but I did manage to convince my then nonreligious husband that the kids needed religious education," says Anna. "We started church shopping, and during that time my husband and I switched roles—he became the religious one, and I became the atheist. My son and I came to the conclusion that there is no god or other supernatural force behind the universe, while my husband accepted Jesus as his personal savior. My daughter's still undecided."

> *My kids have a confidence in their beliefs that I never had as a kid. I think that is because we've allowed them to develop their own identity rather than force one upon them.* —Anna

Anna and Gary's approach has always been broad and deep. "We have Sunday school at home where we learn about all the religions, not just one brand of Christianity. I'm lucky to have a very diverse group of friends to help me with this. They attend other services and places of worship and talk with others of different faiths whenever they can. And even though my husband and I aren't together anymore, we're still committed to letting our kids decide their own religious or nonreligious identity. I'm careful not to push my worldview on my children, so I preface everything with 'This is what I believe.' I do notice that my kids have a confidence in their beliefs that I never had as a kid, and I still struggle with sometimes as an adult. I think that is because we've allowed them to develop their own identity rather than force one upon them.

"That's the vital factor in almost every parenting decision related to the mixed-belief marriage," she says. "Autonomy."

I am sure we will discuss [how to approach religion] in the future. I think our children will be exposed to Hinduism, since I practice it, and they will also be exposed to the way Scott feels about religious identification and practice. In time as they grow and mature, our children can decide for themselves what they wish to practice. —Dhanya, Hindu

We do plan to have children, but I'm still not really sure how we will approach this. I don't mind Dhanya teaching them her [Hindu] practices. I'm just going to be my normal self. I hope to teach them to have a critical and questioning view about life. I'm certainly planning to encourage them about science, math, nature, and learning. We still need to talk about this in detail. —Scott, nonreligious

See **Scott and Dhanya, *Chapter 6***

What Should They Know?

For real religious literacy, these are some basic things your kids should know:

→ *The basic stories and major figures in the Bible (the creation story, Noah and the Ark, Moses and the Ten Commandments, the exodus of the Jews from Egypt, John the Baptist, and the life and death of Jesus)*

→ *The basic beliefs of the five major religions (Judaism, Buddhism, Islam, Christianity, and Hinduism) and where in the world they are mainly practiced, including which religions believe in higher deities and which do not*

→ *The religious backgrounds of their extended families and what their relatives (including their parents) actually believe*

And while you're exploring worldviews, don't forget the nonreligious. The history of atheism and humanism is a fascinating one and includes both intellectual and ethical heroes and stories in every era.

In raising their son, Will, Pete (humanist) and Joan (Catholic) methodically worked out their negotiables and nonnegotiables. "We understood that he would in time develop his own religious orientation," Pete says, "but naturally aimed for a fair balance in his exposure to our beliefs during his most formative years. It seemed reasonable for each of us to freely talk about religion from our own view, always in the context of an understood choice of beliefs, and with guidelines on how to phrase our beliefs: No attempting to convince. Any comment on a religious subject should include 'I believe.' Note the difference between 'God loves you' and 'I believe God loves you,' for example, or between 'There is no god' and 'I see no reason to believe in a god.' And Joan would often take care to add, 'You know, Dad feels differently about this.' As a beleaguered atheist in a huge extended family of Catholics, that always meant a lot to me."

See Pete and Joan, *Chapter 17*

A Subtle Shift for Catholic Parents in Mixed Marriages

Until 1983, the Catholic Church would agree to marry a Catholic and a non-Catholic only once a firm promise was made by both parents to raise any eventual children as Catholics.

In 1983, the Code of Canon Law was revised. Now the Catholic partner is asked to "do all in his or her power"[13] to have their children baptized and raised in the Catholic faith, and the non-Catholic spouse is no longer required to make the same promise—only "to be informed at an appropriate time of these promises which the Catholic party has to make, so that it is clear that the other party is truly aware of the promise and obligation of the Catholic party."[14]

In practice, as with other issues, U.S. Catholics in mixed marriages tend to go even further in the direction of family tolerance and openness. If children are raised in another tradition, says theologian Fr. Robert Hater, "The Catholic parent must show children good example, affirm the core beliefs of both parents' religious traditions, make them aware of Catholic beliefs and practices, and support the children in the faith they practice."[15]

Not a single word of that advice differs from mine.

They also agreed to ask extended family to respect their approach. "We asked family members to honor our compromise," Pete says, "and not upset the hard-won balance by giving religious gifts or talking religious talk to our son."

Keeping the "Hell" Away from Your Kids

There's one major exception to complete openness to religious ideas, an exception nonreligious and liberal religious parents alike can agree on. If you don't want your child's exploration muddied by fear, defuse the idea of hell. Don't ignore it; as Tom and Danielle's story illustrates, most kids in most areas of the United States will hear about hell from peers, especially if their family does not attend church or if it includes an atheist family member. So it's important that kids have this paralyzing idea defused early on in a safe place.

Fortunately, an increasing number of fully religious homes fall into the category of safe places as well. A Pew survey in 2008 found that belief in hell as a place where the wicked are punished has declined to 59% in the United States.[16] Many analysts point to the increasing proximity of people of different worldviews. It's easier to hate and fear people of different religions when we don't know any. Belief in heaven is holding steady, in the mid-70% range.

A fine way for a religious (or even nonreligious) parent to defuse hell is to get God on his side. Invite kids to picture God smacking himself on the forehead saying, "How do they come *up* with these terrible ideas? How can they think I would punish them for honest doubts?"

Coming of Age

When I was about 13, I went through a serious bout of bar mitzvah envy. A Jewish friend had his, and I was hooked. Not with memorizing a chunk of the Torah or having to follow the 613 commandments in the Law of Moses. What attracted me was the idea of going through this formal passage from childhood to adulthood. Sure, I was going through that transition myself already, but gradually. Having a *moment* is different; it's a time when your community says, "Okay, you're not a child anymore. You have more privileges, but we also expect more from you."

Unless you count a particular birthday—the 16th maybe, or 18th, or 21st—the transition into adulthood usually goes unmarked today. The main exceptions are religious denominations, where there's obviously a big religious component. The child isn't just becoming an adult, but also taking on a religious identity.

Confirmation, First Communion, and similar events mark the same kind of moment—coming of age combined with joining a community—in many Christian denominations. To avoid early labeling by a single religion, some couples choose to forgo these. Others go through with them, reminding the child that the ultimate choice of identity is still his or hers, and add exposure to other worldviews in age-appropriate ways.

Mark (a secular humanist raised by Jehovah's Witnesses) worked out a unique solution with his Catholic wife, Mary. "She feels obligated to raise the children as Catholic until they have completed Confirmation," he says. "Now that my daughter has done so, I'm free to take her to religious services of other denominations, as well as nonreligious meetings. I hope to give her, and eventually my son, a broader view of what we as humans believe and how we make sense of the world. If they grow up to be Catholic, I want it to be because they choose it, not because they were born into it."

Some humanist groups around the world have created meaningful, human coming-of-age rituals. The trick as always is to keep the things religion has done well without the belief-pledging and raisin-banning bits. One of the most successful in the world is the Humanist Confirmation program in Norway. Each spring, more than 10,000 15-year-old Norwegians take a course about life philosophies and world religions, ethics and human sexuality, and human rights and civic duties. At the end they receive a diploma at a moving ceremony with music, poetry, and inspirational speeches. They're confirmed not into atheism, but into an adulthood grounded in the human values that underlie civil society.

UUs and Ethical Culture have thoughtful, effective coming-of-age programs that are focused on the things most important in that transition—ethics, civic responsibility, sexuality—without dictating the young person's religious or nonreligious identity. And for those couples who include a Jewish identity, there are bar and bat mitzvahs.

UUs and Ethical Culture have coming-of-age programs focused on the things most important in that transition—ethics, civic responsibility, sexuality—without dictating religious or nonreligious identity.

Teaching Values

Though "values" are often conflated with "beliefs," they're not at all the same. *Beliefs* are opinions about what is true. *Values* are opinions about what is good. "Jesus is the son of God" is a belief, while "It's wrong to harm another person" is a value.

Parents have a responsibility to teach values and ethical behavior, and they will naturally frame those values in their own worldviews. But mixed-belief parents should take special care not to give their kids the message that any one frame is essential. It's the values that matter, and every major moral value can be framed in religious or nonreligious terms.

Every major moral value can be framed in religious or nonre-ligious terms.

The most powerful human moral concept is called the Reciprocity Principle: Treat others as you would like to be treated. Christians will recognize that as the Golden Rule, but it's much more universal than any one religion or philosophy. Here are a few examples, some religious, some secular:

- → **Jainism (nontheistic):** "A man should treat all creatures in the world as he himself would like to be treated."[17]

- → **Buddhism:** "Hurt not others in ways that you yourself would find hurtful."[18]

- → **Platonic philosophy (secular):** "One should never do wrong in return, nor mistreat any man, no matter how one has been mistreated by him."[19]

- → **Hinduism:** "This is the sum of duty: do not do to others what would cause you pain if done to you."[20]

- → **Confucianism (secular):** "Surely it is the maxim of loving-kindness: Do not unto others that you would not have them do unto you."[21]

- → **Christianity:** "Do unto others as you would have them do unto you."[22]

- → **Judaism:** "What is hateful to you, do not do to your fellowman. This is the entire Law; all the rest is commentary."[23]

- → **Islam:** "No man is a true believer unless he desireth for his brother that which he desireth for himself."[24]

→ **Taoism:** "Regard your neighbor's gain as your own gain and your neighbor's loss as your own loss."[25]

→ **Baha'i:** "Lay not on any soul a load that you would not wish to be laid upon you, and desire not for anyone the things you would not desire for yourself."[26]

→ **Wicca:** "An' it harm none, do what thou wilt."[27]

It's the heart of human morality, something people generally figure out on their own by age six. But here's a slice of humble pie for parents: Like most ethical principles, it isn't learned by teaching. As much as we would like to think we're inculcating morality into our kids, that's mostly untrue. Parents have a role; we're just not as central as we think.

Moral development research by such major figures as Joan Grusec, Larry Nucci, and Diana Baumrind has shown that moral understanding comes not from books or teaching but from experience—especially peer interactions. That's why kids start framing everything in terms of fairness around age five, right when most of them are starting to have regular, daily peer interactions—including the experience of being treated fairly and unfairly—and making choices about how they will treat others and feeling the consequences of those choices.

Parents can and should help kids process their experiences and articulate their thoughts about them, but it's the experience itself that provides the main text from which they draw moral understanding—not from a book, and not from us. At least not our words: Our example still speaks volumes.

This should be a major relief to parents who are worried about the implications of a secular/religious marriage for their kids' moral development. As moral development expert Larry Nucci puts it, children's understanding of morality around the world is very much the same whether they're of "one religion, another religion, or no religion at all." There is just one major exception, one way in which parents can actually impede their children's moral growth: "If it's simply indoctrination," Nucci says, "it's worse than doing nothing. It interferes with moral development."[28]

Indoctrination isn't just a religious idea. It happens anytime someone is required to accept an idea without questioning it. When a child asks why he shouldn't hit his little brother and the parent says, "Because I said so," the child gets a very weak understanding of that moral principle. He misses an opportunity to develop his own moral muscle by learning the basic principles behind right and wrong. If instead you encourage empathy ("How would it feel if he hit you?"), you build a more powerful understanding of why we should be good. "Because Mom/Dad/the law/the Bible/the parenting book says so" teaches only the ability to follow rules. If you want a moral thinker, help your child to think about the reasons behind the rules, regardless of your own worldview.

Spare the Rod

Discipline is a point of contention for many couples, even if they share the same worldview. But one topic often divides nonreligious and religious partners: corporal punishment.

"Before David became an atheist, we were typical religious parents and disciplined our kids with spankings," says Hope. It's a common practice in conservative churches, like the one in which Hope and David were raised, which tend to cite Proverbs 13:24: "He that spares his rod hates his son: but he that loves him disciplines him promptly." Influential Christian parenting author James Dobson is one of several voices on the Religious Right who encourages spanking. "Spanking should be of sufficient magnitude to cause genuine tears," he writes in *The New Dare to Discipline*. He recommends using paddles to hit children as young as 18 months old and calls pain "a marvelous purifier."[29]

See Hope and David, *Chapter 7*

Even though much of the support for corporal punishment comes from religious books and spokespeople, corporal punishment isn't a simple secular/religious issue. Many religious parents and parenting experts are horrified by Dobson's advice and reject corporal punishment, including the prominent Christian parenting expert Dr. William Sears. And many nonreligious people engage in the practice as well.

Like me, for example.

Well, not anymore. Like Hope, I was spanked as a child, and I'm sorry to say I continued the practice for the first few years of my parenting. But I stopped abruptly when I learned that research conclusively shows that spanking is less effective than other methods of discipline *and* does significant harm to the child in the long run.

According to an analysis of 88 corporal punishment studies compiled by Dr. Elizabeth Gershoff at Columbia University, 10 negative outcomes are strongly correlated with spanking, including a damaged parent-child relationship, increased antisocial and aggressive behaviors, depression, and the increased likelihood that the child will physically abuse his or her own children.[30]

The study revealed just one positive correlation: immediate compliance, meaning a spanked child will tend to do what you want in the moment. But the many negative consequences simply aren't worth it, especially given the fact that many nonviolent discipline techniques can likewise achieve immediate compliance.

Many people think a no-spanking policy is just plain soft on crime. "Discipline has been one of the most challenging aspects of parenting since my deconversion," David says. "I stopped spanking our kids and Hope still did, and she sometimes saw this as putting the full burden of discipline on her. But I tried to learn other methods, like time-outs and other consequences that I feel are age-appropriate."

One of the alternatives parenting experts recommend is keeping a mental list of your kids' favorite privileges, such as staying up late, reading time before bed, video games, freedom, dessert. If they really are privileges rather than rights (never withhold rights), they can be made contingent on good behavior. Choose well, and the selective granting and withholding of privileges will work better than spanking. Given a choice between a quick spanking or early bedtime for a week, many kids would surely hand Dad the paddle and clench. But if the quick fix is not an option, actual compliance ensues. The key to any discipline plan, of course, is follow-through. If kids learn that your threats are idle, all is lost.

After some time on a different discipline track from her husband, Hope is now moving away from spanking and admits it's a challenge. "David is always there for me when I'm in a bind," she says. "When one of our kids is being stubborn, I'll sometimes call him at work and say, 'What do you think I should do?' Or if he sees one of the kids disrespecting me he is quick to say, 'Listen to your mother.' That's been a big shift. I'm glad we stepped away from spanking. I think so far we've had good results with other forms of discipline."

The Bottom Line

Whether religious or nonreligious, both parents should share the beliefs and practices of their worldviews with their kids while constantly reiterating the invitation to decide for themselves without any fear. Children who are invited to engage in discussing profound questions freely and fearlessly have the best chance of choosing a meaningful and inspiring worldview that fits their vision of themselves. It's a tremendous gift for parents to give that freedom, and mixed-belief parents are in an especially good position to encourage that honest search.

20

Parting Ways

KEY IDEAS

→ Roughly half of all divorces are "good divorces"—relatively amicable and positive.

→ Parenting is the primary source of challenges in a divorce.

→ Any positive parenting agreements reached about religion/irreligion during the marriage should continue to be respected.

→ Children should never be put in the middle of a "religious war." Continue to protect their right to reach their own conclusions.

→ Their relationship with the other parent should be preserved in part by refusing to denigrate that parent's worldview.

No aspect of marriage is more mangled and mythologized than divorce. Start with the common belief that every new marriage has a 50% chance of ending in divorce. The actual percentage, never that high, has been steadily declining since 1981 and is currently estimated to be closer to 33%—the lowest rate since 1970.[1]

But the overall percentage is much less meaningful than the percentages that correlate to real risk factors. Age at marriage is perhaps the most crucial factor in predicting the risk of eventual divorce. The strong tendency in recent generations to wait longer before getting married has paralleled the drop in the divorce rate. The median age of first marriage in 1960 was 21 for women and 24 for men, in 1990 it was 24.5 for women and 26 for men, and today it is 27 for women and 29 for men.[2]

That's an encouraging trend, since the risk of divorce drops sharply if both partners are 25 or older at the time of marriage. Women who marry before age 18 face a 48% chance of divorce within 10 years. The risk is 40% if they wait until 18–19 and drops to 29% if they are 20–24. And if women wait until age 25 or older, their risk of divorce for *any reason* drops to 24%.[3] The reason for this drop is likely the fact that interpersonal and relationship skills are better developed at age 25 than 18, and we tend to have a better idea of what we want and what makes for a healthy relationship.

The mixed-belief marriage rate has more than doubled since the 1950s, from 20% to 45% of all new marriages.[4] If it really did lead to a higher divorce rate, it would temper or even cancel out the declining divorce rate. But as the studies cited in the Introduction make clear, having mixed beliefs will usually have little or no impact on your likelihood of divorce.

Whatever the odds, it will happen for some couples, and in some cases religious difference is among the aggravating circumstances.

Divorce is an incredibly complicated event, one that a single book chapter can't even begin to capture. Fortunately, this chapter is about only one thing: the way worldview difference plays out in the divorce of a secular/religious couple, and a few ways to improve the odds of having it play out well.

A Typology of Divorce

Divorce isn't always a bad thing. Sometimes it ends a relationship that made one or both partners miserable. Other marriages are less dramatic but still driven to end due to incompatibility or "irreconcilable difference" of one kind or another. And the divorce itself is less often a stereotypic stew of hatred and resentment than movies and television would have us believe. Constance Ahrons, author of *The Good Divorce*, estimates that roughly half of all divorces are "good divorces," meaning a marriage ends with a relative lack of acrimony and inflicted emotional harm, and children continue to have two parents.[5]

In her classic study of divorced families,[6] Ahrons identified five different outcomes (with cute names you'll have to forgive):

1. "Perfect Pals"—12% of couples in the study.

PPs are former couples who continue to interact frequently and communicate well. The disappointments of the failed marriage don't overshadow the positive elements of a longstanding relationship. They still call themselves good friends, speak with each other once or twice a week, and are still interested in each other's lives. Trust is high, and each remains connected to the other's extended family. All PPs with children in the Ahrons study had joint custody. Many PPs slide into one of the other categories over time.

2. "Cooperative Colleagues"—38%.

CCs interact less often but still communicate effectively when they do. They don't call themselves friends but cooperate very well around issues concerning the kids. They occasionally cross paths at events like family birthdays or teacher conferences without trouble. Ahrons says they "compartmentalize their relationship," separating out issues related to marriage from those related to parenting. "What's best for the kids" takes precedence over everything else. Within five years, about one in four CCs deteriorate to Angry Associates. The rest (75%) remain cooperative for the long haul.

3. "Angry Associates"—25%.

Here's where it starts to heat up a bit. AAs interact moderately, just like CCs, but they communicate seldom and poorly. All AAs with children in the Ahrons study had some form of sole custody with the noncustodial parent spending some arranged time with the kids. After five years, one-third of AAs are still AAs, one-third improve to Cooperative Colleagues, and one-third decline to Fiery Foes.

4. "Fiery Foes"—25%.

Now we've arrived at the stereotypic "War of the Roses" divorced couple. They rarely interact or communicate, and when they do, they tend to fight. Divorces are often highly litigious, and they cling to resentments, unable to move on. They have the most polarizing arrangements with kids, either exchanging them at the door without a word or including no visitation at all. Two-thirds in this category are still in it after five years.

5. **"Dissolved Duos"—0% (in the Ahrons study).**

Even though the Ahrons study had no couples in this category, they do exist. DDs are couples who split so completely that there is no remaining interaction, communication, or relationship to describe. In most cases, these will be childless couples.

Parenting After Divorce

You'll notice that children are mentioned in almost every category, and for good reason. A couple can come to agreement (with or without legal assistance) about the division of their property and finances, but children are an ongoing, nonnegotiable link between them. If there are no kids, the secular/religious difference usually ceases to matter after the split. If there are kids, it can often intensify—especially if either parent feels his or her religious differences were part of the reason for the split. In those cases it's often tempting for each parent to "purge" the influence of the other parent's views from the lives of their children.

The Custody Question

One of the central pillars of child custody law in the United States is the primacy of the "best interests of the child." Family courts are given wide latitude in deciding when those best interests are threatened, and this principle is sometimes invoked in denying or restricting custody of children to a nonreligious parent.

This violates the free speech clause of the Constitution, says UCLA law professor Eugene Volokh, but happens nonetheless, especially in certain states. "Mississippi is the most serious offender, though I've seen cases since 1990 in Arkansas, Louisiana, Michigan, Minnesota, Pennsylvania, South Carolina, South Dakota, and Texas."[7]

Even religious parents aren't entirely in the clear if their practice is deemed less intensive than their ex-partner's. In 2001, the Mississippi Supreme Court upheld an order giving a mother custody partly because she took the child to church more often than the father did, thus providing a better "future religious example." In 2000, the same court ordered a father to take the child to church each week, citing a 1966 decision in a similar case which reasoned that "it is certainly to the best interests of [the child] to receive regular and systematic spiritual training."[8]

Fortunately, such cases are much less common than they once were because attorneys are increasingly successful in challenging such decisions on constitutional grounds.

"Our religious difference was really not a big deal when we were married," says Laurie, a Christian mother of three with an atheist ex. "We had an agreement that the kids would explore both of our views and make up their own minds. But since the divorce there's this new dynamic, like we're both trying to 'win' the religion thing. I hate it, but I feel like I'm also doing it myself." It's a common theme—once the two worldviews are no longer sharing a home, the kids can become pawns in a religious war between their parents, yet another way of becoming the "right" one in the divorce.

Divorce experts are clear on this one. Couples with a genuine concern for their kids should make a special effort not to denigrate the other parent. In the case of mixed-belief parents, that also means a special effort not to denigrate the other parent's worldview.

Continuity is also crucial for kids. Rules and agreements that held sway in a mixed-belief household should be maintained to the best of the parents' ability after a separation. Allowing kids to come to their own religious conclusions is a best practice for married couples, and it's a best practice for divorced couples.

Of course it's harder to monitor and enforce, and ex-partners on both sides of the divide can start to feel a creeping sense that the other is indoctrinating the kids. "It seems like every time they came back from Mom's house, there was a new joke or criticism of religion," says Brian, a Catholic father of two. But he says his relationship with his agnostic ex-wife is positive enough that they could sit down and discuss it. "I reminded her about the agreement we had before the divorce, and she was very receptive. She's been much more careful and respectful since then."

Lynette is an atheist divorced from a Christian. "Being divorced and raising children in two separate households with two different worldviews is more difficult than raising children in one household in which the parents agree to compromise," she says. "My ex is spending far more time and effort emphasizing religion with our children now than he ever did when we lived together. They sometimes ask about why I don't pray or go to church, and I simply tell them that everyone has different beliefs about God. I don't want to set myself up in opposition to religion and tell them these things are wrong because I don't want it to become something that we fight about as they grow older."

Recently, her six-year-old son came back from Dad's house and said something that broke her heart. "He said, 'Every day when I'm with Papa I pray for you that you will believe in God so that you don't have to die.' This was the most heartbreaking moment of my life, seeing the pain and worry that my lack of belief is causing him. I had no idea how to respond to this, and still don't. I do not want him to spend the rest of his life, or even the next few years, worrying about me or trying to convert me. My biggest fear right now is that he and I will always have different beliefs, and that at some point he may not be able to accept or be close to me because my beliefs are different than his." But she is committed to giving her kids a balanced message so they can make their own choices.

Wayne, a secular humanist dad in Kansas, realized that he didn't have to be as careful talking to his kids about religion after his divorce—he had to be *more* careful. "Before we had a home with mixed beliefs," he says, "but now there's 'the Christian home' and 'the humanist home.' So when I criticize Christian beliefs, it feels much more like I'm criticizing their mom directly. I know it's important for them to keep a positive relationship with her, so I really don't want to do that, and things that I think were really fair game before just aren't now." He also developed a litmus test for anything he says about his ex-wife's religion: "I just flip it around: How would I feel if I heard her saying the same kind of thing about my humanism? It's amazing what that does."

If the relationship between exes is good—either "Perfect Pals" or "Cooperative Colleagues"—they might agree on that litmus test on both ends. And if fairness for the kids isn't enough incentive, many couples report that a heavy-handed approach often backfires in divorce situations. When one parent demands a single way of thinking and being, whether religious or nonreligious, and the other parent encourages openness and free exploration without negative consequences, kids often gravitate toward the more open and relaxed environment.

The Bottom Line

Divorce plays out in countless ways depending on the people and circumstances. But when it comes to divorces between religious and nonreligious partners, parenting is the usual point of contention, and a small number of vital principles apply across the board:

1. Half of all divorces are "good divorces" with healthy ongoing communication and cooperation. You should make use of whatever positive assets your relationship retains after a split, especially for the sake of the kids.

2. Kids should never be put in the middle of a religious conflict between their parents.

3. Best practices during a marriage are also best practices after divorce. Couples should redouble their efforts to preserve the free exploration of religious and nonreligious ideas by their kids.

4. Religious differences are made more visible by the split, so criticism of the other parent's worldview can feel more personal and wounding than before. More care is needed at exactly the time many ex-partners feel *less* is needed.

21

The Positive Side of the Secular/Religious Mix

Despite the general pall that so many commentators cast over religiously mixed marriages of every kind, the picture of the secular/religious marriage is positive and encouraging.

That's not to say it's always positive. After all, we've just spent a great deal of time examining the many issues and tensions that can arise when one partner is religious and the other is not. Helping couples work through such issues is one of the main purposes of this book. But most couples do find the challenges manageable, tension usually decreases over time, and many people find that the benefits outweigh the challenges.

When I asked respondents to my survey to describe any specific benefits or positive results from their secular/religious difference, *fewer than 5% said they couldn't think of any benefits.* The rest offered not only benefits, but many of the same benefits, over and over. This chapter is devoted to that encouraging repetition.

Things That Have Gone Missing Because My Husband Is an Atheist
First-person blog excerpt from "Alise . . . Write!" by Alise Wright
When Jason came out to me about being an atheist, I assumed that there would be a litany of shared interests that would be missing due to

his lack of faith. Some are what you would expect, like attending church together regularly or having a singular vision for our children's spiritual education. To be sure, there are times when I absolutely miss these moments.

But I have also discovered that because of his deconversion, there are other things that have gone missing, many that I didn't expect:

→ ***My assumptions about what atheists think about Christians.***

Obviously I don't know all of the atheists in the world, but my inter-actions with the bulk of the atheists that I've met online and those I've met in person through Jackson have pretty much shattered how I assumed that group felt about Christians. I thought that atheists believed that all Christians were stupid; most simply feel that Christians are wrong. I thought that atheists hated Christians; most don't have any problem with Christians. I thought that atheists were angry; most are considerably more laid back than some of my Evangelical friends. Over and over I've found that my assumptions keep being proved wrong and are slowly disappearing.

→ ***My assumptions about how Christians would treat us.***

When Jackson came out to me, I asked him not to talk about it because I was afraid of how the Christians in our lives would react. I knew that people were going to treat us (and more to the point, me) dif-ferently. What I found, however, was that when we finally told people, most embraced us with even more love. I almost never felt like some-one's project, and I'm certain that at least a few times when I did feel that way, it was more perception than reality. I know that plenty do not have such a positive experience, but I do believe that we need to be more generous with our assumptions about people in general.

→ ***My assumptions about hell.***

Before I was close to someone who had no beliefs about an afterlife, I never really gave it much thought outside of "believers go to heaven, unbelievers go to hell." In the past two and a half years, I have read con-siderably more about hell than I did in the previous 30-something years. I still haven't completely settled on what I believe about the afterlife, but I no longer accept that things are as black and white as I've always been taught. I'm far more hopeful now, not just for me, but for everyone that I meet. Which leads me to the next thing that is missing . . .

→ ***My assumptions about life now.***

Because my beliefs about the afterlife are in flux, this has affected how I view the here and now. When I was sure about who was in and who was out, my primary goal was simply to make sure that everyone ended up in the same place. Now that I'm less convinced of this, I am far more interested in knowing everyone's story. When I can demon-strate that I care about the thoughts of someone I previously saw as being on "the outside" without an agenda, we are able to have a more honest dialogue.

Letting go of assumptions can be difficult. They can feel as comfort-able as many of the more positive areas of our relationships, and when there's already a lot of upheaval, our instinct can be to cling to that which is familiar. But I've found as I loosened my grip on my assump-tions, I haven't really missed them as they've slipped away.[1]

The Positives

What follows is a list of seven specific benefits that are repeatedly experi-enced in the secular/religious marriage.

1. Many partners discover that religious and nonreligious people can share morals and values.

"We both found that each other was not the 'scary atheist' and 'crazy Christian' that we were led to believe," says Julie, a Lutheran married to an atheist. "We both have the same views and morals and outlook on how life should be, how people should treat other people, animals, and the earth. We both want to do good in the world. The only difference is I think there is a God and he does not."

2. Many partners report becoming a better example of their own worldview.

Religious and nonreligious partners alike say that having a spouse on the other side of the aisle has made them smarter, more effective, and more empathetic in their engagement and activism and better examples of their own worldview.

"It may seem strange, but I think I'm a better Muslim than I was before I met my [agnostic] wife," says Fadi. "I used to see things in fairly black and white ways and was very judgmental. She makes me think first about whether I am expressing the true heart of Islam in what I say. I am a better representative of my own faith now than before I met her."

Many nonbelievers feel the same. "Having a wife that is a liberal Christian actually helps me in my activism," says Steven. "She helps me moderate my message and tailor things so that religious people will be more receptive and less offended."

3. Many conservative religious believers adopt more progressive and tolerant social views.

Close experience with difference usually has a liberalizing effect, and it's no different for secular/religious couples. "I have become more liberal in my thinking because of him and changed Lutheran denominations because of that," says Julie. "We both can agree, and I love the Evangelical Lutheran Church of America. In fact, I feel we both have strengthened the other in their views. At least he has for me by questioning why I think what I think. I was able to separate my true beliefs from just believing things because I grew up believing it."

Hope (see Chapter 7) says much the same. "Having my nice little Christian bubble popped has, at the end of the day, been a good thing. I'm more liberal now, and a lot of my friends act like I'm crazy, especially about abortion issues and gay rights. But I think more or less it's a shift for good."

4. Many nonbelievers are better able to let go of paralyzing resentments toward religion.

Many nonreligious partners bring a painful history with religion into the relationship, including some deep resentments. Some have experienced betrayal, rejection, fear, anger, or even complete disowning from religious families and communities. Being in a loving relationship with a religious believer can help the nonbeliever to transcend this unproductive resentment.

"Despite my best friend being extremely religious and my family being fairly religious, I had a very toxic relationship with religion when I met my partner in high school," says Stephanie, an atheist. "I felt it was inferior to atheism, close-minded, and overall a negative influence in the world. Through exploring my husband's [religious] belief system, as well as my own humanism, I've been able to let go of a lot of the resentment I was holding against religion. I've reconciled with myself that people express abstract concepts through religion in good, helpful ways and in bad, harmful ways. I no longer automatically view someone who identifies as religious with derision, and I can in fact admire their faith, and I instead align myself with them based on the larger question of whether or not they are a good person in the broader sense."

5. The difference often leads partners to learn more about each other than they otherwise would have.

Some couples with different worldviews go out of their way to avoid the topic. But if the rest are any indication, including many of my survey respondents, they might be missing out on a good thing. One respondent after another described having deeper conversations with their partners and learning more about each other in the process than they ever did in their shared-belief relationships. "It has caused friction at times," says one, "but it has also ultimately brought us closer together."

"I have had to lose so many assumptions about atheists, and in some cases, about Christians as well," says Alise, an Independent Protestant (and author of the blog post in the sidebar). "My husband and I have had to become much more intentional about the ways that we relate to one another. When you have the same belief, you assume a lot without asking. But I'm often curious about how he sees something differently, so I ask."

Nolan, an atheist married to a former Methodist, echoes Alise. "It's opened up a lot of discussions, and we've learned a lot about each other through conversations about our core beliefs."

Others say the difference has increased their mutual trust. "I'm sure religious differences sometimes tear relationships apart, but ours has only made us trust one another more," says Amanda, an atheist married to a Baptist. "I grew up Baptist, but now I am a closeted atheist in the South. My husband is the only person I have entrusted with my nonbelief, and he has been kind and considerate and loving in a way that I know not even my closest friends or family members would be. And through it all we have realized that our relationship is built on a strong foundation. That foundation just isn't faith. It's trust, respect, communication, cooperation, and friendship."

6. Both believers and nonbelievers find themselves examining their own beliefs more closely.

If you share a belief system with someone, it's easy to leave many of your beliefs unexamined. But living with someone whose beliefs are different—especially someone on the far side of the chasm between the natural and supernatural—makes a person more likely to think deeply and well about what he or she believes. There's an inherent challenge to our complacency, even if not a word is said.

See **Andrew and Lewis,** *Chapter 12*

"It's clearly not good to go through life with intellectually indefensible positions," says Lewis, a Christian. He and his atheist fiancé, Andrew, both feel they've shed some of the weaker opinions and beliefs they once held. "I think it's wonderful that we've been able to help each other shed those positions," Lewis says.

I know I thought much more deeply and intensely about my own beliefs when Becca was still religious, even though we only rarely engaged the questions. Just the presence of the difference was like a whetstone against which I sharpened my mind. I've definitely gotten duller in that area since she changed her mind.

Once again, I'm far from alone:

J.T. (agnostic atheist): "Being close to my partner's religion and attending her [Independent Protestant] church has prompted me to more closely examine what may or may not be the truth. I have joined Meetups and groups (both secular and religious) I would have otherwise never gone to and met some wonderful people."

Patty (former Methodist, now agnostic): "I have been challenged to really think about what I believe. My life is richer and more meaningful as a result of this."

Hannah (Lutheran Mennonite): "I find being married to an atheist a challenge to my personal convictions. I'm more or less forced to delve deep into what I value without hindering my husband with my personal beliefs."

Nalia (atheist): "I think my [Independent Christian] husband feels more free to question his beliefs even if he still accepts them. He asks my opinions after he's attended church with his family on occasion, even taking notes when he goes."

Mandy (Catholic): "When I returned to active Catholicism, my [agnostic] husband was very supportive and was intellectually curious about Church practices, stands, and history. His questions have helped me look deeper into my faith practices."

Amy (secular humanist): "I have found that being the nonreligious partner has motivated me to research and clarify my viewpoints so that I can better describe them to my partner as well as to friends (though the topic does not come up often, if at all, in my presence). Since the birth of my daughters, I have had to take a much closer look at my own worldview in order to be able to explain it to them in terms they can understand and in a way that will not offend my partner."

Religious people with nonreligious partners often describe becoming

→ *more universalist in their views (i.e., everyone is saved, not just believers)*

→ *less fearful and distrusting of atheists, and more comfortable with difference generally*

→ *less convinced that religious belief is a necessary precondition for a moral life*

Nonbelieving people with religious partners often speak of

→ *developing a more nuanced view of religion, seeing a wider range of good and bad among different expressions*

→ *being more willing to coexist with religion and the religious*

→ *being less convinced that religious belief indicates a lack of intelligence*

7. Many partners are now more open-minded and less militant toward the "other side" of the belief gap.

One benefit stood head and shoulders above the rest in the survey: that being married across the secular/religious gap increases a person's tolerance and open-mindedness about the other side of the gap because it is harder to maintain a simplistic cartoon of religious believers, on the one hand, and nonbelievers, on the other. It's harder to dismiss all religious people as unintelligent or all atheists as immoral when you have fallen in love with a flesh-and-blood representative of that worldview.

"It is really helpful to see the other side of the coin for me," says Jack, an atheist married to a Catholic. "I have learned to be able to look at life issues from a different perspective and see why people make the choices they do. I wouldn't have been able to do that as well before."

"My marriage has made me more open-minded," says Hannah, an Independent Christian married to Ken, a secular humanist. "A considerable amount of respect exists in our relationship, and I always feel supported as the religious half to explore and discuss my beliefs. His nonbelief has certainly challenged my thinking about certain religious traditions, which has caused me to think hard about what specifically is important to me and why instead of just something the way everyone in my family has always done it. Ken's character is a testament to the fact that while religion may shape values, it is not the only source—he is a fantastic, good man who shares many of my morals and values."

"I think we have a moderating effect on each other," says Jesse, an atheist, of his Catholic wife, Anna. "Her Christianity has led me to be careful in talking about religious issues, and to self-identify more as UU/secular humanist than atheist. In turn, I think I have led her to more clearly understand some of the points where she and the Catholic Church do not agree."

Sometimes the opening of minds develops slowly over time. "At first I didn't find any value in it at all, but as time has gone by I have learned some valuable things," says Alison, a Mormon. Her marriage neared divorce after her husband left the Mormon church but has since recovered and is now strong. "I have learned to have more tolerance and less control. I have tried to stop changing my husband, and that has given me this sense of freedom because I no longer feel responsible for his decisions. He makes good, logical decisions, even if they aren't the decisions I would make."

The same ideas—greater openness and tolerance and less militancy—echo throughout the survey:

Gary (atheist): "I am more understanding and empathic of religious people, where I was meaner prior to knowing [my wife]."

Kylie (Christian): "I have become much more relaxed about atheists. Unless they're shouting in my face at a party (you know that particular type of Dawkins fan), I am totally cool with whatever."

Paul (atheist): "She has helped me be more moderate when discussions of religion occur amongst friends. I was fairly rabid toward believers prior to meeting her and have become a lot more accepting since. I have really accepted the religious as worthy, whereas I had zero interest in even having a conversation prior."

Sarah (Independent Evangelical): "I saw people mostly in black and white terms before we got together, saved and unsaved. That just doesn't make sense to me anymore, though I'm still every bit as committed to my faith. I think God works in more complex ways than I had given Him credit for."

William (atheist): "I have learned the importance of not imposing my beliefs/nonbelief on anyone as it isn't likely to result in any change. The decision/move from a religious to nonreligious identity is a personal journey that must be initiated by the individual. It is important for me to respect my partner's different views and to allow her to believe as she does with my full respect and support."

Finally there's Brenda, a Mormon in Provo, Utah, whose husband left the church when he decided he was an atheist. "I was very worried at first when he left the church, but now I'm glad he is finding his own beliefs and feels more confident, comfortable, and happy with himself. I am thankful that he has taught me to trust myself and my moral judgment, and to think openly and critically. My mind is a lot more open to what might be out there in the universe, and I am a lot less closed-minded and judgmental of things I don't understand or don't agree with."

My relationship is a constant reminder that Christianity, and religion in general, isn't as toxic as its worst examples. I think this has helped me avoid the Richard Dawkins–esque mentality that we must proselytize our nonbelief and "convert" believers, as if their individual beliefs are somehow a threat to my own. I have a living, breathing example of the good that religious belief can provide for people who believe—even though I don't believe myself. I know that I can live alongside people like my partner, who believes quite strongly, without it impinging on or restricting my atheism. And hopefully, my partner knows that she can live alongside fervent atheists without her beliefs being restricted. That's a microcosm of the world we all want to live in, I think. —Thomas, atheist

Notes

Introduction

1. 2 Corinthians 6:14. And actually, it's not all that clear, since First Corinthians 7:12–16 says the opposite. More on that later.

2. Naomi Schaefer Riley, "Interfaith Marriages Are Rising Fast, but They're Failing Fast Too." Available at http://www.washingtonpost.com/wp-dyn/content/article/2010/06/04/AR2010060402011.html. Accessed March 16, 2014.

3. Margaret Vaaler and C. G. Ellison, "Religious Dissimilarity and the Risk of Divorce: Evidence from Two Waves of the National Survey of Families and Households." Paper presented at the annual meeting of the American Sociological Association, Philadelphia, PA, August 12, 2005.

4. Kalman Packouz, *How to Prevent an Intermarriage* (Nanuet, NY: Philipp Feldheim, 2005).

5. Janice Aron, "Interfaith Marriage Satisfaction Study Yields Answers and More Questions," August 28, 2009, unpublished doctoral research. Synopsis available at http://www.interfaithfamily.com/relationships/marriage_and_relationships/Inter faith_Marriage_Satisfaction_Study_Yields_Answers_and_More_Questions_.shtml. Accessed March 14, 2014.

6. Riley, "Interfaith Marriages."

7. Naomi Schaefer Riley, *'Til Faith Do Us Part: How Interfaith Marriage Is Transforming America* (New York: Oxford University Press USA, 2013), 120.

8. Cited in Naomi Schaefer Riley, "Interfaith Unions: A Mixed Blessing," New York Times op-ed (A-17), April 6, 2013. Figure includes intra-Protestant marriages.

9. Not all in the "unaffiliated" category are nonbelievers. For more on this problematic survey category, read Chapter 3, "Meet the Nonbelievers."

10. U.S. Religious Landscape Survey, Pew Research Center's Religion & Public Life Project, 2007. Compiled data and graphics available online at http://religions.pew forum.org/portraits. Accessed March 7, 2014.

11. Sam Harris, "The Boundaries of Belief," On Faith blog, *Washington Post* online, July 4, 2008. Accessed March 15, 2014.

Chapter 1: The Big Picture

1. "LCMS Participates in Ecumenical Summit on Biblical Marriage, Sexuality," Lutheran Church Missouri Synod press release, May 14, 2013, http://blogs.lcms.org/2013/lcms-participates-in-ecumenical-summit-on-biblical-marriage-sexuality. Accessed March 16, 2014.

2. Interracial marriage statistics from Gallup polling data. See article at http://www.gallup.com/poll/163697/approve-marriage-blacks-whites.aspx, accessed March 7, 2014. Sun orbiting the earth from National Science Foundation survey, available online at http://www.nsf.gov/statistics/seind14/index.cfm/chap ter-7/c7h.htm, accessed March 7, 2014.

3. Pew Social Trends, "Marrying Out," available at http://pewsocialtrends.org/files/2010/10/755-marrying-out.pdf. Accessed March 7, 2014.

4. "A Shifting Landscape: A Decade of Change in American Attitudes About Same-Sex Marriage and LGBT Issues." Public Religion Research Institute survey, November 12–December 18, 2013. ($N = 4,509$).

5. "Changing Attitudes on Gay Marriage," Pew Research Center, Religion and Public Life Project, slide 3 (http://features.pewforum.org/same-sex-marriage-atti-tudes/slide3.php). Accessed April 10, 2014.

6. Naomi Schaefer Riley, *'Til Faith Do Us Part: How Interfaith Marriage Is Transforming America* (New York: Oxford University Press USA, 2013), 6.

7. "Faith in Flux" survey, Pew Research Center's Religion & Public Life Project, April 27, 2009, http://www.pewforum.org/Faith-in-Flux.aspx. Accessed March 9, 2014.

8. Robert Putnam and David E. Campbell, *American Grace: How Religion Divides and Unites Us* (New York: Simon & Schuster, 2012), 134–135.

9. Ibid.

10. Silver, Christopher, and Thomas Silver. "Atheism, Agnosticism, and Nonbelief: A Qualitative and Quantitative Study of Type and Narrative," University of Tennessee at Chattanooga. Research in pre-publication phase as of January 2014. See project description at http://atheismresearch.com/. Accessed March 16, 2014.

11. Data from the McGowan-Sikes survey of secular/religious mixed marriages, conducted in June–July 2013 ($N = 994$).

12. U.S. Census, 2010.

13. Putnam and Campbell, *American Grace*, 522.

14. Ibid., 523.

15. Ibid.

16. Ibid., 526–527.

17. Ibid.

18. This does not include intra-Protestant mixes, such as a Lutheran marrying a Methodist, which would raise the total even higher, to 37% of all current U.S. marriages. U.S. Religious Landscape Survey, Pew Research Center's Religion & Public Life Project, 2007. Compiled data and graphics available online at http://religions.pewforum.org/portraits. Accessed March 7, 2014.

19. "Brides, Grooms Often Have Different Faiths," Pew Research Center's Religion & Public Life Project (2009). Available online at http://www.pewforum.org/2009/06/04/brides-grooms-often-have-different-faiths. Accessed March 7, 2014.

20. Ibid.

21. M. J. Penton, *Apocalypse Delayed: The Story of Jehovah's Witnesses* (Toronto: University of Toronto Press, 2008), 280–283.

22. U.S. Bureau of Justice Statistics, http://www.bjs.gov. Accessed January 6, 2014.

23. http://christianstiredofbeingmisrepresented.blogspot.com/p/about-us.html.

24. "Polarised Voters, or Polarised Choices?" *Economist*, August 10, 2012, http://www.economist.com/blogs/democracyinamerica/2012/08/presidential-race.

25. "Overlapping Pro-Choice and Pro-Life Identities," article and graphic based on Religion, Millennials, and Abortion survey by the Public Religion Research Institute, June 9, 2011. Available online at http://publicreligion.org/2013/01/graphic-of-the-week-overlapping-pro-choice-and-pro-life-identities. Accessed March 7, 2014.

26. More on the Belief-O-Matic in action in Chapter 9.

27. Pew Research Center, "The States of Marriage and Divorce," available online at http://www.pewresearch.org/2009/10/15/the-states-of-marriage-and-divorce/. Accessed March 7, 2014.

28. Naomi Schaefer Riley, *'Til Faith Do Us Part: How Interfaith Marriage Is Transforming America* (New York: Oxford University Press USA, 2013), 11.

Chapter 2: Meet the Believers

1. U.S. Religious Landscape Survey, Pew Research Center, 2008. Compiled data and graphics available online at http://religions.pewforum.org/portraits. Accessed March 7, 2014.

2. Cited in Robert Putnam and David E. Campbell, *American Grace: How Religion Divides and Unites Us* (New York: Simon & Schuster, 2012), 538.

3. McGowan-Sikes survey, 2013.

4. "Faith in Flux" survey, Pew Research Center's Religion & Public Life Project, April 27, 2009, http://www.pewforum.org/Faith-in-Flux.aspx. Accessed March 9, 2014.

5. Catechism of the Catholic Church, n. 2357, 2370, 2384, 2271, respectively.

6. "Catholic Attitudes on Gay and Lesbian Issues," Public Religion Research Institute report, March 2011. Once again, even the papacy has shown a marked shift on the issue. In 2005, Benedict XVI wrote that homosexuality constituted "a strong tendency ordered toward an intrinsic moral evil." In 2013, his successor, Francis, responded to a question about homosexuality by saying, "If someone is gay and he searches for the Lord and has good will, who am I to judge?"

7. Gallup Values and Beliefs survey, May 3–6, 2012.

8. "Catholic Voters' Views on Health Care Reform and Reproductive Health Care Services: A National Opinion Survey of Catholic Voters," Beldon, Russonello, & Stewart Research and Communications report, September 2009.

9. Pew Research Center for the People and the Press, July 2009.

10. Sacraments Today: Belief and Practice Among U.S. Catholics, 2008.

11. U.S. Religious Landscape Survey, Pew Research Center, 2007. Compiled data and graphics available online at http://religions.pewforum.org/portraits. Accessed March 7, 2014.

12. "Report Examines the State of Mainline Protestant Churches," The Barna Group. December 7, 2009.

13. Putnam and Campbell, *American Grace*, 112.

14. Pew Research Center's Religion & Public Life Project data, available at http://religions.pewforum.org/portraits. Accessed March 7, 2014.

15. Aggregated data from Pew Research Center's Religion & Public Life Project annual polls as of 2013.

16. Ibid.

17. Ibid., data through March 2014.

18. Public Religion Research Institute/Religion News Service survey, September 14–18, 2011.

19. The version of the Baptist Faith and Message used by her church is available at http://www.travis.org/what-we-believe. Accessed January 6, 2014. The official, unabridged version of the creed is available at the website of the Southern Baptist Convention: http://www.sbc.net/bfm/bfm2000.asp. Accessed March 31, 2014.

20. Sergio DellaPergola, "World Jewish Population, 2010," in *Current Jewish Population Reports*, ed. Arnold Dashefsky and Ira Sheskin. (Storrs, CT: North American Jewish Data Bank).

21. Quoted in Naomi Schaefer Riley, *'Til Faith Do Us Part: How Interfaith Marriage Is Transforming America* (New York: Oxford University Press USA, 2013), 20.

22. "The World's Muslims: Unity and Diversity," Pew Research Religion and Public Life Project survey, 2011.

23. Ibid.

24. Ibid.

25. U.S. Religious Landscape Survey, Pew Research Center's Religion & Public Life Project, 2007. Compiled data and graphics available online at http://religions.pew forum.org/portraits. Accessed March 7, 2014.

26. Public Religion Research Institute survey, June 9, 2011.

27. U.S. national survey conducted by the Pew Research Center's Religion & Public Life Project from July 31 to August 10, 2008.

Chapter 3: Meet the Nonbelievers

1. Faith Matters survey, Roper Center for Public Opinion Research, conducted June 29–August 29, 2006 ($N = 3,100$).

2. Kosmin, Barry. American Religious Identification Survey, Graduate Center of the City University of New York, 1990 and 2012.

3. Personal conversation with Christopher Silver, August 13, 2014.

4. Silver, Christopher, and Thomas Coleman. "Atheism, Agnosticism, and Nonbelief: A Qualitative and Quantitative Study of Type and Narrative," University of Tennessee at Chattanooga. Qualitative interviews ($N = 59$), follow-up testing, and quantitative survey ($N = 1,153$) completed June 6, 2013. Research at this writing is pre-publication. Executive summary available at http://www.atheismresearch.com. Accessed March 9, 2014.

5. A favorite personal saying, inscribed on Huxley's memorial at Ealing, quoted in *Nature* XLVI (30 October 1902), 658.

6. Susan B. Anthony, "On the Campaign for Divorce Law Reform" (pamphlet, 1860).

7. Interview with Empire Online, available at http://www.empireonline.com/inter views/interview.asp?IID=1192. Accessed March 27, 2014.

8. Christopher Hitchens, *Letters to a Young Contrarian* (New York: Basic Books, 2009), 55.

9. Jonathan Rauch, "Let It Be," *The Atlantic* 291, no. 4 (May 2003), 34.

10. Alain de Botton, *Religion for Atheists: A Nonbeliever's Guide to the Uses of Religion* (New York: Vintage Books, 2013), 14.

11. Silver and Coleman, "Atheism, Agnosticism, and Nonbelief."

12. Personal conversation with Christopher Silver, August 13, 2014.

13. Ibid.

14. From executive summary of Silver and Coleman, "Atheism, Agnosticism, and Nonbelief," at http://www.atheismresearch.com. Accessed March 9, 2014.

15. Ibid.

16. Ibid.

17. Robert Altemeyer and Bruce Hunsberger, *Atheists: A Groundbreaking Study of America's Nonbelievers* (Amherst, NY: Prometheus Books, 2006), 59–68.

18. Ibid., 66.

19. Sunstein, Cass. *Going to Extremes: How Like Minds Unite and Divide.* (New York: Oxford University Press, USA; Reprint edition, 2011).

20. U.S. Religious Landscape Survey, Pew Research Center's Religion & Public Life Project, 2007. Compiled data and graphics available online at http://religions.pew forum.org/portraits. Accessed March 7, 2014.

Chapter 4: What Helps, and What Doesn't

1. J. J. Lehmiller, "Perceived Marginalization and Its Association with Physical and Psychological Health," *Journal of Social and Personal Relationships* 29 (2012), 451–469.

Chapter 9: Finding a Meeting Place

1. See Chapter 1 for more on the Belief-O-Matic Quiz.

2. Taken from http://www.uua.org/beliefs/principles/. Accessed January 4, 2014.

Chapter 11: The Unequally Yoked Club

1. A longer version of this first-person account first appeared in serial form in Cassidy's blog "Roll to Disbelieve" at http://rolltodisbelieve.wordpress.com. Accessed December 26, 2013.

Chapter 12: Trivial Differences, Common Values

1. Adult male fandom of this children's show has grown into a sizable phenomenon in recent years. Known as "bronies," the fans are often considered part of the New Sincerity trend, an attempt to counter modern trends toward cynicism and irony by encouraging appreciation of simple and straightforward emotion in art and entertainment.

Chapter 13: Discovering the Difference

1. More on her differences from Baptist doctrine in Chapter 2.

2. U.S. national survey conducted by the Pew Research Center's Religion & Public Life Project from July 31 to August 10, 2008.

3. McGowan-Sikes survey, 2013.

4. R. Gaunt, "Couple Similarity and Marital Satisfaction: Are Similar Spouses Happier?" *Journal of Personality* 74, no. 5 (2006), 1401–1420.

5. Designed by social psychologist Dr. Brittany Shoots-Reinhard for this book. Although drawing from research on values and relationships, this quiz has not been scientifically validated as an independent instrument.

6. C. D. Lomore, S. J. Spencer, and J. G. Holmes, "The Role of Shared-Values Affirmation in Enhancing the Feelings of Low Self-Esteem Women About Their Relationships," *Self & Identity* 6, no. 4 (2007), 340–360.

7. Gaunt, "Couple Similarity"; S. S. Hendrick, "Self-Disclosure and Marital Satisfaction," *Journal of Personality and Social Psychology* 40, no. 6 (1981), 1150–1159; C. J. Lutz-Zois, A. C. Bradley, J. L. Mihalik, and E. R. Moorman-Eavers, "Perceived Similarity and Relationship Success Among Dating Couples: An Idiographic Approach," *Journal of Social and Personal Relationships* 23, no. 6 (2006), 865–880.

8. E. C. J. Long, "Maintaining a Stable Marriage," *Journal of Divorce & Remarriage* 21, no. 1–2 (1994), 121–138; E. C. J. Long and D. W. Andrews, "Perspective Taking as a Predictor of Marital Adjustment," *Journal of Personality and Social Psychology* 59, no. 1 (1990), 126–131.

9. J. P. Meyer and S. Pepper, "Need Compatibility and Marital Adjustment in Young Married Couples," *Journal of Personality and Social Psychology* 35, no. 5 (1977), 331–342; S. G. White and C. Hatcher, "Couple Complementarity and Similarity: A Review of the Literature," *American Journal of Family Therapy* 12, no. 1 (1984), 15–25.

Chapter 14: Tying the Knot Across the Gap

1. A Sanskrit word meaning "Hail!" Also the name of Agni's wife, who presides over all burnt offerings. Always chanted during Hindu fire rituals.

2. Khalil Gibran, *The Prophet* (New York: Alfred A. Knopf, 1929).

3. 1 Corinthians 13:1–8. Translation from the *New American Standard Bible.*

4. Neale Donald Walsch, *Conversations with God,* Book 3 (Newburyport, MA: Hampton Roads Publishing, 1998), 239.

5. "A Portrait of Jewish Americans," Pew Center's Religion & Public Life Project, October 1, 2013.

6. Ibid.

7. U.S. Religious Landscape Survey, Pew Research Center's Religion & Public Life Project, 2007. Compiled data and graphics available online at http://religions.pew forum.org/portraits. Accessed March 7, 2014.

8. Ibid.

9. Ibid.

10. Carl Olson, *The Many Colours of Hinduism: A Thematic-Historical Introduction* (New Brunswick, NJ: Rutgers University Press, 2007), 9.

11. Available online at www.sacred-texts.com/bud/btg/btg21.htm. Accessed March 11, 2014.

12. Though attributed to Native American tradition, this lovely passage was actually penned for the 1947 novel *Blood Brother* by Elliott Arnold.

13. Available online at www.beliefnet.com/Prayers/Other-Faiths/Marriage/When-Two-People-Are-One.aspx. Accessed January 6, 2014.

14. Available online at ocean.otr.usm.edu/~w312788/comprel/summer/KrishnaRadha.htm.

15. See Naomi Schaefer Riley, *'Til Faith Do Us Part: How Interfaith Marriage Is Transforming America* (New York: Oxford University Press USA, 2013), 74.

Chapter 15: Church, Prayer, Holidays, and More
1. McGowan-Sikes survey, 2013.

2. To compare apples to apples, I have compared claimed attendance of the cohort to claimed attendance of the general population. Actual attendance for both is likely much lower than the claims—around 20% for the general population. See M. Chaves, K. Hadaway, and P. Marler, "Overreporting Church Attendance in America: Evidence That Demands the Same Verdict," *American Sociological Review* 63, no. 1 (February 1998), 122–130.

3. Excerpted from Leith Anderson, *Winning the Values War in a Changing Culture* (Ada, MI: Bethany House, 1994).

4. In the wake of an outcry from Barna's fellow Evangelicals, the Barna study was removed from public access but is cited in detail at http://divorce.lovetoknow.com/Divorce_Statistics_by_Religion. Accessed January 4, 2014.

5. Chaeyoon Lim and Robert D. Putnam, "Religion, Social Networks, and Life Satisfaction," *American Sociological Review* 75, no. 6 (December 2010), 914–933.

6. Quoted in Stephanie Pappas, "Why Religion Makes People Happier (Hint: Not God)," LiveScience, http://www.livescience.com/9090-religion-people-happier-hint-god.html. Accessed March 11, 2014.

7. Ibid.

Chapter 16: Who Are You?
1. Institut de la statistique Québec: http://www.stat.gouv.qc.ca/statistiques/index_an.html.

2. Chaeyoon Lim and Robert D. Putnam, "Religion, Social Networks, and Life Satisfaction," *American Sociological Review* 75, no. 6 (December 2010), 914–933.

3. Psalm 14:1.

Chapter 17: Communication and Respect

1. Quotes from Pete and Joan's story first appeared in Pete Wernick, "Parenting in a Secular/Religious Marriage," in *Parenting Beyond Belief*, ed. Dale McGowan (New York: AMACOM, 2007).

2. Ibid.

3. Gottman, John. *The Seven Principles for Making Marriage Work* (New York: Harmony Books, 2000), 27–32.

4. Robert Altemeyer and Bruce Hunsberger, *Atheists: A Groundbreaking Study of America's Nonbelievers* (Amherst, NY: Prometheus Books, 2006).

5. Ibid., 60.

6. Ibid.

7. Examples include Lawrence Kurdek, "Dimensionality of the Dyadic Adjustment Scale: Evidence from Heterosexual and Homosexual Couples," *Journal of Family Psychology* 6, no. 1 (September 1992), 22–35; and Patricia Fishman, "Interfaith Marriage, Religious Orientation, and Dyadic Adjustment." Master's thesis, Northern Illinois University, 2010.

8. Study cited in Francine Russo, "How Not Talking About Conflict Could Help a Marriage Last," *Time*, July 2, 2013.

9. Ibid.

10. McGowan-Sikes survey, 2013.

11. A reference to the subtitle of Hitchens's book *God Is Not Great: How Religion Poisons Everything* (New York: Twelve Books, 2007).

12. Pete Wernick, "Parenting in a Secular/Religious Marriage," in *Parenting Beyond Belief*, ed. Dale McGowan (New York: AMACOM, 2007).

Chapter 18: Extended Family

1. Christopher R. Agnew, Timothy J. Loving, and Stephen M. Drigotas, "Substituting the Forest for the Trees: Social Networks and the Prediction of Romantic Relationship State and Fate," *Journal of Personality and Social Psychology* 81, no. 6 (2001), 1042–1057; P. E. Etcheverry and C. R. Agnew, "Subjective Norms and the Prediction of Romantic Relationship State and Fate," *Personal Relationships* 11 (2004), 409–428.

2. J. J. Lehmiller, "Perceived Marginalization and Its Association with Physical and Psychological Health," *Journal of Social and Personal Relationships* 29 (2012), 451.

3. Cited in Naomi Schaefer Riley, "Interfaith Unions: A Mixed Blessing," *New York Times* op-ed (A-17), April 6, 2013. Figure includes intra-Protestant marriages.

4. In roughly a third of these, there was no tension because the couple shared the same faith at the wedding.

5. McGowan-Sikes survey, 2013.

6. Robert Putnam and David E. Campbell, *American Grace: How Religion Divides and Unites Us* (New York: Simon & Schuster, 2012), 526–527.

7. First Amendment and Article 18, respectively. For more on the Universal Declaration of Human Rights, see Chapter 19.

8. Nontheists who consider religion *in general* to be harmful or abusive should seek the opinion of a credible third party in determining whether a given practice qualifies.

9. See Marshall Rosenberg, *Nonviolent Communication: A Language of Life* (Encinitas, CA: Puddledancer Press, 2003).

Chapter 19: Kids in the Mix
1. J. H. Kellogg. "Solitary Vice," in *Plain Facts for Old and Young* (Burlington, IA: Segner and Condit, 1881).

2. Available at http://pediatrics.aappublications.org/content/103/3/686.full. Accessed January 4, 2014.

3. Available at http://www.aafp.org/patient-care/clinical-recommendations/all/circumcision.html. Accessed January 4, 2014.

4. Douglas Gairdner, "The Fate of the Foreskin: A Study of Circumcision," *British Medical Journal* 2 (1949), 1433–1437. Available at http://www.cirp.org/library/general/gairdner/. Accessed January 4, 2014.

5. Book of Common Prayer, 298.

6. Book of Occasional Services (2003), 159.

7. Website of the Episcopal Diocese of New York, "Concerning Baptism," http://www.dioceseny.org/pages/228. Accessed January 4, 2014.

8. Speech to the national convention of Atheist Alliance International, September 29, 2007.

9. Universal Declaration of Human Rights, available online at www.un.org/en/documents/udhr. Accessed January 4, 2014.

10. "Raising Children in Two Faiths," op-ed by Rabbi Joshua M. Davidson, *New York Times*, November 6, 2013, A28.

11. Pew Research Religion and Public Life Project, Religious Knowledge survey, conducted May 19–June 6, 2010.

12. McGowan-Sikes survey, 2013.

13. Catholic Code of Canon Law 1125, available online at www.vatican.va/archive/ENG1104/_P41.HTM. Accessed January 4, 2014.

14. Ibid.

15. Fr. Robert J. Hater, *When a Catholic Marries a Non-Catholic* (Cincinnati, OH: St. Anthony Messenger Press, 2006).

16. Pew Research Religion and Public Life Project, Religious Landscape survey, Chapter 1, p. 33, available online at http://religions.pewforum.org/pdf/report2reli gious-landscape-study-chapter-1.pdf. Accessed March 16, 2014.

17. Sutrakritinga; Wisdom of the Living Religions #69, I:II:33.

18. Udanavarga 5, 18.

19. Plato, Crito (49c).

20. Mahabharata 5, 1517.

21. Confucius, Analects 15, 23.

22. Matthew 7:12.

23. Talmud, Shabbat 3id.

24. Azizullah, Hadith 150.

25. T'ai Shang Kan Ying P'ien.

26. Baha'u'llah, Gleanings, LXVI:8.

27. The Wiccan Rede.

28. Quoted in Beth Pearson, "The Art of Creating Ethics Man," *The Herald* (Scotland), January 23, 2006.

29. James Dobson, *The New Dare to Discipline* (Carol Stream, IL: Tyndale Momentum, 1996), 6, 35, 65.

30. Elizabeth Gershoff, "Corporal Punishment by Parents and Asociated Child Behaviors and Experiences: A Meta-Analytic and Theoretical Review," *Psychological Bulletin* 128, no. 4 (July 2002), 539–579.

Chapter 20: Parting Ways

1. "Divorce Rate Drops to Lowest Rate Since 1970," *USA Today*, May 11, 2007. Available online at http://usatoday30.usatoday.com/news/nation/2007-05-11-divorce-decline_N.htm. Accessed March 16, 2014.

2. U.S. Census data, available online at www.census.gov/hhes/socdemo/marriage/data/acs/ElliottetalPAA2012figs.pdf. Accessed March 16, 2014.

3. Tara Parker-Pope, *For Better: How the Surprising Science of Happy Couples Can Help Your Marriage Succeed* (New York: Plume, 2011), 9–12.

4. Cited in Naomi Schaefer Riley, "Interfaith Unions: A Mixed Blessing," New York Times op-ed (A-17), April 6, 2013. Figure includes intra-Protestant marriages.

5. Constance Ahrons, *The Good Divorce* (New York: HarperCollins, 1994), 2–5.

6. Ibid. 50–59.

7. Personal blog of Eugene Volokh, available online at http://www.volokh.com/posts/1125342962.shtml. Accessed March 16, 2014.

8. Supreme Court of the State of Mississippi, *McLemore v. McLemore*, 762 So.2d 316 (2000), and *Hodge v. Hodge*, 186 So.2d 748, 750 (1966). Available at http://www.leagle.com/decision/20001078762So2d316_11075.xml/McLEMORE% 20v.%20McLEMORE. Accessed March 20, 2014.

Chapter 21: The Positive Side of the Secular/Religious Mix

1. First appeared on Alise Wright's blog Alise . . . Write! at http://alise-write.com, May 29, 2012. Accessed March 16, 2014.

Index